Sport and Society

Series Editors
Benjamin G. Rader
Randy Roberts

Books in the Series Sport and Society

A Sporting Time: New York City and the Rise of Modern Athletics, 1820–70
Melvin L. Adelman

Sandlot Seasons: Sport in Black Pittsburgh
Rob Ruck

West Ham United: The Making of a Football Club
Charles Korr

Beyond the Ring: The Role of Boxing in American Society
Jeffrey T. Sammons

John L. Sullivan and His America
Michael T. Isenberg

Television and National Sport: The United States and Britain
Joan M. Chandler

The Creation of American Team Sports: Baseball and Cricket, 1838–72
George B. Kirsch

City Games: The Evolution of American Urban Society and the Rise of Sports
Steven A. Riess

Reprint Editions

The Nazi Olympics
Richard D. Mandell

Sports in the Western World
William J. Baker

The Creation of American Team Sports

The Creation of American Team Sports

Baseball and Cricket, 1838–72

George B. Kirsch

University of Illinois Press
Urbana and Chicago

Manufactured in the United States of America
C 5 4 3 2 1

This book is printed on acid-free paper.

Library of Congress Cataloging-in-Publication Data

Kirsch, George B.
The creation of American team sports.

(Sport and society)
Bibliography: p.
Includes index.
1. Baseball—United States—History. 2. Cricket—United States—History. 3. Sports—United States—History. I. Title. II. Series.
GV863.AIK57 1989 796′.0973 88-14209
ISBN 0-252-01560-6 (alk. paper)

For
Susan Lavitt Kirsch

Contents

Preface

THIS book grew out of two long-term passions: sports—especially baseball—which I have loved since the age of five; and American history, which I have studied intensively since my junior year in college and have taught for more than fifteen years. Sometime during the late 1970s I decided to merge these two interests, and I began to browse in the subject of sport history. My fascination with baseball, football, basketball, soccer, and other team and individual sports moved me to investigate the origins of modern athletics in the United States during the middle years of the nineteenth century. This study represents my efforts to understand the beginnings of a movement that has become such an important part of contemporary American life.

As a social history of the early development of American baseball and cricket, this volume presents a comprehensive, comparative narrative of the early years of both sports. The discussion of the rise of baseball in Chapters 3, 4, 9, and 10 synthesizes my own findings with the scholarship of Harold Seymour, David Voigt, Melvin Adelman, Warren Goldstein, and many others who have written excellent accounts of the emergence of America's national pastime. I concentrate on the amateur era and the sport's transition into commercialism and professionalism because I believe that these topics deserve more detailed consideration than they have received in the existing works; thus, I end this study with the organization of the first professional baseball league in 1871. This volume also presents a complete narrative and analysis of early American cricket, with Chapters 2, 4, and 9 carrying the story of that sport up to the early 1870s. A brief overview of the subsequent fate of the English game in the United States is offered in the Conclusion. Chapter 5 discusses the competition between baseball and cricket in America and explains why baseball became the favored game on this side of the Atlantic.

The second purpose of this book is to analyze those aspects of baseball and cricket that were significant in the social and cultural life of nineteenth-century American cities. Over the past decade many scholars have studied such aspects of urban life as work and play, the family, group ethnic and racial experience, and residential and workplace patterns. While a few popular culture studies have appeared, there has been relatively little serious work on recreation and sport within the new social and urban history. Chapter 1 introduces the rise of modern American ball games, and Chapters 6, 7, and 8 treat the players, clubs, and spectators that created the first team sports in the United States. I explain the meaning of baseball and cricket for most of the social and economic classes that populated America's cities and towns during this era and, through the use of both qualitative and quantitative sources and methodologies, reveal the experiences of artisans, factory workers, small shopkeepers, clerks, managers, professionals, and many others who enjoyed playing ball either informally or as members of organized clubs. I deal with all regions and all sizes of communities in the United States but concentrate on New York City, Brooklyn, Newark, Jersey City, Philadelphia, Boston, Chicago, and Cincinnati. I stress both the internal developments in each sport in each place and also the interdependence of cities and towns in the United States. In short, in this book I contribute to our knowledge of organized American cricket and baseball and also the recreation of the people who lived in America's cities from 1838 to 1872.

Acknowledgments

During the years that I worked on this project many people helped and encouraged me in numerous ways. My first thanks go to the playmates of my childhood, adolescence, and college years; the fun we had nurtured my love of sport and laid the foundation for my present academic interest in athletics. In particular I recall countless happy hours of good sportsmanship and fellowship with my brother, Daniel Kirsch, and my friends Barry Cohen, Henry Cenicola, Richard Prager, Barry Vasios, Kevin Clermont, Steven Wexler, and Martin Leeds.

In academe I owe the most to the members of the North American Society for Sport History. They welcomed me warmly, criticized my papers and manuscripts, and exhorted me to keep trying. I especially appreciate the support offered by Alan Metcalfe, Randy Roberts, Stephen Hardy, Jack Berryman, Ron Smith, and Nancy Struna. Steven Riess, Melvin Adelman, Allen Guttmann, and Benjamin Rader gave me expert criticism on my articles and on various drafts of this book. Tom Jable served as an invaluable collaborator and astute evaluator, and he kindly and very generously permitted me to use his data on Philadelphia cricketers.

Research grants have helped me a great deal and have shortened the time required to complete this study. A 1980 National Endowment for the Humanities award for a Summer Seminar for College Teachers introduced me to Professor Murray Murphey of the University of Pennsylvania. He assisted me in formulating some of my ideas at an early stage of this project. A 1984 stipend from the New Jersey Historical Commission and summer grants from Manhattan College in 1981 and 1986 were also extremely helpful. For their patience, accuracy, and diligence I must thank my research assistants, Frank Curci, Robert Burnett, and Michael Quinn; for teaching me how to use the computer and SPSS I am indebted to Bro. Anthony Flynn, Denis McCornac, and Mary Ann Groves.

During the course of my research many people on the staffs of numerous historical societies and libraries have assisted me, especially at the New Jersey Historical Society, the New-York Historical Society, the Historical Society of Pennsylvania, the New York Public Library, the Christopher C. Morris Cricket Collection at Haverford College, and the Cardinal Hayes Library at Manhattan College. I wish to acknowledge in particular Carl Lane, Murray Haines, Rotan Sargent, Capt. George Dalton, Catherine Shanley, Maire Duchon, and Dominick Caldiero.

I am grateful to all of the people at the University of Illinois Press who helped with the publication of this book. I especially appreciate the encouragement and friendship of Lawrence J. Malley, editor in chief, who knows that sport can be both fun and the subject of serious scholarship. I thank Theresa L. Sears for her rigorous copyediting and careful supervision of the production of this volume. Her suggestions and support were simply first-rate.

Finally, I wish to extend my love and appreciation to my parents, Nathan S. Kirsch and Anne Rizack Kirsch, who continue to nurture me more than four decades after they gave me life. This book and my son were conceived at just about the same time. Adam has made the past six years exciting and fulfilling, even if he sometimes slowed me down a bit. Finally I offer a special tribute to my wife, Susan, the most important person in my life. I thank her for twenty years of love together.

The Creation of American Team Sports

CHAPTER

1

The Rise of Modern Ball Games

IN early July 1867 the Louisville Base Ball Club journeyed to Cincinnati to play a match against the hometown Red Stockings. The game inaugurated the new grounds leased and improved by the Union Cricket and Cincinnati Base Ball clubs at an expense of about $10,000. A high fence enclosed a well-manicured field of eight acres. The ballpark featured a beautiful two-story pavilion, with a veranda and raised seats for the accommodation of the ladies. This facility was conveniently accessible by streetcars, which on the day of the contest "were packed with their human freight like sardines in a box," as excited spectators made their way to the park. A capacity crowd admired the guests from Louisville, who arrived with their friends and female companions in six omnibuses, each drawn by four horses. The visitors sported uniforms of blue (jean) pants, blue shirts trimmed with red, and caps and belts of red and white. The hosts wore the hose that would distinguish their team when they became baseball's first legendary nine. The game proved to be satisfying to the home fans, as Cincinnati won easily, 60–24. The telegraph flashed the news around the nation; within a few days an inning-by-inning account of the action appeared in local newspapers and national sporting journals published in New York City and Philadelphia.[1]

By contrast, imagine another ball game played decades earlier in a remote rural setting. A columnist for a southern newspaper recalled that on Saturday afternoons "the neighborhood boys met on some cropped pasture, and whether ten or forty, every one was to take part in the game." He explained that "self-appointed leaders" chose sides and whirled a bat that decided who would hit first. The ball "was usually made on the spot by some boy offering up his woolen socks as an oblation, and these were raveled and wound round a bullet, a handful of strips cut from a rubber overshoe, a piece of cork or almost anything." The field might have four, six, or seven bases, which "were not equidistant, but were marked by any fortuitous rock, or shrub, or depression in the ground where the steers were wont to bellow and paw up the earth." Home plate was "the den." In addition, "there were no masks, or mitts, or protectors. There was no science or chicanery, now called 'head-work.'" The pitcher's object "was to throw a ball that could be hit. . . . There was no umpire, and very little wrangling. . . . The score was kept by some one cutting notches in a stick, and the runs in an afternoon ran into the hundreds."[2]

In 1867 the Philadelphia correspondent of the *New York Tribune* reported on the deliberations of the National Association of Base Ball Players (NABBP), lamenting how much the game of baseball had changed in just a few years. He recalled that as a boy he and his playmates took five minutes to choose sides and determine which team would bat first. "No advertising, no challenging, no costume, no excursions, no waste of time, no betting, no gambling, no drinking, drunkenness, fighting, or nonsense. This was play—genuine, hearty, healthful boy's play. The folly and crime of riper years never entered into those youthful sports." Back then the newspapers ignored these games; but now, he wrote, grown men "play the games of boyhood, demoralized by practices happily unknown to the innocence of school-days. Now bats and balls, grounds and club rooms, costumes and trainers, matches and excursions, meetings and conventions, are patented, purchased, erected, devised, made, maintained and organized at a waste of time, money, and strength, that in earlier and purer times would have been pronounced downright wickedness."[3]

Only a generation or two separate these two types of ball playing, but each belongs to a very different era in the development of American civilization. The Louisville-Cincinnati contest and the 1867 gathering of the NABBP represent early modern baseball, while the country boys' sport was a premodern pastime. A comparison of these types raises two important questions concerning the nature of ball games in nineteenth-century America: What are the characteristics of each type? What explains the transition from the premodern to the modern? To answer the first question requires a brief review of traditional ball playing for children and adults in the United States before 1840, followed by a summary of the modern form. The second question demands a consideration of how changes in American society—especially in the areas of industrialization, transportation, communication, urbanization, and ideology—influenced the creation of the first modern American team sports.

According to most sport historians, ball playing was not a very significant feature of early American athletics because of the rural nature of society, the tradition of individualism, and religious objections to such amusements. This viewpoint maintains that while children sometimes enjoyed early versions of cricket and baseball, adult men rarely competed in these sports. While this interpretation may be true for the colonial and revolutionary eras, its validity is highly doubtful for the early nineteenth century.

Proof of the widespread popularity of ball games for the period 1800–1840 may be found in many published reminiscences and newspaper editorials. Such pastimes were popular among schoolchildren and college students, and some adults braved public disapproval to join in the fun, especially on holidays and other special occasions such as barn raisings. From deep in Dixie in 1841 the *New Orleans Daily Picayune* reported: "Playing ball is among the very first of the 'sports' of our early years. . . . who has not played 'barnball' in his boyhood, 'base' in his youth, and 'wicket' in his manhood?" In 1858 the *New York Daily Times* noted that "baseball was one of the games we read of, and remembered as in pretty nearly the category of the blind-man's bluff, goal, and tag, that so delighted us when we were quite young gentlemen." *Harper's Weekly* questioned whether baseball was a popular game at all in the interior of the United States or in any part of the country except a few great cities, to which a reader from Steuben County, New York, replied, "For twenty years . . . baseball has been a 'popular game' wherever I have lived." He assured the editor that the game was "a popular one in nearly all the villages and among rural districts of Western New York" and asked, "Who that has attended country 'raisings' does not know this, and dwell with a pleasant remembrance on the game of ball that was sure to follow after the building or frame was raised?" He also reported that the sport was played in Ohio, northern Indiana, and Michigan. Although he admitted that rural areas had no organized clubs, he explained that country people (especially children) played and enjoyed folk versions of the pastime: "It is *the* game at our district schools during the intermission hours, and often engaged in by youths of both sexes."[4]

The great variety of ball games in the United States before the 1850s shared some common characteristics that place them in the category of folk or premodern recreations. These simple amusements lacked formal club organization and uniform rules, with participants mediating disputes. Natural factors determined the shape and size of the field, and there were no limits on the number of players. Equipment was homemade and rudimentary. Except for the pitcher and catcher, there was very little specialization by position. Players were unskilled, and brute force counted more than finesse. Individualism took precedence over teamwork. Spectators were few, and media coverage was nonexistent. While someone always tallied runs scored, there was no interest in keeping statistics or permanent records.

Although this kind of recreation persisted in parts of rural America long after the Civil War, by 1870 the modern pattern of ball playing had become dominant in most cities, towns, and villages across the United States. In the new version formal clubs played according to a detailed code formulated by a sport association. Standardized regulations fixed the dimensions of the field, the size and weight of the bats and balls, and the number of contestants on each side. Factories manufactured sporting goods for the masses. Athletes perfected highly specialized batting and fielding techniques and were trained for specific roles. Expert managers taught skilled players the teamwork that would turn them into an efficient machine. Finesse and trickery replaced brute force as the keys to victory. Clubs traveled hundreds (even thousands) of miles by railroad and steamboat to compete against their rivals. Spectators paid up to a half dollar to watch their heroes in action, while the telegraph and the printing press kept millions abreast of the latest results. Journals and yearbooks recorded statistics and compiled records. Rationalization, bureaucratization, specialization, regional and national competition, extensive media coverage, and a fascination with numbers all characterized modern ball playing.[5]

The preceding comparison of premodern and modern ball games illustrates the dimensions of change that marked the creation of team sports in nineteenth-century America, but it does not explain that transformation. The modernization model is helpful in defining the precise nature of the two types of recreation, and it does shed some light on the development of American cricket and baseball after the 1840s. But a more complete understanding of the rise of modern athletics involves a careful investigation of the influence on earlier forms of ball playing of specific transformations in many dimensions of American life. The middle decades of the nineteenth century witnessed a series of revolutions in industry, transportation, communication, urban life, and values. These innovations provided the preconditions that made modern cricket and baseball possible in the United States. Men and women who lived through these developments at first tried to maintain their traditional patterns of play and leisure. Yet the changes in most areas of their lives forced them to abandon their older practices or adapt them to new circumstances. Americans transformed traditional recreation or invented new forms to suit their new needs. Their desire to play remained strong, but it was expressed in new contexts and in new ways.[6]

While sport historians have recognized the broad impact of industrialization on the growth of athletics in America, they have not been precise about how it shaped the leisure experiences of all classes. Scholars once argued that the coming of the machines increased the free time available for the average person, but it now appears that this is a gross oversimplification. In fact, industrialization undermined premodern patterns of work and play. In the kind of traditional society that characterized the United States until the early 1800s, farmers and townspeople broke up long hours of hard labor with periods of sociability and relaxation. Much work was cyclical and seasonal in nature, and its tempo was irregular. Intense preoccupation with crops, crafts, or cargoes gave way to days or weeks of relative inactivity. A typical year also included religious and political holidays, family celebrations, and other diversions. Moreover, in traditional society an individual had very little choice in selecting nonwork activities that did not involve some kind of group obligation. If one defines true leisure as a free activity a person selects without regard to work, family, religious, or social responsibilities, then there was precious little leisure in early America.

The advent of the new technology did not revolutionize agricultural life patterns in the United States before the Civil War, but it did drastically transform the culture of cities and towns. The logic of capitalism and the increasing use of machines eliminated the traditional casual workday of sporadic labor. As the tyranny of the clock took over factories and countinghouses, work and free time became more distinct. Recreation now had to come before or after work on weekdays or else on weekends. But since most people worked six days a week, and since Sunday amusements were either prohibited or discouraged in many localities, free time was in very short supply. Thus one of the major effects of industrialization was to deprive people of traditional rest periods and compel them to schedule special time for nonwork activities.[7]

The industrial revolution transformed the lives of all city dwellers and townspeople, but its effects varied considerably according to occupation. For the sake of clarity, it is convenient to discuss the impact of industrialization on leisure by referring to five groups: high white-collar (industrial capitalists, managers, professionals), low white-collar (petty proprietors and clerks), skilled artisans, semiskilled workers, and unskilled workers. It is obvious that the coming of machines enriched a few captains of industry and enabled them to enjoy more leisure time as well as spend a great deal of money on recreation. Many of these men patronized the elite sports of thoroughbred horse racing and yachting, but a few either played or supported cricket and baseball. In Philadelphia, the Wister and Newhall families promoted the Philadelphia and Germantown cricket clubs, while in Hoboken, New Jersey, the Stevens family (especially John C. Stevens) helped both ball games by donating grounds on the Elysian Fields to New York clubs. Many prosperous lawyers and merchants followed their example and endorsed the new pastimes.

City dwellers were more directly involved in commercial than industrial pursuits, but they also felt the increased pressures of the new work discipline of industrial capitalism. Low white-collar merchants, grocers, small shopkeepers, clerks, and bookkeepers labored through long hours in stores, offices, banks, and countinghouses, trying to keep pace with the paperwork generated by expanding business. These sedentary workers naturally sought relief from their toil, many flocking to ball fields during early morning hours, after work, or on Saturday afternoon.

Artisans experienced the cruelest effects of the industrial revolution, which dramatically altered their premodern habits of work and play. Yet the impact of metropolitan industrialization varied enormously on the different crafts and their workers. Some trades, such as carpentry, blacksmithing, food preparation, and shipbuilding, retained their traditional structures throughout the mid-1800s. Skilled craftsmen employed in these fields had sufficient income and time for leisure, and many of them played baseball or cricket. For example, butchers' hours ended before noontime, and they often occupied their afternoons and early evenings with sports or drinking. However, other less fortunate artisans wound up in shops where new systems of production broke down traditional skills into a series of more specialized and simpler tasks.

Workers who labored under the direction of master craftsmen to produce clothing, shoes, hats, furniture, and other items found that the advent of the first machines and the new organization of manufacturing standardized and often speeded up the pace of work. They experienced deteriorating conditions as they performed repetitious tasks in tight quarters with little or no break before lunch or the end of the day. Hatters, shoemakers, trunk makers, and others in such trades sought recreation on ball fields; sometimes their bosses cooperated and even joined in the action. Heavy manufacturing and large-scale factories were not yet dominant in America's cities before 1870, but some crafts (such as printing) were far along in the use of technological innovations. Given the nature of the work of compositors and pressmen and their relatively high wages, it is not surprising that many of them took up baseball or cricket.

Factory laborers and outworkers who sweated at home doing piecework suffered much more than the independent mechanics and shop artisans from the changes of this period. Most of them were too preoccupied with the struggle for survival and too poor to participate in the athletic boom of the times. Semiskilled and unskilled immigrants and natives in manufacturing, as well as carmen, laborers, waiters, coachmen, and others on the lowest rungs of society, found an escape in taverns and burlesque halls, but very few played cricket or baseball.[8]

As industrial technology and the expansion of commerce forced city people to adjust their work and play habits, mass production and new inventions in transportation and communication facilitated modern forms of sport. Factories manufactured large quantities of bats, balls, bases, uniforms, and other sporting goods at a range of prices, thus providing a reasonable quality and selection of supplies that most players could afford. The railroad and steamboat made intercity and interstate competition possible, permitting the playing out of traditional urban, state, and regional rivalries on ball grounds. Brooklyn's Excelsior Base Ball Club could easily steam up the Hudson for a July excursion to play a Newburgh nine, and Cincinnati's Red Stockings could crisscross the nation seeking victory after victory. The telegraph and high-speed printing presses allowed daily and weekly newspapers to recount the excitement of major matches while they were still fresh in people's minds. Philadelphia's *Sunday Mercury,* the *New York Clipper, Wilkes' Spirit of the Times,* and other journals brought the scores and commentary to remote parts of practically every state in the Union.[9]

While the industrial, transportation, and communications revolutions profoundly shaped the early development of modern American sport, urbanization was a more critical factor. As Stephen Hardy demonstrates, the nineteenth-century city influenced new forms of athletics in many complex ways. City dwellers could not enjoy many traditional rural recreations and suffered from an increasingly oppressive, congested, and unhealthy environment. The new types of amusements they created were not merely a reaction to the negative features of city life; rather, they were also a positive product of many dynamic forces. Borrowing from the pioneer work of Louis Wirth and Oscar Handlin, Hardy explains that the city may be viewed as a physical structure, social organization, or state of mind. Each of these three aspects of urbanization affected the growth of modern sport in the United States in general and ball games in particular. Furthermore, it is essential to emphasize the interdependence of America's cities during the mid-1800s. Alan Pred's work on the building of city-systems focuses on demographic and economic topics, but it is relevant for social and cultural life as well. One cannot understand the rise of modern American sport simply by looking at discrete cities; one must also appreciate the athletic interactions among many large and lesser cities, towns, and villages.[10]

The physical development of mid-nineteenth century American cities had two major implications for the modernization of sport. First, the deteriorating environment bred sickness and psychological stress that endangered the people's corporal and mental health. Huge population increases, higher density, and inadequate housing created staggering disease problems, as municipalities struggled to supply better water, sewerage, and sanitation services. The public health crisis naturally forced many to lobby for more healthful recreation for the masses. Second, as expanding cities encroached upon traditional amusement areas, residents had to organize formal associations to acquire and maintain playing grounds. New York, Boston, and other cities improved parks for public recreation, while sportsmen joined together to rent or purchase space for cricket, baseball, yachting, and other athletic clubs. The modern city thus threatened the physical well-being of its inhabitants as well as their premodern patterns of informal and spontaneous play.[11]

The social organization of these cities also contributed a great deal to the rise of modern sport. As native and European migrants flooded into Brooklyn, New York City, Newark, Boston, Philadelphia, and other places, these metropolitan centers grew more diverse in race, religion, and ethnicity. Communities became fragmented as social and class relations were strained. Many urbanites sought a sense of identity and fellowship in voluntary associations for political, religious, cultural, or sporting purposes. Since Americans enjoyed a long heritage of grouping themselves into private organizations, it is not surprising that cricketers and baseball players followed this practice. Because of the complex social structure of these cities, men could group themselves by neighborhood, vocation, wealth, or membership in some common social or religious association. Sportsmen who banded together to acquire some playing space for themselves were also trying to preserve and strengthen their social identities in an increasingly impersonal environment.[12]

The population explosion and the accompanying trend toward pluralism in American cities of this era also contributed to the expansion of modern forms of leisure and especially to their commercialization. Since the urban masses were now cut off from most of their former modes of recreation, they sought diversion through whatever activities the new urban life could provide. Their sizable numbers not only filled the rosters of hundreds (even thousands) of clubs but also supplied audiences for all types of amusements. Entrepreneurs satisfied the growing demand for entertainment by creating the modern business of leisure. P. T. Barnum and his followers gave the populace the circus, the minstrel and burlesque shows, and the popular drama. Patrons flocked to theaters, saloons, race tracks, and ball parks, as well as the bordellos and cockfighting and ratting pits frequented by the "sporting fraternity." The modern city offered a selection of high- and low-brow excitement through a dazzling variety of free-time activities. While only the privileged few had such choices in premodern society, now all classes had some freedom over how to spend their time and money after work. Thus the modern U.S. city was the birthplace of the leisure revolution, which in turn made possible the commercialization of baseball.[13]

Cities exist not only in their streets, blocks, buildings, and avenues, or in the social, political, economic, and cultural relations among their residents. They live also in the minds of their inhabitants. Urban symbolism was a powerful force in the United States of the 1800s as communities searched for identities that would distinguish them from their neighboring and distant rivals. Upstart towns competed for political and economic supremacy; local boosters puffed up their settlements and denigrated competitors. Modern sport both reflected and intensifed boosterism and intercity rivalry. This was especially apparent in the growth of baseball, but these themes also appear in the early development of cricket.

The twin trends of urban imperialism and interdependence are also intimately linked to the rise of modern American sport. All nineteenth-century American cities tried to extend their political, economic, and cultural influence over as wide an area as possible. Through this process of urban imperialism each sought to retain and expand its hinterland. By the 1850s New York City had become the most powerful metropolis in the United States, while

Boston, Philadelphia, Baltimore, New Orleans, St. Louis, and other cities struggled to hold their power over their respective regions and to increase their influence across the nation. Chicago and San Francisco were newcomers to this game, with bright prospects. But while each community vied with its rivals, each also depended on them as well. The cities were part of a dynamic, complex system that exchanged people, produce, and finished products and shared information, expertise, and political power.

This system of cities helped to promote modern ball games in many ways. It fostered standardized rules across the United States as well as the formation of regional and national associations and leagues. Urban interdependence facilitated player and club mobility as well as communication about sport. Thus, in both the internal development of cities and their mutual interdependence, urbanization and the modernization of cricket and baseball were closely related.[14]

The final prerequisite for the development of modern American sport was the appearance of an ideological justification of athletics that would supercede the traditional religious and social objections to sport in the United States. Until the middle of the nineteenth century, most Protestant clergymen, educators, newspaper and magazine editors, and business leaders discouraged physical exercise and sport on the grounds that they were immoral, useless, and socially improper. Although Puritan ministers had usually tolerated moderate amusements to refresh one for work and study, they were always deeply suspicious of idle play and were especially hostile toward the gambling that frequently accompanied such premodern pastimes as horse racing and cockfighting. As late as the 1850s, some churches disciplined their members for participating in ball games. In 1859 a Maryland congregation expelled several young men for playing cricket and warned a few others not to follow their example.[15]

School and college teachers and administrators, journalists, and businessmen also frowned upon sport. In 1859 *Harper's Weekly* noted: "Men of thirty can remember well that when they were at school, proficiency in the athletics games of the play-ground was regarded rather as a drawback than a merit." Most schoolteachers still discouraged games "as tending to interfere with 'legitimate studies,'" it added. "As with our boys, so with our men. Bank clerks, young merchants, mercantile aspirants, all seem to think time devoted to any exercise wasted, and the model clerk him who drudges six days of every week at his desk without an hour of physical labor." The magazine questioned whether, during the late 1830s, "any leading family journal would have dared to intimate that it is perhaps as important for boys to learn baseball as prosody or conic sections."[16] The *New York Times* reported that many old lawyers and merchants suffered from "dyspepsia and neuralgia, and gout, and gravel, and liver complaint." They "despair of cure, and find distraction in intense devotion to business." Their young counterparts who followed suit and scorned vacations and exercise viewed health as "discreditable, as it indicates laxity of devotion to business."[17]

While these attitudes persisted during the mid-1800s, a new viewpoint toward physical fitness and athletics came into being during this period and eventually replaced the older ideas. The damaging effects of industrialization and urbanization on health, coupled with changes in philosophical and religious thought, contributed to this ideological shift. The negative economic and social consequences of modernization certainly moved many to reconsider earlier notions about exercise and play. Within this changing social context, physicians, physical educators, Romantics, Transcendentalists, Unitarians, and reformers propounded a positive philosophy of sport. These theorists believed that American citizens required athletics to meet the challenges of an uncertain future. While most were optimistic, many were deeply worried about the latest developments in politics, industry, urban growth, and social structure. In their view, physical training, recreation, and sport would help people cope successfully with these changes.[18]

The most influential champions of the new ideology of sport were the prominent molders of public opinion in antebellum America—namely, journalists, public officials, educators, businessmen, and ministers. It is not surprising that the editors of the national sporting weeklies published in New York City and Philadelphia were ardent advocates of the new gospel of sport. William T. Porter, Frank Queen, George Wilkes, Henry Chadwick, William Meeser, and others had a vested interest in amusements and athletics, for the more the masses believed in their message, the more their publications would prosper. It is significant that daily newspapers and weekly and monthly family periodicals also actively promoted physical fitness and sport. Dozens, perhaps hundreds, of local papers supported athletics in countless editorials, and magazines such as *Harper's Weekly* followed suit. Municipal officials in New York, Boston, and other cities endorsed the new thinking by planning and building the first public parks in the United States. Schools and colleges added more recreation and physical education to their curricula. Some enlightened businessmen even allowed their employees a few extra holidays and dismissed them early on summer Saturday afternoons.[19]

To win over the dominant Protestant middle class to the new attitudes, the approval of the clergy was critical. While some pastors remained skeptical, many used their pens and pulpits to preach the new gospel of "muscular Christianity." Perhaps the most famous was Thomas W. Higginson, a Harvard graduate, minister, and president of the Lincoln Cricket Club in Worcester, Massachusetts. In 1858 he published the influential article "Saints and Their Bodies" in the *Atlantic Monthly*.[20] More important, many less prominent ministers delivered sermons to their congregations in which they praised ball games and other sports. For example, the Reverend C. H. Everett of East Brooklyn's Puritan Church devoted a Sunday homily to physical education in which he praised the benefits of baseball. In Philadelphia and other cities more clergymen appeared on baseball diamonds and cricket pitches. There were even a few clubs whose rosters were exclusively pastors.[21]

Propagandists for the new philosophy of athletics aimed their message at children and women as well as men. Frank Queen's *New York Clipper* praised those colleges that were encouraging physical fitness because they gave their students a better hope of a long life as they reaped their academic honors. The journal maintained that "the physical . . . should be studied before the mental" and that from the age of five bodily training should accompany schooling. It concluded that the results for the grown-up men and women would be "the excellencies of mind and body in union."[22] The *Brooklyn Eagle* declared that "it would be an addition to every school, that would lead to great advantages to mental and bodily health, if each had a cricket or ball club attached to it, as in England."[23] The *Clipper* applied traditional ideas of women's roles to argue for female fitness, praising young ladies who rowed and skated. Those girls who glided gracefully on the ice "would be much better fitted to become mothers of American children. . . . If the children are born of puny mothers, the race degenerates, mentally and physically. . . . whatever then will tend to render the mothers of future generations robust and hearty, will conduce immensely to the well being of the race."[24] It was also boldly suggested that "a day's exercise on the cricket field would not be such a breach of manners. . . . even for ladies . . . such amusement . . . will be found quite as salutary in its results, as a night's frolic in a ball-room."[25]

The writers and preachers who championed the cause of athletics attacked the American obsession with work and money making and the poor physical condition of the populace and urged all citizens to find escape and relief in sport. The *Boston Saturday Dispatch* called for more city games because "the tendency toward city life is always towards physical degeneracy." It declared that "constant indoor employment . . . works sad havoc. . . . We need . . . something to take us out and away from our killing seclusion and labor."[26] The *Brooklyn Eagle* agreed: "We pay far too much attention to our desks, counters, and offices than the laws of Dame Nature will admit of without the accompanying penalty of ill health."[27] *Porter's Spirit of the Times* reported that "the Base Ball epidemic has carried off its thousands from the ranks of our over-worked and too-little-exercised population." In club competition it saw "a moral, as well as physically healthful substitute for the enervating excitement attendant upon 'runnin wid de masheen,' with its accompanying abuses, and injurious and fatal results to the health and morals of our city youths."[28]

The *Clipper* praised pioneer California cricketers and noted with pleasure that "while some are absorbed in the endeavor to 'make their pile' others are looking after their health and doing their utmost to establish this invigorating game." It claimed that sport (not the frontier) was "the greatest safety valve of society," especially when periodic depressions caused public disorders. "Work! work! work! grates harshly on the ear of those who seldom if ever get time to devote to anything else, the consequence of which is, that a general moroseness pervades those classes of society so situated, and no sooner does 'hard times' put in an appearance, than we are treated to such scenes as have of late been witnessed in our parks and public squares, instead of which it were just even more easy that the contrary should be the case, by . . . *a proper encouragement* of sport."[29]

The crusaders for fitness and sport stressed that exercise promoted good physical, mental, and spiritual health, fostered proper moral and social conduct, and drew young men away from more sordid amusements. A correspondent to Jersey City's *Daily Courier and Advertiser* wrote: "Our young men are beginning to learn that the sound mind in the sound body is the great desideratum."[30] Frank Queen repeatedly argued that "sports and amusements are not incompatible with gentlemanly deportment and a high state of learning, or even antagonistic to the proper fulfillment of the duties of the pulpit." He praised Higginson and other ministers who endorsed cricket and baseball, asking: "Is it to be supposed that a man . . . taking part in the exercises on the base-ball or cricket field . . . is less likely to 'Remember his Creator' than when shut up in the office, work shop, or laboratory? or that religious feelings cannot be elsewhere entertained than within the walls of the sanctuary?"[31]

Porter's Spirit noted that Brooklyn was known as the "City of Churches" but was "fast earning the title of the 'City of Base Ball Clubs.'" It added that the baseball fever would "work no harm to the church interests of pious Brooklyn" because the ball clubs furnished "both innocent amusement and healthful exercise" and were "valuable adjuncts to the church, inasmuch as a healthy bodily condition is undoubtedly essential to the enjoyment of a peaceful and religious state of mind."[32] Queen wrote that the old Puritan suppression of sport "led to sensual indulgences and solitary vices, far worse . . . than any supposed evils which might possibly arise from attending out-door games or athletic sports." Reverend Everett lauded baseball in part because it attracted men away "from the vices and places of bad repute, depopulating the saloons so numerous in the city," and supplied "the right kind of strength and amusement."[33]

Finally, those who propounded the new philosophy of sport maintained that physical activity instilled character traits and strengthened the bonds of society. They believed that athletics would help to preserve order and the future prosperity of a rapidly changing American culture. Writers were particularly sensitive to the issue of adult men playing children's games, so they stressed the "manliness" of athletics in general and cricket and baseball in particular. The *Fulton* (New York) *Democrat* stated that cricket required "courage, activity, and perseverance" and rejected the idea that sports were "too puerile for the adult, and perpetuate the pastimes of our infancy."[34] *Porter's Spirit* insisted that in cricket, "patience, fortitude, self-denial, order, obedience, and good-humor, with an unruffled temper, are indispensable." The sport taught "a love of order, discipline, and fair play, for the pure honor and glory of victory." That journal also praised cricket's democratizing influences: "On the cricket-field . . . we can waive, for awhile, the precedence of wealth and position."[35] Queen emphasized that a man who joined a club "at once enlarges the sphere of his business acquaintance," while gaining friends who would remember him after his death. He also believed that athletics would not foster dissipation and disorder but rather would promote law and stability in society.[36]

Industrialization, transportation and communication innovations, urbanization, and a new positive ideology of athletics—these were the preconditions for the rise of modern cricket and baseball in nineteenth-century America. By the 1850s they were all present in the largest American metropolitan centers as well as in many of the lesser cities and towns across the country. What remains to be explained is the exact timing for the appearance of adult ball playing by the masses. While a few sportsmen founded cricket and baseball clubs during the 1830s and 1840s in several communities, the vast majority of residents had no interest in either pastime. That state of affairs changed dramatically after 1855, as a cricket mania swept Philadelphia and a baseball craze engulfed New York, Brooklyn, the adjoining counties in northern New Jersey, Westchester, Long Island, and the Boston vicinity.

The year 1857 was a particularly critical one for the expansion of ball playing in each of these regions. Why that season witnessed the phenomenal growth of both sports (but especially baseball) remains a mystery. Perhaps all of the critical factors discussed here simply came together at that time, or perhaps the business depression of that year played some decisive role. One could speculate that the economic slowdown idled many merchants, managers, and artisans, who chose to spend some of their unwanted free time on ball fields. For whatever reasons, men who had enjoyed premodern pastimes as youngsters now decided that they could amuse themselves playing cricket and baseball as adults. Within a few short years what had been a novelty became commonplace: grown men competing on baseball diamonds and cricket pitches.

Economic, social, urban, technological, and ideological forces continued to shape the development of both team sports after their first growth spurts of the late 1850s. Yet it should be emphasized that the future of cricket and baseball in the United States depended not only on these external factors but also (and, perhaps, more important) on the institutional requirements and the peculiar nature of each sport. The following chapters present a narrative and an interpretation of the major features of each pastime. While cricket and baseball shared many characteristics, they differed markedly in their respective degrees of popularity and modernization. Social forces combined with the unique qualities of each to determine their respective fates in nineteenth-century America.

NOTES

1. Newspaper clipping, July 4, 1867, Henry Chadwick's scrapbooks, vol. 11, Albert G. Spalding Collection, New York Public Library.

2. Quoted in Albert G. Spalding, *America's National Game* (New York, 1911), 41–42.

3. Quoted in *Ball Players' Chronicle,* December 26, 1867, 2.

4. Quoted in Dale Somers, *The Rise of Sports in New Orleans, 1850–1900* (Baton Rouge, La., 1972), 48; quoted in *New York Clipper* (hereafter cited as *Clipper*) 6 (September 18, 1858): 172; *Harper's Weekly* 3 (October 15, 1859): 658; (November 5, 1859): 707. Melvin Adelman agrees with the view that ball playing was not a main American sport prior to 1840. He points to the weakness of the kind of ritualistic, deferential, traditional, and communal society that had fostered ball playing in the Old World. He also notes the absence of a landed gentry and a feudal shire system, which seem to have promoted these amusements in England. See *A Sporting Time: New York City and the Rise of Modern Athletics, 1820–70* (Urbana, Ill., 1986), 97–100.

While it appears that England had a stronger tradition of ball playing than did the United States before 1840, there is much evidence that such recreation was more common among American youth and adults than Adelman and other historians suggest. While communal activities and rituals were less important in America than in England, there was a tradition in the United States of ball playing on election and fast days and at barn raisings. For examples of youngsters and adults playing early versions of baseball during the era from 1800 to 1840, see Robert W. Henderson, *Ball, Bat, and Bishop* (New York, 1947), 146–60. See also Jennie Holliman, *American Sports: 1785–1835* (Durham, N.C., 1931), 64–68; Harold Seymour, "How Baseball Began," *New-York Historical Society Quarterly* 40 (October 1956): 369–85; Samuel Hopkins Adams, *Grandfather Stories* (New York, 1955), 143–56. A type of baseball played in Oxford County, Ontario, Canada, in 1838 had two characteristics that are strikingly similar to the version developed by the New York Knickerbockers in 1845. Both games separated fair and foul territory and placed the batter and home base at the same spot. See Robert K. Barney and Nancy B. Bouchier, "The Baseball Reminiscence of Adam E. Ford: A Source Analysis" (paper presented at the conference of the North American Society for Sport History, Columbus, Ohio, May 1987).

5. Several sport scholars have adapted the ideas of Max Weber to develop models that identify the characteristics of premodern and modern sport. I synthesize their formulation with my own. See Eric Dunning, "The Structural-Functional Properties of Folk-Games and Modern Sports: A Sociological Analysis," *Sportwissenschaft* 3 (1973): 215–32; Allen Guttmann, *From Ritual to Record: The Nature of Modern Sports* (New York, 1978), 15–55; Alan G. Ingham, "Methodology in the Sociology of Sport: From Symptoms of a Malaise to Weber for a Cure," *Quest* 31 (1979): 187–215; Adelman, *A Sporting Time,* 5–6.

6. Adelman's *A Sporting Time* is the most thorough and sophisticated work that applies the modernization model to the rise of modern sport in nineteenth-century America. It is particularly strong in its descriptions of the characteristics of various recreations at different stages of their transition into modern sport. For thoughtful critiques of modernization theory, see Raymond Grew, "Modernization and Its Discontents," *American Behavioral Scientist* 21 (November/December 1977): 289–312; Raymond Grew, "More on Modernization," *Journal of Social History* 14 (Winter 1980): 179–87; Peter N. Stearns, "Modernization and Social History: Some Suggestions, and a muted Cheer," *Journal of Social History* 14 (Winter 1980): 189–209.

7. Michael R. Marrus, ed., *The Emergence of Leisure* (New York, 1974); Keith Thomas, "Work and Leisure in Pre-Industrial Society," *Past and Present* 29 (1964): 50–66; "Work and Leisure in Industrial Society: A Conference Report," *Past and Present* 30 (1965): 96–103; Sebastian

de Gazia, *Of Time, Work, and Leisure* (Garden City, N.Y., 1964); E. P. Thompson, "Time, Work-Discipline, and Industrial Capitalism," *Past and Present* 38 (1967): 56–97.

8. For further discussion of the ideas in this and the preceding three paragraphs, see Sean Wilentz, *Chants Democratic: New York City and the Rise of the American Working Class, 1788–1850* (New York, 1984), chap. 3; Steven J. Ross, *Workers on the Edge: Work, Leisure, and Politics in Industrializing Cincinnati, 1788–1890* (New York, 1985), chaps. 5, 7; Susan Hirsch, *Roots of the American Working Class: The Industrialization of Crafts in Newark, 1800–1860* (Philadelphia, 1978), chap. 2.

9. John R. Betts, "The Technological Revolution and the Rise of Sport, 1850–1900," *Mississippi Valley Historical Review* 40 (September 1953): 231–56; "Sporting Journalism in Nineteenth-Century America," *American Quarterly* 5 (1953): 39–56.

10. Stephen Hardy, "The City and the Rise of American Sport: 1820–1920," *Exercise and Sport Sciences Reviews* 9 (1981): 183–219; *How Boston Played: Sport, Recreation, and Community, 1865–1915* (Boston, 1982), chap. 1; Louis Wirth, "Urbanism as a Way of Life," *American Journal of Sociology* 44 (July 1938): 1–24; Oscar Handlin, "The Modern City as a Field of Historical Study," in Oscar Handlin and John Burchard, eds., *The Historian and the City* (Cambridge, Mass., 1963), 1–26; Allan R. Pred, *Urban Growth and the Circulation of Information: The United States System of Cities, 1790–1840* (Cambridge, Mass., 1973); *Urban Growth and City-Systems in the United States, 1840-1860* (Cambridge, Mass., 1980).

11. Adelman, *A Sporting Time,* 7.

12. Benjamin G. Rader, "The Quest for Subcommunities and the Rise of American Sport," *American Quarterly* 29 (1977): 355–69.

13. Arthur H. Cole, "Perspectives on Leisure-Time Business," *Explorations in Entrepreneurial History* (2d ser.) 1 (supplement; 1964): 1–38; Fritz Redlich, "Leisure-Time Activities: A Historical, Sociological, and Economic Analysis," *Explorations in Entrepreneurial History* (2d ser.) 3 (1965): 3–24; Dale Somers, "The Leisure Revolution: Recreation in the American City, 1820–1920," *Journal of Popular Culture* 5 (Summer 1971): 125–47; Foster Rhea Dulles, *A History of Recreation: America Learns to Play,* 2d ed. (New York, 1965).

14. For further discussion of the ideas in this and the preceding paragraph, see Daniel Boorstin, *The Americans: The National Experience* (New York, 1965); Richard Wade, *The Urban Frontier* (Chicago, 1964).

15. *Clipper* 7 (December 3, 1859): 258. For a more detailed analysis of the press and the ideology of modern sport, see Adelman, *A Sporting Time,* 269–86.

16. *Harper's Weekly* 3 (October 15, 1859): 658.
17. *New York Times,* October 11, 1859.
18. John R. Betts, "American Medical Thought on Exercise as the Road to Health, 1820–1860," *Bulletin of the History of Medicine* 45 (1971): 138–45; "Mind and Body in Early American Thought," *Journal of American History* 54 (March 1968): 787–805; Guy Lewis, "The Muscular Christianity Movement," *Journal of Health, Physical Education and Recreation* 37 (May 1966): 27–42; John A. Lucas, "A Prelude to the Rise of Sport: Antebellum America, 1850–1860," *Quest* 11 (December 1968): 50–57; Roberta Park, "The Attitudes of Leading New England Transcendentalists toward Healthful Exercise, Active Recreations and Proper Care of the Body: 1830–1860," *Journal of Sport History* 4 (Spring 1977): 34–50; Peter Levine, "The Promise of Sport in Antebellum America," *Journal of American Culture* 2 (Winter 1980): 623–34.
19. See Hardy, *How Boston Played,* chaps. 2, 3.
20. Thomas W. Higginson, "Saints and Their Bodies," *Atlantic Monthly* 1 (March 1858): 582–95; Lucas, "Prelude to the Rise of Sport," 54–55; *Clipper* 6 (April 24, 1858): 4; (June 26, 1858): 25; *Porter's Spirit of the Times* (hereafter cited as *Porter's Spirit*) 4 (April 24, 1858): 117.
21. Newspaper clipping entitled "A Sermon on Baseball," undated, Chadwick's scrapbooks, vol. 5.
22. *Clipper* 7 (August 27, 1859): 148; (February 18, 1860): 348.
23. Quoted in the *Spirit of the Times* (hereafter cited as *Spirit*) 28 (March 27, 1858): 78.
24. *Clipper* 7 (November 19, 1859): 242.
25. *Clipper* 5 (October 31, 1857): 220. See also *New York Times,* August 11, 1859.
26. Quoted in *Clipper* 5 (May 30, 1857): 42.
27. Quoted in *Spirit* 28 (March 27, 1858): 78.
28. *Porter's Spirit* 5 (November 27, 1858): 196.
29. *Clipper* 5 (August 29, 1857): 148; (December 12, 1857): 268.
30. *Jersey City Daily Courier and Advertiser,* September 20, 1860.
31. *Clipper* 5 (May 30, 1857): 42; 6 (April 24, 1858): 4.
32. *Porter's Spirit* 2 (June 20, 1857): 245.
33. *Clipper* 7 (April 30, 1859): 12; newspaper clipping entitled "A Sermon on Baseball," undated, Chadwick's scrapbooks, vol. 10.
34. Quoted in *Porter's Spirit* 2 (May 30, 1857): 19.
35. *Porter's Spirit* 6 (May 14, 1859): 164.
36. *Clipper* 7 (April 23, 1859): 4; 7 (April 30, 1859): 12.

CHAPTER

2

Early American Cricket

ALTHOUGH a few cricket clubs were organized in the British colonies and during the inaugural decades of the new republic,[1] the sport's modern era in America did not really begin until the 1830s. Several groups in the Albany (N.Y.) vicinity played earlier formal matches,[2] but the St. George Cricket Club of Manhattan, founded in 1838, claimed to be the first regular outfit governed by rules and regulations. During the fall of 1838, several sides of Englishmen resident in New York and Brooklyn played two matches that led to the founding of the St. George club. On September 20, former residents of Nottingham and Sheffield contested at Brooklyn for a stake of $100; on October 22 and 23, eleven cricketers from the New York Cricket Club traveled to Brooklyn to play eleven Long Islanders and won $500.[3] One account of the origins of the St. George club gives its birthdate as July 1838 and lists this New York victory as the Dragon Slayers' first match. The club was more formally organized in 1839 and was finally christened on St. George's Day (April 23) in 1840, in the rear of a tavern on the old Bloomingdale Road in Manhattan.[4]

In the spring of 1844 the St. George club found itself with a new rival in the field, the New York Cricket Club. John Richards, the English-born publisher of the *Spirit of the Times,* was the club's founding father and his editor, William T. Porter, served as the club's first president. They recruited many members from the *Spirit*'s staff and others from New York's literary and artistic communities. Thanks to the generosity of John C. Stevens, the club secured a fine playing ground near Hoboken's Elysian Fields across the Hudson River in New Jersey. Soon it boasted fifty members and within a few years began an intense rivalry with the Dragon Slayers for cricketing supremacy in New York.[5]

Although New York and its neighboring cities dominated American cricket during the sport's formative years,[6] Philadelphia was destined to become the cricket capital of the United States. Natives of the City of Brotherly Love were treated to cricket demonstrations by groups of affluent and working-class Englishmen. As early as 1831, several members of the Tichnor family played on a ground on the west bank of the Schuylkill River. A few years later a group of mechanics competed on the Kensington commons. About 1840 a party of hosiery weavers at Wakefield Mills scheduled matches on Whitmonday, holidays, and Saturday afternoons. The Union Cricket Club, founded in 1843 when Robert Waller of the St. George club moved to Philadelphia and brought together several English importers, a few Kensington men, and a sprinkling of American townball players, was the first to play on its own specially leveled and turfed ground, at Camden, New Jersey. Although businessmen dominated the new outfit, it also enlisted several respected mechanics, including a saw maker, a frame smith, and a wood turner.[7] This mixture of white- and blue-collar workers was unusual for antebellum American clubs but is understandable considering the short supply of cricket talent in the area.

The Union club followed many of the English customs connected with cricket, such as sending out invitations for interclub contests and providing tent accommodations for ladies and collations for players on match days. These Philadelphia sportsmen did break with one important English custom in that they did not, "as a Club, *under any circumstances,* engage in a game of Cricket where there [was] a *single dollar* at stake," although they knew that their matches stimulated considerable private wagering. When a combined squad of Union and St. George men challenged a Canadian team in 1846, they refused to play for money, but their opponents were "well aware, from private information, that 'considerable blunt' [would] be sported on the occasion by friends of the combined clubs."[8]

William Carvill, a gardener, encouraged an interest in cricket among students at Haverford College in Pennsylvania as early as 1834. This club, probably the first composed entirely of Americans, lasted only a few years, but the college fielded two new elevens in 1848. The Union club gave a big boost to the future of the game in the United States when it sponsored the Junior Cricket Club at the University of Pennsylvania in the mid-1840s. The older Union players recruited William Rotch Wister, then a student at the university, who rounded up about forty fellow scholars. For an annual fee of fifty dollars, these young men sublet the Union's clubhouse and playing ground for one afternoon a week. In 1845 they played a series of matches with another junior club, this one led by John Wister and composed of young schoolboys and the sons of local English weavers.[9]

These bright beginnings for Philadelphia cricket soon dimmed, for the Union club vanished after the 1846 season, a victim of financial problems and dissension among members. When Robert Waller returned to New York, the club lost one of its driving forces. Also, most of the active players were of "humble circumstances," and the club incurred debts it was unable or unwilling to pay. To make matters worse, sharp conflicts appeared between men from the north and south of England, who sometimes resorted to "hard blows" to resolve their differences. With the loss of its patron and ground, the Junior Cricket Club also disbanded, in Wister's words, "to the sincere rejoicing of the fathers of most of the members, who, while tolerating the game, yet constantly dreaded that their sons might be carried by it into dissipation."[10] For the next seven years small groups of cricketers kept the sport alive with informal play in Germantown and Kensington, joined by pioneering sportsmen in several cities in the Northeast, South, and West.

A new era of American cricket dawned in 1854 when a few gentlemen launched the Philadelphia Cricket Club. These sportsmen, who had been playing Saturday scrub matches, decided that to enjoy their favorite pastime to the fullest they required a more formal structure, including a regular schedule of practice and intrasquad and interclub competition and a better playing field. To this end they founded the Philadelphia club at William R. Wister's office. A revived Germantown club appeared six months later, composed of young men who were at least sixteen years old. In 1855, when the members of the Germantown club denied admission to their younger brothers and friends, the upstarts launched the Young America club, which soon grew into a powerhouse of juvenile cricket.[11]

During the two decades that preceded the Civil War, enthusiasts for American cricket promoted their pastime throughout the United States. To assess their efforts and to survey the status of the sport and its geographical extent as of 1860, it is necessary to focus on five key factors: geographical mobility and the willingness of the English immigrants to teach cricket to younger and older Americans; the New York City sporting journals and the local dailies; intercity competition; the New York City cricket conventions; and special all-star and international matches. As a result of these forces, American cricket showed considerable strength on the eve of the great sectional conflict, even as it faced some serious internal problems and a powerful rival in the upstart sport of American baseball.

Many of the Englishmen who founded the first American cricket clubs were merchants, professionals, or representatives of their government. A love of cricket, coupled with a high degree of personal mobility, motivated them to assist in the formation of new clubs and to teach novices. Robert Waller of the St. George club was instrumental in founding Philadelphia's Union Club in 1843, while two other Dragon Slayers, Robert Bage and George Wheatcroft, organized a group of skilled craftsmen into the Newark Cricket Club in 1845. George Aitken, the British consul in San Francisco, founded that city's first modern sporting organization in March 1852 when he launched the San Francisco Cricket Club. Several British players helped in the formation of the Lowell (Mass.) club, whose secretary wrote in 1857 that "we Americans never saw a game of cricket played, and knew nothing of it, until we formed a club and got some Englishmen to learn us."[12] And sometimes elevens were formed by club members who found it more convenient to play closer to home, such as the Dorchester (Mass.) club, which was "one of the satellites of the Boston club." Members of the latter "residing in the environs of the city, [liked] to have cricket at home, so [started] clubs on their own hooks."[13]

During the 1850s several prominent cricketers headed west to seek their fortunes and to play the game of cricket in their spare time. William M. Bradshaw of Philadelphia moved to Cincinnati, John Hardcastle of King's County (Brooklyn) played in St. Louis, and Harry Groom and George Stead made it all the way to San Francisco.[14] In reporting an 1857 California contest, the *Clipper* pointed out that "one or two of the players have often hurled the leather and wielded the bat on the favorite play ground at Hoboken."[15]

The admirers of cricket realized that the future of the sport in America rested with the younger generation of Americans, but they had to contend with the prevailing attitude that exercise and sport did not mix with education. A few British and American schoolteachers boldly introduced the game to their pupils, perhaps led by S. R. Calthrop, an immigrant from Cambridge, England, who founded a boarding school in Bridgeport, Connecticut, where he used cricket as part of the curriculum to build character in his charges. His object was "not to make mere bookworms of his boys, but to make men of them—men of courage, coolness, patience, endurance." He had faith that "the best cricketer in his school will be likely to excell also in all other things."[16]

Some senior cricketers tried to foster a love of the game among boys and young men by admitting them as limited, nonvoting members of their clubs. The 1854 constitution of the Philadelphia Cricket Club provided that "persons under the age of twenty-one years may be elected Junior Members," exempt from the obligation of an entrance fee and not allowed to vote or hold office but still liable for special assessments. In May 1858 the New York Cricket Club established a "Novitate's Eleven" for lads under the age of eighteen. The Brooklyn Cricket Club followed suit, organizing a "Junior Class" for youths under eighteen, who paid less than one-half the regular dues. The St. George Cricket Club also sponsored a junior eleven. In 1861 the New York Cricket Club organized matches for youngsters who were at least seven years old, with instruction provided. In general, however, the New York City region lagged far behind both Philadelphia and New Jersey in popularizing cricket among its youth, partly due to the habit of permitting older, more experienced players to dominate batting practice during club play days. Although this helped the first-eleven cricketers prepare for interclub contests, it limited a novice's chance to learn the sport well enough to become addicted to it.[17]

While English and American-born cricketers spread their gospel across the land, daily and weekly newspapers gave valuable coverage to America's first modern team sport. Local periodicals provided only limited announcements and results for hometown clubs, but the New York City sporting journals granted extensive space to cricket news. John Richards's *Spirit of the Times* nurtured American cricket during its infancy, while he and William Porter led the New York Cricket Club to a prominent position among the city's sporting crowd. During the 1850s the *Clipper* and Richards's, Porter's, and George Wilkes's versions of the *Spirit* published editorials extolling the merits of the game, announcements of upcoming contests, detailed stories and box scores, names of club officers, official rules of the Marylebone Cricket Club of London (the powerful governing institution of English cricket), model constitutions and bylaws,[18] summaries of the proceedings of the annual cricket conventions, and year-end reviews of club records as well as batsmen's and bowlers' averages.

New York City's sporting journals also tried to promote the regional spread of cricket throughout the South and West, with mixed results. A case in point is Frank Queen's efforts to popularize the sport in Richmond, Virginia, in 1857.[19] Local players did form a cricket club that year, but it was apparently defunct in 1858. Meanwhile, the New York weeklies applauded the introduction of cricket into Baltimore, New Orleans, St. Louis, Chicago, Detroit, Milwaukee, San Francisco, and numerous other towns across America.[20]

Although these journals' publishers and editors sincerely wished to encourage wholesome and healthy amusements in America, they also had a material interest in the rise of modern sport: namely, they knew that sportsmen enjoyed seeing their names and exploits in print, and that cricket and baseball reports boosted subscriptions to their publications. Queen served his readers in Philadelphia by printing numerous pieces on local cricketers, including the results of boys' street games. When one reader questioned whether these informal affairs deserved such attention, Queen encouraged the youngsters to "send on their scores . . . for their publication gives additional interest to their games" and might help to recruit "some valuable acquisitions to the ranks of cricketers."[21] Most cricket and baseball clubs showed their appreciation with special toasts to the press at club dinners. It was customary on these occasions for a representative of a daily or weekly newspaper to respond to the toast with a speech that invariably complimented the members and praised the virtues of their sporting endeavors.[22]

The box scores and year-end statistics published by the various New York papers are especially significant for two reasons. First, they reveal the high degree of modernization achieved by American cricket before the Civil War. Second, they indicate the cricketers' interest in comparative performances and improvement of their skills. The *Spirit* published English and a few New York averages during the 1840s,[23] while all of the journals showed a more scientific approach to sport statistics by the late 1850s. In May 1857, for example, the *Clipper* called itself the "cricketers' chronicle" and invited club secretaries to forward all match results so that the paper could compile this data "in a systematic manner." That year the *Clipper* also prepared a form for use in the preparation of key statistics and printed a comparison of English and American batsmen's and bowler's averages. Although they conceded the obvious problems in comparing these numbers, the editors hoped that such a study would encourage American cricketers to copy the English and to correct their deficiencies.[24] Thus, before 1861 American cricketers clearly displayed a fascination with statistics and an urge to set and break records—two key characteristics of modern sport.

Most newspapers claimed to be neutral in their accounts of sports, and it did make good business sense not to take sides in interclub disputes. But there were some journals that favored or criticized certain clubs. The *Spirit* naturally leaned toward the New York Cricket Club, especially when it engaged its arch-rival, the Dragon Slayers. The most serious feud between a sporting paper and a cricket club reached a peak in 1860, when the *Clipper* repeatedly criticized the St. George club for what it deemed its exclusiveness and lack of cooperation in promoting American cricket. It censured the club's managers for allowing "the prejudices and partiality of the few, to control the opinions of many," and, while claiming to be impartial, pointedly noted, "It is not to be presumed that we are to shower praise upon those who are forever trying their best to injure us by their constant abuse of our paper."[25] The sporting press sometimes exhibited the partisan spirit that was so characteristic of mid-nineteenth-century journalism, but the weeklies generally printed far more words of praise and encouragement than of censure.

While the New York City periodicals advertised the benefits of cricket, they also helped to foster intercity competitions that stimulated the founding of new clubs and heightened interest in the sport. The keen rivalry between the St. George club and Philadelphia's Union club, begun in the mid-1840s, intensified during the 1850s. Other teams from New York, Brooklyn, Philadelphia, and Boston traveled throughout the Northeast to engage their respective adversaries. After the Brooklyn Star Club defeated a Syracuse eleven at the loser's ground in 1846, "a few spirited old cricketers" invited them to stop off at Utica (N.Y.) on their return trip. After a day's play the Uticans organized their own club "and requested the Brooklynites to christen 'the baby,' which they did, by the very appropriate name of 'Star of the West.'" The Brooklyn team disbanded after a few years, but in 1851 a Utica player reported that "her child in the West still shines on in her brilliant career, eclipsing all the other little orbs around, and throwing them entirely into the shade."[26] The Utica club carried on the series with Syracuse begun by the Brooklyn eleven.

The West also had many intercity cricket matches, which both reflected and intensified that region's traditions of urban rivalry and boosterism. In 1846 the *Spirit* remarked, in reporting an intracity Cincinnati contest, "if Pittsburgh, Louisville, Dayton, or any of the western villages could raise a club and play Cincinnati, the game would be much more exciting."[27] During the 1850s cricketers pitched wickets in the West for clubs representing Cleveland, Pittsburgh, Chicago, Cincinnati, and Milwaukee, among others. An 1853 encounter between two Chicago and Milwaukee clubs prompted spokesmen for each city to reflect upon the value of the sport for the townspeople and the cities. The Chicagoan praised the health and moral advantages of cricket but noted that the local club was not as well supported by the city's leading citizens as was the Milwaukee club. "Now, Chicago claims to be a little ahead of anything in the West for enterprise," he wrote, "and why let Milwaukee outstrip her in this one thing." A *Milwaukee Sentinel* editor also endorsed the physical and mental benefits of the sport and elaborated on another reason for supporting the local cricket club: "Every match which our Milwaukee Club has played has been duly chronicled in the *Sentinel,* thence transferred to the N.Y. *Spirit of the Times,* and been copied, in many instances, from that paper into the English Journals. All of this helps not a little to keep our city before the public, and our Cricket Club is one of the attractions which draws emigrants from Old England hither; as our Musical Society does many Germans."[28] Local boosters were enthusiastic about sporting events that might give some free publicity and perhaps a competitive edge to their hometowns in the struggle for supremacy among frontier communities.

While these intercity challenges demonstrated the potential for the growth of American cricket in the mid-nineteenth century, the game's advocates realized the need for a national association that would nurture and promote cricket throughout the United States. From 1857 to 1860 the leaders of American cricket held a series of conventions in New York City that aimed at creating such an organization. It was an ambitious and important undertaking, and the difficulties encountered reflected many of the problems of early American cricket. William Lacy of Albany and Thomas Facon of Philadelphia called the first session with the hope that the delegates would "centralize the game of cricket, and . . . give it a truly national scope." *Porter's Spirit* believed it likely "that there [would] soon be formed a State Central or U.S. Central Club, which [would] act as the Grand Umpire and law-giver for the sport throughout the country, after a fashion of the Marylebone Club in England."[29]

While the delegates obviously looked to the great English club as a model, they were also willing to discuss "what measures [might] be most suitable for the furtherance of the game of cricket among Americans." The *Clipper* praised the inaugural meeting as "the first important step towards placing the noble game on a sure and permanent basis in America." It noted with pleasure that "we shall now have a source of authority to be looked up to as the representative of the great cricket fraternity" and anticipated the time "when the game, to some extent, [would] be adopted as one of our national sports, and form one of the connecting links of that bond of brotherhood which ought to exist between the sons of old England and Young America."[30] Expectations were high and prospects seemed bright for the growth of England's national pastime on this side of the Atlantic.

The first cricket convention in 1857 addressed the sensitive subject of adapting the sport to conditions in the United States. Daniel W. Baker, an American-born cricketer and former president of the Newark (N.J.) club, explained that "there were many things connected with the game which Americans could not understand. They knew only that it was an English game, and that was enough not to touch it." He wanted to "Americanize it—to make it an American game," and he expected the following year's meeting to adopt "some plan by which we also might have our Marylebone Club, or supreme power, to devise and arrange laws for the government of the game in America." But his proposal met a cool reception, as several men objected to any alteration of the rules of the Marylebone club, as if by changing anything "the game would cease to be cricket."[31] Indeed, this feeling was so strong that *Porter's Spirit,* in announcing the 1858 meeting, declared: "We cannot . . . see how a convention can form a better set of the Laws of Cricket, than those of the Marylebone Club. If they should succeed in reforming or improving the code for this meridian, how can they induce the clubs at a distance to adopt the amendments." Baker himself seconded a motion, which was unanimously approved at the 1858 convention, to adopt the Marylebone code as the standard for American cricket.[32]

Many American cricketers, Baker among them, were less concerned with changing the laws of cricket than with revising some of the local customs of selecting participants for interclub matches. They did not approve of any club's use of professionals, but they were more upset about "the unfair custom of cricketers, who belonged to different clubs, for the purpose of playing in matches." Baker pointed out that the practice of permitting multiple-club membership created a monopoly by the few talented players and that "clubs were never certain whom they had to play against." In 1858 the convention delegates agreed to exchange club membership rosters, from which the contending elevens would be chosen one week prior to a match. On a related point, they required that professionals be played as such, not as members of clubs for which they were engaged.[33]

These conventions served the needs of cricketers from the Middle Atlantic region but failed to create a truly national organization to nurture the English pastime in other parts of the country. Participants were most successful in appointing the committees that picked the players for the all-star events of each season. The two most important of these were the match in which eighteen Americans challenged eleven Englishmen, normally scheduled for June or early July, and the international contest between Canada and the United States, usually held in August. In truth, these special events primarily served the cricketers of New York, Philiadelphia, and vicinity.[34] Several delegates lobbied unsuccessfully for an East-West challenge, including H. A. Bury of Cleveland, who in 1858 proposed an annual intersectional match with professionals barred and alternate games in Chicago and Hoboken. He argued that railroad fare discounts and playing only one match a year would save expenses, but the convention delegates rejected his plan as "inexpedient." W. H. Coolidge, president of the Union Cricket Club of Cincinnati, charged that the convention did little if anything to benefit the game in the West and, angered by the decision to meet again in New York in 1859, suggested a more central location for the group's deliberations.[35]

Increasing controversy and dissatisfaction marked the last two cricket conventions before the Civil War. The leading issue at the 1859 meeting was the efforts of the Brooklyn club to resolve a bitter dispute between the New York and St. George clubs. That feud resulted from a disagreement over whether an 1857 match should have been completed on its second day after the appointed time for suspension of play had been passed. Several members of the Brooklyn club believed that the convention delegates had the power and the duty to resolve this pernicious quarrel, which they felt had "done more to prejudice the course of Cricket in this vicinity than would the total abolishment of both the clubs." They asked that the delegates hear each side's case, take a vote, and render a binding decision. The proposal was rejected, prompting one Brooklyn delegate to accuse them of being afraid that "one of their mighty clubs would frown upon them for daring to discuss a subject, when it was the wish of the Great Moguls of Cricket that it should be laid upon the table." The *Clipper* countered that by avoiding the question the convention prevented a disgruntled faction from destroying the entire group.[36]

The situation was worse in 1860, when the convention deteriorated into several heated exchanges between the officers of the St. George, the New York, and other clubs. Robert Waller of the Dragon Slayers opened the session by moving to abolish its constitutional rule for an annual meeting and then declared that his club would no longer participate in "any amalgamated matches," including the annual Canada contest. A dispute erupted over a proposal to change the special match between English and American cricketers to eleven on each side, with all professionals barred, and then digressed into a discussion of the role of professional cricketers and the St. George club's policy of charging an admission fee for matches at its newly enclosed ground. Waller argued that his club instituted these changes to support the professionals he believed were essential to the future of American cricket. Henry Sharp, a former president of the New York club, attacked these innovations as "striking at the very root of the prosperity of cricket . . . by checking public interest in the game." James Higham, another prominent New Yorker, pointed out that "nothing was ever heard of this suddenly manifested deep interest in the welfare of professional cricketers, on the part of the St. George's, previous to their obtaining their new enclosed ground."[37] The *Clipper* joined in criticizing America's premier club, accusing some of its members of "having a great desire to obtain a controlling influence in all matters appertaining to cricket" and argued that the Dragon Slayers' enclosed ground and full treasury proved that they were too exclusive and not sufficiently interested in promoting American cricket.[38]

In evaluating the overall record of these New York–based cricket conventions, it is apparent that, while they did arrange several successful all-star contests, they did not introduce any distinctive American adaptations to the sport nor generate additional interest in the game outside of New York and Philadelphia. Their inability to soothe the acrimony between the New York and St. George clubs was probably the delegates' biggest failure. Also, none of the conventions attracted sufficient representation to justify any claim to being a national body. In 1859 one critic called that year's meeting "a farce," in part because it was composed of only twelve clubs, including seven from the New York City vicinity, with seventeen of thirty-five delegates from the St. George or New York clubs. He asked, "Does any sane person call this a general convention of Cricketers of the United States?"[39] The 1860 meeting, which drew delegates from eighteen clubs (ten from the New York area, two from Albany, and six from Philadelphia), ended in dissension. Had the Civil War not intervened, the group would have met in Philadelphia in May 1861, where the *Clipper* predicted it would achieve permanency in its new home "and be properly conducted . . . which . . . cannot be justly said of it hitherto."[40]

While these cricket conventions did not achieve all of their goals, the special events they arranged attracted players and other enthusiasts and did much to popularize the sport in the United States before the Civil War. As American-born cricketers became more prominent, they began to schedule all-native contests to show that they could play a tolerable standard of cricket without the assistance of Englishmen. In August 1854 the Newark club arranged the first exclusively American match, splitting a home-and-home series with the New York club. The *Spirit* praised the New Jerseyans, gratified to see that "this English game, like most other good English customs, has now gained a permanent footing in this country."[41] By the late 1850s many of the prominent clubs had all-native elevens, which played intrasquad contests against their English clubmates and also challenged American elevens of rival organizations.[42]

By 1856 there were sufficient skill and interest among hometown players for an all-star challenge match between eighteen Americans and eleven Englishmen. In spite of their numerical advantage, the Americans lost the first four annual matches, prompting *Porter's Spirit* to suggest, no doubt facetiously, that the next game be played with even sides, as "a defeat under such circumstances would not be accompanied with the unpleasant associations it is with eighteen in the field."[43] The Americans achieved their first triumph on July 4–5, 1860, at Philadelphia, with a side that included seventeen young cricketers from that region and one from Amsterdam, New York. The *Clipper* reported the triumph with pride but also noted its preference for even sides, stating that "we had better suffer defeat under such circumstances than win with odds in our favor."[44]

While the American versus English matches highlighted the late 1850s, the premier event each season was the annual United States versus Canada contest. This series began in 1840 and was the first international competition in the history of cricket. Since the U.S. representatives were apparently all English-born, it must be conceded that these contests were not strictly between Americans and Canadians. From 1840 to 1846, members of the St. George club, Philadelphia's Union club, and the Toronto and Montreal clubs competed in several contests that generated considerable excitement (and gambling) on both sides of the border. Unfortunately, these events also produced a number of misunderstandings and disagreements. While they clearly demonstrated the willingness of the participants to travel great distances to test their best elevens, they also revealed the ill will that frequently marred early American cricket.

The series got off to an embarrassing start in August 1840 when the St. George club accepted an invitation to journey to Canada to play the Toronto Cricket Club. Upon their arrival the Dragon Slayers discovered that an imposter had issued a bogus challenge. Fortunately, the Toronto club remedied the situation by hastily arranging a match for $250 per side. The trip ended happily for the New York contingent, which won the contest and celebrated with a scrub game and a dinner arranged by their hosts.[45] The Toronto players traveled to New York in September 1843 and defeated the Dragon Slayers.[46] A return match, scheduled for July 1844 in Toronto, never took place. The Toronto club refused to play against the St. George eleven because it included three cricketers from Philadelphia's Union club. Negotiations broke down, and the visitors made the long trip back to New York in disgust. In early August they issued a fresh challenge to "any Eleven Players in Canada . . . for any sum $100 to $1000." The Toronto club accepted, to prove that they had not backed out of the previous match and "to vindicate their good name." They agreed to play for $1,000, which they won in late September on the St. George ground in Manhattan. Several newspapers judged the crowds at 4,000–5,000 persons, with estimates of total bets reaching $50,000.[47]

The two games that were played in 1845 might technically be called the first truly international contests, since both elevens included men from more than one city. Apparently the St. George and Philadelphia cricketers had tasted defeat enough at the hands of Toronto, for they chose to play a side that included mostly men from the Montreal Cricket Club. However, they fared no better, losing both encounters.[48] In the following year, the match at New York ended abruptly in a controversy caused by a fight between opposing players. Samuel Dudson, a "sturdy, strong, and rough" Philadelphia artisan, was knocked down by a Canadian batsman while attempting to catch an opponent's fly ball. Enraged, he threw the ball at the Canadian, with the result that the visitors withdrew from play and refused to finish the match. After the home side claimed victory, some of the Canadians paid their bets under protest. Still, later that day the players dined together, and the *Spirit* reported that "every unfriendly feeling appeared to have been buried, and all was good humor and conviviality." But this ugly incident must have soured many on these international matches, for the series was interrupted for seven years.[49]

U.S.-Canadian matches were resumed in 1853, with the Americans winning five of seven contests through 1860 (there was no match in 1855). These events generated more publicity and drew larger crowds than any other cricket contest, with the exception of the all-England visit in 1859.[50] Unlike the encounters of the 1840s, they were relatively free of ill will on the part of the contestants, although there was considerable disagreement on both sides of the border over the selection of the respective elevens. In Canada, bad feeling between the Toronto and Montreal clubs led to the exclusion of all of the eastern (Lower Canada) cricketers in 1858 and 1859. In the United States, the feud between the New York and St. George clubs ended in a partial boycott by the Dragon Slayers in those same two years. St. George cricketers refused to participate "as a club" but did permit a few members to play as individuals. The Montreal and St. George clubs staged an alternative international match in 1860, with a few outsiders participating to lend it an all-star flavor.[51] As always, the Dragon Slayers' sharpest critic was the *Clipper*, which gloated over the United States victories, gained without the support of America's oldest cricket club, and scolded the club members for their lack of courtesy toward the Canadians. The editors hoped that the St. George club had been taught a lesson, "that cricket matches of the *best description* can be arranged, and carried out" without its assistance.[52]

Also at issue was the composition of the United States eleven, especially the nationality of participants. Only a few American-born cricketers played for the United States in the 1859 contest.[53] The annual convention's selection committee picked five Americans from the Philadelphia vicinity for the 1860 challenge, and their participation gave the United States victory a more native flavor. The *Clipper* pointedly observed that the removal of the influence of the St. George club brought about a more liberal policy toward choosing Americans: "American cricket . . . stands fairer and higher, and more independent at the close of this match than at any previous hour of its history."[54]

By far, the most celebrated episode in antebellum American cricket was the visit of the All-England Eleven to Hoboken, (N.J.), Philadelphia, and Rochester (N.Y.) in 1859. Competition between the United States and Great Britain was keen throughout the nineteenth century in political and cultural life, and the world of sport and games was no exception. Americans were proud of victories over Englishmen by Commodore John C. Stevens in yachting, Richard Ten Broeck in horse racing, and Paul Morphy in chess. In 1851 the *Spirit* bragged: "We whip the British in most things: they can't reap with us; nor yacht with us; their Australian gold ain't as good as our Californian gold. . . . why should we not be able next season to 'try it on' at cricket?"[55] Rumors began circulating in 1859 of a proposed visit by professional English cricketers, provided that money could be raised to meet their terms. Although Frank Queen was at first outraged at the idea of paying foreigners to come here to play,[56] most sportsmen endorsed the plan. Robert Waller of the St. George club joined with an officer in Montreal to negotiate an agreement with the All-England Eleven. To reduce expenses, Waller subcontracted half of the St. George's share of the expenses to the Philadelphia club. Edwin A. Stevens gave part of his family's estate at Hoboken to the Dragon Slayers for their new ground and raised $2,000 to prepare it for the great match.[57]

As it became clear during the summer of 1859 that the all-England team would in fact cross the Atlantic to play, anticipation reached fever pitch in New York, Philadelphia, and many other cities. The British eleven agreed to play five matches against Canadian and American sides of twenty-two players each, with two contests scheduled in Canada and three in the United States.[58] Proponents of American cricket predicted many positive benefits from this foreign invasion. The *Clipper* stated that the games would improve the Americans' skills, win over baseball players, attract large crowds, popularize cricket in the United States, and advance international goodwill.[59] The *Spirit* noted that "numbers of baseball players are joining Cricket Clubs in order to fully enjoy the great matches." *Wilkes' Spirit* used the visit to propose the creation of an All–United States Eleven, which it felt would stimulate more interest in the sport across the nation.[60] A South Carolinian welcomed competition on the cricket field but hoped that England and America would never again be at war.[61] *Porter's Spirit* predicted victory for the United States, considering its two-to-one advantage in manpower and the quality of its players. *Clipper* editors thought such an outcome was improbable but hoped for an upset, "since it would give a great impetus to cricket in this hemisphere."[62]

The celebrated British athletes arrived in Canada in September, led by their captain, George Parr, known as the best batsman in Great Britain. They opened their tour at Montreal with an easy victory over players from Lower Canada, then journeyed to New York for a match against twenty-two players chosen by the St. George club. Ideal weather and intense interest attracted thousands of spectators to Hoboken's Elysian Fields for the three-day match in early October. While everyone enjoyed a fine spectacle, the United States suffered a crushing defeat, as the Englishmen triumphed by sixty-four runs without even batting in their second innings. The *Clipper* was quick to point out that this "ignominious" setback should not be viewed as an American defeat, for only three of the U.S. cricketers were natives; of the rest, at least half were not even American citizens, "*never having been naturalized,* and probably not having the remotest idea of renouncing their allegiance to the British Crown." Frank Queen sharply criticized the local sportsmen: "In common parlance, the leading players of the

New York and St. George clubs have had the starch taken out of them, completely." He urged them "to go to work in earnest, forget about the past differences, build up their clubs on a permanent footing, eschew all old fogyism and its supporters, and encourage Young America."[63]

The next stop for the Englishmen was the City of Brotherly Love, where the Philadelphia club selected nine New Yorkers and thirteen local players to compete against them. William R. Wister's side, with ten Americans, made the best showing of any of the opponents of the All-England Eleven, losing by only seven wickets. Although poor weather on the first day held down the crowds, a large turnout for the concluding days made the match a financial success. Despite the loss, it was also something of a sporting triumph for the United States' native contingent, who outscored their English teammates. The *Clipper* viewed the result as proof of the superiority of Philadelphia cricketers over "the coxcomb and conceited individuals in New York." While its publisher was certainly biased against the St. George club, he was right when he concluded that Philadelphia had taken "the lead in the United States as the fountain head of cricket." Fred Lillywhite, the captain of the English team, and *Bell's Life in London* also praised the Philadelphians for their skill (especially in fielding), energy, and enthusiasm.[64] After a week's play in Philadelphia, the British continued their circuit of North America with a victory at Hamilton against a western Canadian side. In early November they concluded their sweep with still another lopsided win over a combined United States–Canadian team at Rochester (N.Y.), playing in the cold and snow.[65]

As many had hoped, the skill of the English cricketers did attract the attention of many baseball players. During the latter part of the trip, a delegate from New York's baseball fraternity issued a challenge: that the cricketers play a three-game baseball series against a New York all-star nine. The baseball enthusiasts were willing to raise $5,000 to compensate the Englishmen, but the latter's agents asked for more money and travel expenses, which did not materialize. The cricketers were also reluctant to take on the New Yorkers at their own sport. Lillywhite said that baseball resembled English rounders "as played by school-boys" and observed that the rule that a ball caught on the first bound constituted an out made it "a very childish game." One of the Englishmen explained that they chose not to accept the challenge "on the ground of not being acquainted with [baseball], at the same time offering to engage even in that game if [the Americans] would give them twelve months to practice at it." While in Rochester the All-England Eleven did play a pick-up baseball game with mixed sides that included local players. Shortly thereafter they sailed for home with an unblemished record for their first excursion outside the British Isles.[66]

The all-England visit had an immediate and positive impact on those in America who were already enamoured of the sport, but it is more difficult to determine the long-term effects. The exhibition of skill displayed by the English cricketers impressed the leading New York and Philadelphia clubs, which resumed play in the spring of 1860 with renewed spirit. The club members also benefited from a detailed critique of their play written by one of the visitors and published in March 1860 in *Wilkes' Spirit.* At the twenty-second anniversary dinner of the St. George club, President Robert Bage referred to the recent one-sided defeat as "a gain to the game of cricket." He believed that it showed the Dragon Slayers "what bowling, wicket-keeping, and fielding is" and that it took "the conceit out of us pretty effectually." A Philadelphian wrote: "The visit of the English Eleven has imparted fresh life and vigor to the professors and amateurs of this manly healthy game." Local cricketers diligently worked on the batting and bowling techniques learned from the all-England match. In New York, a number of baseball players joined cricket clubs in 1860, and *Wilkes' Spirit* noted that the success of the English professionals provided some impetus to "our good old national game of Base Ball," encouraging a new proficiency among players, especially in their fielding.[67]

The complete domination by the All-England Eleven and their agents' concern for turning a profit detracted somewhat from the beneficial results of their trip. In Frank Queen's view, "they [had] come, seen, and conquered; and . . . reaped a golden harvest," and he hoped they would return in 1860 without the "speculating agents" from both sides of the Atlantic. Queen believed that the positive benefits of the tour had been largely nullified by the "uniform result" and also "by the exclusive behavior of those who had [the cricketers] in charge."[68] While he was a bit too harsh in his assessment of the representatives of the Montreal and St. George organizations who handled the business aspects of the trip, many others no doubt shared his feeling that there was too much emphasis on making money and not enough amateur spirit in the whole sporting enterprise.[69]

On the eve of the Civil War, then, England's national game had taken root in American soil, though Thomas Dodsworth, speaking at a St. George club anniversary dinner, was probably too optmistic in predicting that "the time will come when every nook and corner of the continent, where the English language is spoken, will have its cricket club; when the lovers of the game will be numbered by tens of thousands."[70] Indeed, the strength of American cricket in 1860 varied considerably from region to region and city to city.

Cricketers had founded clubs throughout New England's factory towns and larger cities during the 1850s, including a few in Maine, New Hampshire, and Rhode Island and many more in Massachusetts and Connecticut. Competition between New York City and Massachusetts clubs excited interest, and the formation of the Boston Cricket Club in 1857 boded well for the game in that area. However, a series of defeats suffered by the Boston club at the hands of Roxbury and Lowell elevens so demoralized its players that dissolution of the club appeared imminent in 1860. But after losing several prominent members, it was saved by a merger with a strong junior outfit, the Bay State club. The newly reorganized group deserted Boston Common for a new ground in East Cambridge and ultimately outlasted all antebellum rivals.[71]

The Middle Atlantic states provided cricket's greatest concentration of activity, as the sport thrived in New York, New Jersey, and Pennsylvania. Upstate New Yorkers from Albany, Utica, Rochester, Syracuse, and other cities emulated their downstate rivals, while across the Hudson River, New Jersey fielded at least two dozen clubs between 1845 and 1860.[72] Manhattan and Staten Island boasted six active clubs in 1860, with Brooklyn and adjacent Long Island adding another half dozen, yet baseball mania threatened to overwhelm cricket completely in the New York City vicinity. As the *Clipper* reported with regret, "the large majority of our ballplayers know as much about cricket as they do hieroglyphics of Egypt, and what is worse, care less if anything."[73]

While cricket in New York City and Brooklyn ranked a distant second in popularity to baseball in 1860, there were some prominent players of the latter sport who wished to see England's national game flourish in the United States. In the fall of that year a few officials of Brooklyn's leading clubs joined with some Long Island cricketers to organize the American Cricket Club of Long Island. The goal of the club's founders was to popularize the sport by speeding up play and inaugurating other changes they believed would attract more Americans to the game. The new club restricted its membership to those who were native-born or who had been permanent residents of the United States since the age of five and were also citizens. It prohibited its members from playing in matches for any other club, "save as representatives of the American club," and pledged itself to play only its own members in its challenges. By rejecting what was then known as the "revolver system," the new club banned a custom still commonplace among English cricketers.[74]

The American club got off to a rousing beginning with forty members enrolled and an inaugural victory over a local eleven of Englishmen. But the outbreak of the Civil War shortened its season of 1861, and the following spring it was forced to suspend several of its rules to prevent dissolution. It now allowed its members to join other elevens and admitted foreign-born members provided they were naturalized U.S. citizens. The club struggled through the summer of 1862, then passed into oblivion, its demise severely retarding the prospects for popularizing cricket among the Brooklyn and New York masses.

Before 1861 Philadelphia had clearly established itself as the cricket capital of the United States, with by far the most clubs and the largest contingent of American-born players. In 1857 an explosion of interest added dozens of elevens to the pioneer organizations of that city. The *Philadelphia Evening Journal* commented on "a perfect mania, now in regard to this game, affecting all ages, from the stripling of a half a dozen years to his greyheaded grandfather." A subscriber to *Porter's Spirit* reported: "The cricket fever is . . . raging in Philadelphia. . . . Everybody plays cricket in Philadelphia from the child to the old man."[75] In that city and its environs, cricket had eclipsed the old game of townball and had not yet been challenged seriously by the New York version of baseball. Cricket had also spread to rural and western Pennsylvania, where it was often a highlight of county fairs.[76]

American cricket caught on below the Mason-Dixon line and beyond the Appalachians before 1860. More than a dozen southern towns produced clubs for at least one season, including Richmond, Baltimore, Savannah, and New Orleans. Baltimore had at least four and perhaps as many as six clubs in 1859, and in New Orleans two sides of the Crescent City Cricket Club played "the first set encounter at the 'noble game' that [had] ever taken place in the extreme South."[77] Cricket was far more prevalent in the West than in the South, with at least twenty-five communities fielding elevens in Ohio, Illinois, Michigan, Wisconsin, Minnesota, Iowa, Kentucky, Missouri, and California. In 1857 *Porter's Spirit* noted that the love of the game had spread with the "advance of civilization" and soon expected that "in the distant regions of Kansas and Nebraska the stumps will be pitched and scores made by the new settlers."[78] Cricket reached the Pacific as early as 1852, and within a few years San Francisco boasted at least three clubs, with a few British diplomats and transplanted easterners leading the way. The Golden State players were too far from the center of cricket to have much impact on the New York and Philadelphia clubs, but the midwestern cricketers did try to influence the easterners. Officials in Cleveland, Cincinnati, and Chicago, who wished to be consulted and included in the conventions as well as the major all-star and international matches, were annoyed when they were ignored or excluded.[79]

Cricketers played in at least twenty-two states and more than 125 cities and towns in the antebellum United States. *Wilkes' Spirit* estimated the number of clubs at 1,000 in 1859, but a more realistic figure would probably be about 500 prior to the Civil War. According to William R. Wister, there were "too many for the good of the game, looking at the expense of procuring a suitable ground and equipping a proper club," and many of them survived only one to three years. *Porter's Spirit* claimed that about 6,000 cricketers lived within one hundred miles of New York City in 1859.[80] If we include those in the Philadelphia area and everyone who played only on practice days, that number is reasonable. Indeed, it is possible that there were 10,000 men and boys in the United

States in 1860 who had played the game actively for at least one season.

Despite its successful beginnings, American cricket faced some serious problems as it concluded the 1860 season. First, the meteoric rise of baseball in Massachusetts and New York overshadowed its progress and limited its chances to recruit large numbers of young people in those states. Furthermore, many citizens still viewed the sport as a disreputable one patronized by gamblers and saloon frequenters. Proof of its continued poor image in the 1850s appears in a few cases where cricketers competed under assumed names. Wister wrote that "the standing of the game was injured by such subterfuge, and the fashion was not followed in Philadelphia." Despite efforts by Wister and others to downplay the wagering on cricket matches, it is clear that the practice persisted on a large scale.[81]

A low standard of play also hurt cricket in America, especially in the area of fielding, which was one of the most attractive features of baseball for spectators. Poor grounds also detracted from the sport's progress, since "to play well on bad ground is an impossibility, and makes cricket positively dangerous. . . . Its scientific points are all but destroyed, thereby, precision and calculation being together out of the question, in every branch of it." To many old-time Englishmen, the tendency of American players to argue with umpires and of clubs to feud with each other was ruining their beloved sport and retarded cricket's growth during its formative years in America.[82]

Thus American cricket had its share of strains and weaknesses that accompanied its impressive development during the antebellum era. Unfortunately for the sport's aficionados, in 1860 the nation was on the brink of a devastating civil war that would profoundly affect cricket's future in the United States.

NOTES

1. In 1809 the Boston Cricket Club played once a week, charged fees, limited its membership to thirty, and regulated its players' behavior, but it apparently did not engage in interclub competition. See *Wilkes' Spirit of the Times* (hereafter cited as *Wilkes' Spirit*) 9 (December 5, 1863): 211.

2. The *Spirit of the Times* reported on a series of contests in 1837 and 1838 among New York elevens from Albany, Schenectady, and Troy. In August 1838 it noted: "A few years since there was a famous Cricket Club in this city, which compromised [*sic*] some of our most eminent citizens, and we should be glad to see it revived." See *Spirit* 7 (September 23, 1837): 249; (October 7, 1837): 272; 8 (August 25, 1838): 220; (September 15, 1838): 246.

3. *Spirit* 8 (October 13, 1838): 278–79; (October 27, 1838): 292; *Clipper* 5 (March 13, 1858): 372.

4. *Porter's Spirit* 6 (March 26, 1859): 52. See also *Albion,* August 29, 1840, 283; William R. Wister, *Some Reminiscences of Cricket in Philadelphia before 1861* (Philadelphia, 1904), 140–41. The St. George members were mostly English import merchants and agents for British houses. The club's first professional was Sam Wright, a recent arrival from Sheffield and father of Harry and George Wright, who later were famous in both cricket and baseball. Its first ground was on East Thirty-first Street, near First Avenue. In 1846 the Dragon Slayers moved uptown to the Red House field on Third Avenue in Harlem. Five years later they followed the New York club across the Hudson River to Hoboken, New Jersey. See John I. Marder, *The International Series: The Story of the United States versus Canada at Cricket* (London, 1968), 16; *Spirit* 16 (April 18, 1846): 90; (June 27, 1846): 207; 20 (August 3, 1850): 288; 21 (April 26, 1851): 115.

5. *Spirit* 14 (May 25, 1844): 150; (June 1, 1844): 162, 15 (April 18, 1846): 90; (September 19, 1846): 351; (September 26, 1846): 363, 25 (September 29, 1855): 391.

6. During the 1840s the Union Star and King's County clubs played in Brooklyn, and a few more clubs were founded in Manhattan, Jamaica (Long Island), Albany, and Syracuse. See *Spirit* 14 (June 1, 1844): 162; 16 (April 18, 1846): 90; (April 25, 1846): 102; (August 1, 1846): 267; 17 (June 19, 1847): 191; (July 31, 1847): 263; (November 20, 1847): 455; 18 (June 10, 1848): 186; (June 24, 1848): 297. Across the Hudson, the Newark Cricket Club began competing in 1845. These Jerseymen were "mostly Sheffielders" and "nearly, if not quite all, Yorkshiremen." See *Spirit* 15 (October 25, 1845): 411; (November 1, 1845): 428; *Newark Daily Advertiser*, October 28, 1845. The *Spirit* reported clubs at Macon (Ga.), Natchez (Miss.), Louisville (Ky.), Boston, and Wilmington (Del.). Cincinnati fielded two clubs—the Western and Queen City—that entertained several hundred ladies and gentlemen with a spirited series in 1845. See *Spirit* 14 (April 20, 1844): 90; 15 (August 23, 1845): 302; (September 13, 1845): 339; (October 4, 1845): 380; (October 25, 1845): 411; (November 15, 1845): 447.

7. Wister, *Reminiscences,* 5–11; John A. Lester, ed., *A Century of Philadelphia Cricket* (Philadelphia, 1951), 9–13.

8. *Spirit* 16 (April 11, 1846): 75; (August 8, 1846): 279. See Lester, *Philadelphia Cricket,* 9–13; *Spirit* 13 (June 3, 1843): 162; (June 24, 1843): 193; (September 16, 1843): 339; (October 14, 1843): 387.

9. Lester, *Philadelphia Cricket,* 11–14; Wister, *Reminiscences,* 12–14; *Spirit* 15 (September 27, 1845): 363; (October 4, 1845): 380; 16 (November 21, 1846): 459. See also *Jones Wister's Reminiscences* (Philadelphia, 1920), 113–21.

10. Wister, *Reminiscences,* 14–15.

11. Wister, *Reminiscences,* 18–31. The proceedings of the early meetings of the Philadelphia Cricket Club are in the club's Minute Book, Historical Society of Pennsylvania.

12. *Clipper* 5 (May 9, 1857): 19. See also *Spirit* 18 (June 24, 1848): 297.

13. *Porter's Spirit* 4 (August 7, 1858): 356.

14. *Porter's Spirit* 6 (March 26, 1859): 52; (May 7, 1859): 149; *Spirit* 15 (October 25, 1845): 411; Roberta J. Park, "British Sports and Pastimes in San Francisco, 1848–1900," *British Journal of Sports History* 1 (December 1984): 304.

15. *Clipper* 5 (August 29, 1857): 148; (October 17, 1857): 205.

16. *Spirit* 26 (October 18, 1856): 421. For other examples of high school cricket clubs in Indianapolis and in Sterling, Massachusetts, see *Clipper* 6 (June 19, 1858): 69; 8 (June 25, 1859): 79.

17. *Porter's Spirit* 4 (May 15, 1858): 164; *Clipper* 6 (May 15, 1858): 28; 9 (July 20, 1861): 108; (July 27, 1861): 119; Minute Book, Philadelphia Cricket Club.

18. *Clipper* 5 (April 27, 1857): 8; (August 29, 1857): 148; 6 (May 8, 1858): 20; 7 (May 14, 1859): 28.

19. *Clipper* 5 (April 11, 1857): 402; 6 (June 26, 1858): 75.

20. *Spirit* 29 (November 19, 1859): 481; *Porter's Spirit* 6 (June 11, 1859): 228; (July 16, 1859): 309; *Clipper* 5 (August 29, 1857): 148; (October 17, 1857): 205; 7 (May 28, 1859): 47; (June 4, 1859): 51, 52; (November 26, 1859): 252.

21. *Clipper* 5 (June 6, 1857): 52.

22. One of the traditional toasts was to the press, "the Score Book of the Universe." *Spirit* 26 (November 22, 1856): 487.

23. *Spirit* 13 (November 4, 1843): 423; 15 (July 19, 1845): 244; (November 15, 1845): 445; 17 (November 27, 1847): 471; 19 (December 8, 1849): 494.

24. *Clipper* 5 (May 2, 1857): 10; (October 24, 1857): 212; (December 26, 1857): 283; *Porter's Spirit* 3 (January 2, 1858): 281; 5 (November 27, 1858): 196.

25. *Clipper* 8 (January 7, 1860): 300.
26. *Spirit* 21 (August 23, 1851): 318.
27. *Spirit* 16 (October 3, 1846): 376.
28. Quoted in *Spirit* 23 (August 27, 1853): 332.
29. *Spirit* 27 (May 9, 1857): 150; (June 6, 1857): 199; *Porter's Spirit* 2 (May 9, 1857): 153.
30. *Clipper* 5 (May 9, 1857): 19.
31. *Porter's Spirit* 2 (May 9, 1857): 156.
32. *Porter's Spirit* 4 (March 13, 1858): 21; *Clipper* 6 (May 8, 1858): 19.
33. *Porter's Spirit* 2 (May 9, 1857): 156; *Clipper* 6 (May 8, 1858): 19.
34. The 1857 meeting planned two other special matches—the best of New York City against "Thirty States of the Union" and a New York State eighteen versus a New York City eleven. While the first match stirred some interest, the lopsided victory by the New Yorkers and poor weather sent the small crowd home disappointed.
35. *Porter's Spirit* 2 (April 25, 1857): 125; (June 6, 1857): 212; (June 13, 1857): 228; *Spirit* 27 (June 20, 1857): 228; *Clipper* 5 (April 25, 1857): 3; (May 2, 1857): 10; (June 20, 1857): 68; (January 9, 1858): 298; (April 13, 1858): 397; 6 (May 8, 1858): 19; (May 29, 1858): 44.
36. *Clipper* 7 (May 7, 1859): 19; (May 21, 1859): 37; (May 28, 1859): 49; *Porter's Spirit* 7 (May 7, 1859): 148.
37. *Clipper* 8 (May 19, 1860): 37; *Wilkes' Spirit* 2 (May 19, 1860): 173.
38. *Clipper* 8 (May 19, 1860): 37.
39. *Clipper* 7 (May 28, 1859): 48.
40. *Clipper* 8 (May 19, 1860): 37.
41. *Spirit* 24 (August 12, 1854): 306; (August 26, 1854): 336.
42. *Porter's Spirit* 1 (October 18, 1856): 117.
43. *Porter's Spirit* 6 (July 16, 1859): 309; 2 (June 20, 1857): 245.
44. *New York Times,* July 9, 1860; *Wilkes' Spirit* 2 (July 14, 1860): 301; *Clipper* 8 (November 3, 1860): 225.
45. Marder, *International Series,* 12–14.
46. *Spirit* 13 (August 26, 1843): 306; (September 16, 1843): 339; (September 23, 1843): 351; *Albion,* September 2, 1843, 435; September 16, 1843, 460; September 23, 1843, 472.
47. *Spirit* 14 (August 3, 1844): 265; (August 10, 1844): 276; (September 14, 1844): 282; (September 28, 1844): 348; *Albion,* August 3, 1844, 375; August 10, 1844, 387; September 14, 1844, 448.
48. *Spirit* 15 (August 9, 1845): 279; (September 6, 1845): 323.
49. Marder, *International Series,* 22–23; *Spirit* 16 (September 5, 1846): 327; (October 31, 1846): 428; Wister, *Reminiscences,* 6. Marder's book

is the most useful and complete account of this series, but it contains a few errors and some confusion on the 1843 and 1844 matches. See also Melvin L. Adelman, *A Sporting Time: New York City and the Rise of Modern Athletics, 1820-70* (Urbana, Ill., 1986), 102–3. He considers the 1845 contest to be the first international match because the newspapers designated the opposition as "all-Canada" rather than Toronto.

50. For a summary of the series see Marder, *International Series,* 36–65. See also *Porter's Spirit* 1 (September 20, 1856): 37; 4 (August 7, 1858): 356–57; (August 14, 1858): 371; 6 (August 19, 1859): 373; *Wilkes' Spirit* 2 (August 11, 1860): 364; (August 18, 1860): 379; *Spirit* 23 (September 3, 1853): 342–43; (October 8, 1853): 402; 24 (July 29, 1854): 283; 26 (September 20, 1856): 379; 27 (August 29, 1857): 343.

51. *Clipper* 8 (September 8, 1860): 163; *Wilkes' Spirit* 3 (September 8, 1860): 5.

52. *Clipper* 7 (August 13, 1859): 131; (July 30, 1859): 115.

53. *Clipper* 8 (July 28, 1860): 114.

54. *Clipper* 8 (August 11, 1860); 130; (August 18, 1860): 140.

55. *Spirit* 21 (September 27, 1851): 379.

56. *Clipper* 6 (November 20, 1858): 244.

57. *Wilkes' Spirit* 1 (January 28, 1860): 326–27; *Porter's Spirit* 6 (July 2, 1859): 281.

58. *Wilkes' Spirit* 1 (September 17, 1859): 21, 29.

59. *Clipper* 7 (July 16, 1859); 98; (September 10, 1859): 164.

60. *Spirit* 29 (July 23, 1859): 282; *Wilkes' Spirit* 1 (October 1, 1859): 57.

61. Speech by John B. Irving in *Spirit* 29 (November 26, 1859): 496.

62. *Porter's Spirit* 6 (July 2, 1859): 281; *Clipper* 7 (September 17, 1859): 170.

63. *Clipper* 7 (October 15, 1859): 202; *New York Times,* October 3–8, 10, 1859; *Wilkes' Spirit* 1 (October 15, 1859): 83. After their regular match the cricketers played an exhibition for the benefit of the English athletes, followed by a gala dinner at the Astor House. See *New York Herald,* October 4–6, 1859; Fred Lillywhite, *The English Cricketers' Trip to Canada and the United States* (London, 1860), 32; John B. Irving, *The International Cricket Match Played October 1859 in the Elysian Fields at Hoboken* (New York, 1859).

64. *Clipper* 7 (October 22, 1859): 210; *New York Times*, October 11, 13–15, 1859; *Wilkes' Spirit* 1 (October 22, 1859): 110; (October 29, 1859): 116; *Philadelphia Press,* October 11, 13–15, 1859; Lester, *Philadelphia Cricket,* 17–21; Lillywhite, *English Cricketers' Trip,* 40–43. Some ill will developed at Philadelphia after a benefit match in that city drew a disappointingly small crowd. Apparently the English players

blamed the poor turnout on their hosts' lack of publicity. See *Wilkes' Spirit* 1 (October 29, 1859): 116.

65. *Wilkes' Spirit* 1 (October 29, 1859): 117; (November 5, 1859): 132.

66. *Wilkes' Spirit* 1 (October 29, 1859): 116; (November 5, 1859): 121, 133; (January 7, 1860): 285; Lillywhite, *English Cricketers' Trip,* 50–53; *Clipper* 7 (November 12, 1859): 234; *New York Times,* October 21, 1859. The negotiations were complicated by an unauthorized agent who claimed to represent the New York and Brooklyn baseball communities.

67. *Wilkes' Spirit* 2 (March 24, 1860): 43; (April 7, 1860): 68; (April 21, 1860): 101; 1 (October 15, 1859): 89; (January 28, 1860): 327.

68. *Clipper* 7 (November 5, 1859): 226.

69. Some of the United States cricketers were upset by the remarks of a member of the All-England Eleven, who criticized the hospitality of the American hosts. See *Wilkes' Spirit* 1 (February 25, 1860): 387, 392.

70. *Porter's Spirit* 6 (April 9, 1859): 84.

71. *Clipper* 7 (December 18, 1858): 277; 8 (August 18, 1860): 140; Charles Peverelly, *The Book of American Pastimes* (New York, 1866), 532–35.

72. For evidence of the growth of New Jersey cricket, see *Brooklyn Daily Eagle,* August 26, 1858; *Jersey City Daily Courier and Advertiser,* August 13, 1858; *Newark Daily Mercury,* June 26, 1857. The *Clipper* acknowledged that Newark had "long been famous for cricketers of the first water." *Clipper* 3 (January 26, 1856): 311.

73. *Clipper* 7 (October 22, 1859): 212.

74. For baseball players trying cricket, see *Porter's Spirit* 3 (November 21, 1857): 180; 4 (July 17, 1858): 309; *Clipper* 8 (May 5, 1860): 19. See also chapter 5 in this volume. For the American Cricket Club, see *Clipper* 8 (September 15, 1860): 170; (September 22, 1860): 179; (September 29, 1860): 186; (October 13, 1860): 204; (October 27, 1860): 219, 221; 9 (August 17, 1861): 143; (September 7, 1861): 162; (September 14, 1861): 171; 10 (June 21, 1862): 74; *Wilkes' Spirit* 4 (August 10, 1861): 357; 5 (September 7, 1861): 4; 6 (June 21, 1862): 244; (June 28, 1862): 269; (July 26, 1862): 333; (August 9, 1862): 355. The Anglo-American Cricket Club was announced in the fall of 1862, apparently patterned after the American club, but there is no other reference to its existence. See *Clipper* 10 (October 11, 1862): 203.

75. Quoted in *Spirit* 27 (May 16, 1857): 162; *Porter's Spirit* 2 (May 23, 1857): 180.

76. *Clipper* 7 (October 22, 1859): 212; 8 (March 10, 1860): 372. For a cricket tournament at the Schuylkill County Fair, see *Clipper* 6 (October 23, 1858): 213.

77. *Porter's Spirit* 6 (June 11, 1859): 228; (July 16, 1859): 309; *Clipper* 6 (June 19, 1858): 67; (June 26, 1858): 75; 7 (May 28, 1859): 47; (June 4, 1859): 51, 52; (September 10, 1859): 163; Dale Somers, *The Rise of Sports in New Orleans, 1850–1900* (Baton Rouge, La., 1972), 48-49.

78. *Porter's Spirit* 2 (June 6, 1857): 212.

79. *Clipper* 5 (August 8, 1857): 123; 7 (October 22, 1859): 57; Park, "British Sports and Pastimes," 304.

80. *Wilkes' Spirit* 1 (October 1, 1859): 57; Wister, *Reminiscences,* 71; *Porter's Spirit* 6 (July 23, 1859): 329.

81. Wister, *Reminiscences,* 57, 59.

82. *Clipper* 6 (January 15, 1858): 308; letter from W. Russell, March 21, 1859, in *Porter's Spirit* 6 (March 26, 1859): 52.

CHAPTER

3

The Emergence of Baseball

On December 30, 1907, Abraham G. Mills, the fourth president of professional baseball's National League, issued the final report of the special commission that had been charged with deciding the true origins of America's national pastime, that is, whether baseball derived from the English schoolyard game of rounders or whether it was a purely native product. Henry Chadwick, a prominent sportswriter for fifty years who was known in many quarters as the "father of baseball," argued for the rounders theory, which had prevailed before the 1880s.[1] He had played the game as a boy in England, before he emigrated with his parents to the United States, and after a half century of watching and promoting the rise of baseball, he was convinced that rounders and the young American sport were closely related because they shared essential principles. As he explained to the commission, which consisted of former ball players and officials, as well as two United States senators, both were "played by two opposing sides of contestants, on a special field of play, in which a ball was pitched or tossed to an opposing batsman, who endeavored to strike the ball out onto the field, far enough to admit his safely running the round of bases, so as to enable him to score a run to count in the game—the side scoring the most runs winning the game." Although Chadwick conceded that the two sports differed in "methods and details of play," he claimed that they were quite close in fundamental structure.[2]

Albert G. Spalding, an American-born baseball star and sporting goods magnate, countered Chadwick's view, declaring that baseball was "of purely American origin and no other game or country has any right to claim its parentage." He recognized that rounders and baseball shared certain features, but he stressed the many differences in rules: for example, by the late 1880s the two sports had diverged in the size and shape of the fields (square versus diamond); the number of players on a side (eleven versus nine), innings in a match (two versus nine), and outs in an inning (eleven versus three); the mode of scoring runs (total bases versus crossing home plate); and the size and shape of the bats (smaller and flat in rounders) and the balls (smaller in rounders). Spalding argued that rounders was closer to cricket than to baseball, that it was never played in the United States, and that any similarity between rounders and the American national pastime was simply a coincidence. A patriot at heart, he could not believe that in 1840 "our national prejudices would permit us to look with favor, much less adopt any sport or game of an English flavor."

Spalding believed that baseball descended from the colonial game of "old cat," in which a player batted a ball and ran to one or more bases. According to him, "old cat" evolved into the townball matches that were popular on village holidays in many early nineteenth-century American communities, and modern baseball was simply a modification of townball. Endorsing the testimony of Abner Graves, who credited Abner Doubleday with the invention of the modern rules of baseball at Cooperstown, New York, in 1839, Spalding admitted: "It certainly appeals to an American's pride to have had the great national game of Base Ball created and named by a Major General in the United States Army."[3]

The Mills Commission also weighed evidence concerning the founding of New York's Knickerbocker Base Ball Club in 1842 and its first written rules of 1845. John M. Ward, a star player for the Providence Grays and the New York Giants during the late nineteenth century, informed Spalding that several prominent Manhattan business and professional men had turned to the boys' game of baseball for exercise. "There was not a code of rules nor any written records of that game," he wrote, "and their only guide to the method of playing was their own recollection of the game as they themselves, when boys, had played it and the rules of the game then in existence, which had come down, like folklore, from generation to generation of boys." Spalding forwarded Ward's letter to the commission, which also considered a statement by Duncan Curry, an original Knickerbocker, who testified that "a diagram, showing the ball field laid out substantially as it is today, was brought to the field one afternoon by a Mr. Wadsworth."[4]

In the end, Mills himself chose among Chadwick's case for rounders, Spalding's and Graves's argument for Doubleday perfecting townball, and the Knickerbocker claim for their New York City version. While he did not feel that the American origins of baseball should be sustained simply on "patriotic ground," he did not find the rounders theory to be very persuasive. Instead, he endorsed Graves's story, while noting that it was possible to link the Doubleday and Knickerbocker diagrams of 1839 and 1845. He concluded: "First, that 'Base Ball' had its origins in the United States. Second, that the first scheme for playing it, according to the best evidence obtained to date, was devised by Abner Doubleday at Cooperstown, N.Y., in 1839."[5]

Robert Henderson, Harold Seymour, and other scholars have since debunked the Doubleday-Cooperstown myth, which nonetheless remains powerful in the American imagination due to the efforts of major league baseball and the Hall of Fame in Cooperstown. For the record, however, one must acknowledge that research has proven that Abner Doubleday enrolled as a cadet at West Point in the fall of 1838 and possibly never even visited Cooperstown. Although he may have played ball with Graves during his boyhood, in his published writings he never mentioned anything about his role in the creation of modern baseball. Furthermore, Mills had known Doubleday ever since their service in the Civil War, but his friend had apparently never told him about his notable brainstorm in Cooperstown. Finally, Mills's verdict rested entirely on an octogenarian's recollection of an event that had occurred sixty-eight years earlier.[6]

If Abner Doubleday did not invent baseball, then who did? The answer, of course, is that no single person created the sport; rather, it evolved in stages from earlier bat and ball games. Historians today believe that Chadwick was correct in linking baseball to English rounders. Henderson, for example, has shown that early nineteenth-century American sports books printed rules for rounders under the heading "Base, or Goal Ball." Townball seems to have been an Americanized variation of rounders, and both probably developed as team versions of the traditional game of "old cat." Strictly speaking, modern baseball is a refined, United States variety of townball and therefore is certainly an indigenous sport. While its ancestry is English, its essence is clearly American. Chadwick made this point as early as 1860 when he wrote that, although baseball was "of English origin, it has been so modified and improved of late years in this country, as almost to deprive it of any of its original features beyond the mere groundwork of the game."[7] In 1864 *Wilkes' Spirit* compared the children's pastime of rounders with the adult sport of baseball, describing the former as "a very simple game, and designed only for recreation during the intervals from study in schools, and . . . entirely devoid of the manly features that characterize base-ball as played in this country."[8]

Despite their different views on the linkage of rounders and baseball, Spalding, Chadwick, and sporting journalists agreed that a distinctly American process of modernization changed a traditional folk game into a late nineteenth-century sport. This transformation began in Philadelphia, Boston, and New York City during the period 1830–60, as each of these cities developed a distinctive version of baseball. During the 1850s these types competed for dominance throughout the United States, and by the Civil War the New York City variety had established itself in most parts of the nation.

A few young sportsmen began a new era of Philadelphia ball playing in 1831, when they crossed the Delaware River for regular contests of "two old cat" at Camden, New Jersey. Before long they had recruited enough players for Saturday afternoon townball, despite being "frequently reproved and censured by their friends for degrading themselves by indulging in such childish amusement." These ball players competed on public grounds, where neither rent nor permission was required, and made their own bats and balls. After another group of townball enthusiasts joined them in 1833, the two formally merged and organized the Olympic Ball Club, drawing up a constitution and field rules to govern their play.[9]

These pioneer athletes were principally merchants and "respectable and well-known citizens of Philadelphia," several of whom later distinguished themselves in their city's business and professional life. They were remembered as a "conservative and temperate body of gentlemen who enjoyed mixing their sports with good conversation, wit, food, and drink."[10] A highlight of each season was the Fourth of July celebration, when their president read the Declaration of Independence and the members sang songs and heard "an address delivered for the perpetuation of the Stars and Stripes." Townball thus remained popular through the late 1850s in the Philadelphia area, with several clubs in Camden and Germantown joining the Olympics, Excelsiors, and Athletics of that city. There is some evidence that emigrants from the City of Brotherly Love carried their sport to Cincinnati, Ohio, and neighboring towns in northern Kentucky, where townball flourished before the Civil War.[11]

Yankee varieties of townball were called "base" or "roundball." In 1856 a Boston enthusiast described that sport as "truly national," a game that "is played by the school boys in every country village in New England, as well as in the parks of many of our New England cities." He continued: "Base used to be a favorite game with the students of the English High and Latin Schools of Boston, a few years ago. . . . Base is also a favorite game upon the green in front of village school-houses in the country throughout New England; and in this city, on Fast Day . . . Boston Common is covered with amateur parties of men and boys playing Base." Boston's truckmen attracted large crowds of spectators, who admired their "supply of muscle that renders them able to outdo all competitors in striking and throwing."[12]

This "Massachusetts game" generally matched sides of eight to fifteen men on a square field with bases or tall stakes (up to five feet high) at each corner. The batter stood midway between first and fourth (home) base and tried to hit a ball "made of yarn, tightly wound round a lump of cork or India rubber, and covered with smooth calf-skin in quarters . . . the seams closed snugly, and not raised, lest they should blister the hands of the thrower and catcher." The round bat varied from three to three and a half feet in length and was often "a portion of stout rake or pitchfork handle

. . . wielded generally in one hand by the muscular young players at the country schools." The pitcher threw the ball swiftly overhand (not underhand, as in the New York version), "with a vigor . . . that made it whistle through the air, and stop with a solid *smack* in the catcher's hands." The receiver had to be able "to catch expertly a swiftly delivered ball, or he would be admonished of his inexpertness by a request from some player to 'butter his fingers'!" The batter could strike the ball in any direction, there being no foul territory.[13] James D'Wolf Lovett recalled that when he played as a boy for a junior club near Boston, batters sometimes shortened up on the bat, grasping it near the middle, "and by a quick turn of the wrist [struck] the ball, as it passed them, in the same direction in which it was thrown, thus avoiding the fielders and giving the striker a good start on the bases." After hitting the ball, the striker ran around the bases until he was put out or remained safely on a base. He could be retired if the catcher caught three missed balls, or if a hit ball was caught on the fly, or if he was struck by a thrown ball while running the bases (called "soaking" or "burning" a runner). Usually one out ended the inning, and the first team to score a fixed number of runs won the game.[14]

The first modern baseball organization in Massachusetts was the Olympic Club of Boston, whose members began play in 1854, formally established the club in 1856, and published rules and regulations in 1857. That year brought many spirited intrasquad games and matches against newly formed clubs on Boston Common. In late June about 2,000 spectators attended the informal Massachusetts championship between the Olympics and the Wassapoag Ball Club of Sharon. Each team had twelve men to a side, twenty-five runs were needed to win a game, and three victories decided the match. Wassapoag defeated the Olympics but then lost to the Unions of Medway. A dispute over rules canceled the return contest and eventually led to the Massachusetts Baseball Convention, called for Dedham in May 1858, at which the Massachusetts Association of Base Ball Players was created and a constitution, bylaws, and rules and regulations were approved. Although the Tri-Mountain club representatives argued for the New York version, the new rules called for a game similar to traditional New England townball, with a square field, overhand pitching, no foul territory, ten to twelve men per side, one out to retire all, and victory belonging to the team that first scored one hundred runs.[15]

The convention's labors bore fruit, for during the years remaining before the Civil War the "Massachusetts game" flourished. In September 1858 a Boston correspondent to the *Clipper* reported a sharp increase in public interest in both cricket and baseball, which he attributed in part to the favorable notices from the local press and the cooperation of city merchants who closed their doors on summer Saturday afternoons. He also credited much of the excitement to the recent formation of the state association of baseball players, adding: "Base Ball is getting to be the most predominant institution of this State. Clubs are now forming in every country town and village, and a great many matches have been played this season." Proof of the baseball fever sweeping New England was evident in a September 1859 match played for the Massachusetts state championship between the Unions of Medway and the Winthrops of Holliston. Several railroads issued excursion tickets to Boston's Agricultural Fair Grounds, where a large crowd bet heavily on the two-day encounter, won by the Unions, 100–71.[16]

While the Massachusetts form of baseball thrived during the late 1850s, it faced a formidable rival in the New York City version, which mushroomed in popularity during these years. Modern baseball derives most immediately from the latter, created by the Knickerbockers during the mid-1840s. As Melvin Adelman has shown, the majority of these sportsmen were prosperous (but not affluent) middle-class merchants, bankers, doctors, lawyers, clerks, and other white-collar workers. None belonged to the city's elite, although a few ranked just one rung below New York's aristocracy. These first ball players sought health, exercise, and good fellowship in their sport and were not very much interested in seeking out other nines for interclub competition. Perhaps because of their defensiveness about playing a child's game, or because they valued privacy, they did not seek publicity in the city's daily or weekly papers.[17]

The driving force behind the Knickerbockers in 1845 was Alexander J. Cartwright, Jr. Later a member of the Hall of Fame, he deserves far more credit than Doubleday for the creation of baseball. The son of a shipping proprietor, Cartwright began his business career as a clerk and then joined with his brother to open a bookstore and stationery shop during the mid-1840s. He belonged to a volunteer fire company and played baseball with friends and fellow firefighters on the east side of Manhattan.[18] Some baseball historians believe that Cartwright was the one who first suggested that the Knickerbockers try a diamond instead of a square for the bases, with the batter standing at home plate. It is more certain that he was the chief organizer of the club and the man responsible for the codification of its first rules—namely, that the ball had to be pitched underhand, not thrown; that a ball knocked outside the range of first or third base was foul; and that a player was out if a hit ball was caught on the fly or first bounce, or if a fielder held the ball on a base before the runner arrived, or if, between bases, a fielder touched the runner with the ball. "Soaking" the runner was prohibited, three outs retired the side, and twenty-one aces (runs) decided the game, provided each side had an equal number of outs.[19]

The Knickerbockers played intrasquad games in the Murray Hill section of Manhattan, then moved to the Elysian Fields of Hoboken, New Jersey, in 1846. There they competed in a few matches against other nines, including a semiorganized outfit called the New York Club.[20] The Gothams (originally named the Washingtons), the next formal baseball club, began play in the early 1850s at the St. George Cricket Club ground in Harlem. The Eagles (1852) and the Empires (1854), both of New York City, and the Excelsiors (1854) of South Brooklyn increased to five the number of teams playing by the Knickerbockers' rules before 1855.[21] During the next six years a veritable baseball mania overtook the greater New York City region, as more than 200 junior and senior clubs sprang into action in Brooklyn, Queens, Manhattan, Westchester, and northern New Jersey.[22]

Before 1861, then, the three leading centers of adult organized ball playing in America were Philadelphia, Boston, and New York. It became apparent that the "New York game" was rapidly invading New England, the Philadelphia area, and even southern and western states in a drive to become the nation's most popular team sport. How exactly did the New York version of the game spread? Why did it surpass competing versions of ball playing? And why did it prevail over cricket, which was firmly established in many American cities and towns before baseball burst upon the sporting scene? This chapter addresses the first two questions; the third one is considered more fully in Chapter 5.

Many of the factors that helped to popularize American cricket before the Civil War also shaped the early development of New York–style baseball. Yet there were also important differences in the influence of personal mobility, intercity competition, urban-rural interaction, newspaper publicity, New York City conventions, and feature events. A review of these forces reveals how and why the "New York game" spread across the United States during the late 1850s. It also provides a geography of early American baseball and suggests why the New York variety became the nation's leading team sport.

While English immigrants were introducing cricket into dozens of communities in antebellum America, native New York City baseball enthusiasts were teaching the rules of their game to friends in neighboring towns and distant cities. Social historians researching mobility patterns in nineteenth-century America find it difficult to trace obscure citizens from city to city, but it is possible to track down a few Manhattan and Brooklyn ball players who promoted their sport through their travels or by entertaining guests at home. For example, Edward G. Saltzman, a member of the New York Gothams, helped to found Boston's Tri-Mountain Base Ball Club in 1857. He became president of the new organization and taught the members the New York rules, which were new to Boston and which the club adopted. Also, the treasurer of the Tri-Mountains, while visiting New York, watched the Empires practice and was invited to play with the Gothams. Personal contact and visits helped to plant the "New York game" in Baltimore as well. In 1858 Joseph Leggett of the famous Brooklyn Excelsiors invited George Beam, a wholesale grocer in Baltimore, to see a game in New York. Beam became a baseball enthusiast and organized a ball club (also named the Excelsiors) in his home city, made up primarily of businessmen. Within one year there were several other nines in Baltimore.[23]

Long-distance geographical mobility brought New York baseball to the Midwest and the West Coast. Theodore Frost (from Rochester College) and Mathew M. Yorston introduced baseball to Cincinnati in 1860, recruiting high school students and businessmen to form the Live Oak Base Ball Club. They worked hard to demonstrate the superiority of this new game over townball, and before long the city's Excelsior and Buckeye townball clubs adopted the rules of the "New York game."[24] Alexander Cartwright crossed the Great Plains in the late 1840s, apparently teaching the game he helped to invent to interested sportsmen. (He stayed only briefly in northern California before moving on to Hawaii.)[25] The first California club was organized in San Francisco in 1858; two years later, M. E. Gelston of New York's Eagles, an all-star player in the 1858 New York versus Brooklyn series, became captain of a San Francisco nine, which renamed itself the Eagle club in his honor. At a November 1860 tournament Gelston's team defeated a Sacramento club, captained by E. N. Robinson, formerly of the Putnams of Brooklyn.[26] (Thus an old New York–Brooklyn rivalry was re-enacted on the Pacific Coast, perhaps a foreboding of the more famous migrations of entire New York and Brooklyn clubs nearly one hundred years later). Gelston and Robinson were followed by many other easterners who took the sport along on their journeys to the Golden State. William and James Shepard, two New Yorkers who had played with famous ball stars of the 1850s, crossed the Plains on their way to San Francisco in 1861, where they continued to enjoy the game they had learned in the East.[27]

Intercity competition was another means of popularizing the "New York game" before the Civil War. While baseball nines were not as mobile as cricket elevens during this era, there were a few urban rivalries that gave the new sport a big boost. Perhaps none was more intense than that between New York and Brooklyn clubs. Since civic pride was keen on both sides of the East River, it was only natural for the leading Brooklyn teams to challenge their New York City counterparts to a three-game series between their best players. In 1858 *Porter's Spirit,* in a burst of hyperbole, predicted that a crowd of 100,000 would see "one of the grandest tournaments that has ever been witnessed in the history of the world."[28] The *Clipper,* in reporting the 22–18 victory of the Manhattan team in the first contest in July, declared that the excitement before the game was "so intense that it has been made the chief topic of conversation," with much speculation concerning who would win.[29]

Brooklyn avenged its defeat with an easy 29–8 triumph in the return match in August, which set the stage for a deciding encounter in September, won by the New Yorkers, 29–18. While the Manhattan men carried off the laurels, the "New York game" in general benefited enormously. Thousands of people witnessed the games, while probably more than a million followed the series in newspapers across America.[30]

Despite their 1858 setback, Brooklyn's baseball fraternity soon established its dominance over neighboring clubs by sweeping all of the early-season interclub contests in 1859. *Porter's Spirit* appealed to the New York teams to reverse this trend, asking: "Is New York to rank second to the village over the other side of the river?"[31] The Brooklynites, however, surpassed all rival cities in both the number of clubs and the quality of their performances. As the *Brooklyn Daily Eagle* crowed, "Nowhere has the National game of Baseball taken firmer hold than in Brooklyn and nowhere are there better players." That paper noted every triumph over a New York club, at one point proclaiming: "If we are ahead of the big city in nothing else, we can beat her in baseball."[32] With the Manhattan-Brooklyn rivalry as a model, Newark, Bloomfield, Jersey City, New Brunswick, and other New Jersey towns inaugurated spirited intercity baseball competitions.[33] Nines from Baltimore and Washington, D.C., followed suit in 1860.[34] Whenever baseball fever infected a new city, it was only a short time before its best teams looked elsewhere for other nines to conquer.

Outside the greater New York metropolitan area the 1860 tours of the Brooklyn Excelsiors excited thousands of sportsmen throughout upstate New York, Baltimore, and Philadelphia. In July this "crack club" visited Albany, Troy, Buffalo, Rochester, and Newburgh, and news of its victories flashed across the state's telegraph wires. Albert Spalding believed that these exhibitions inspired young men to hope "that they might win for their cities a glory akin to that which had been achieved for [Brooklyn]."[35] While Spalding probably exaggerated the impact of the Excelsiors, they did make quite an impression wherever they played. For example, after crushing their namesakes before a large audience in Baltimore, the Brooklyn celebrities were wined and dined by the hometown club. According to the *Clipper,* the Excelsiors' visit advanced baseball in Baltimore by three or four years, and the paper predicted that their excursion would stir up interest in the sport in other cities further south.[36] The Excelsiors concluded their travels in Philadelphia, where they defeated a select nine from the local clubs which had adopted the New York rules that season. Partly because of this visit, Philadelphia baseball exploded in popularity, leaving townball a quaint relic of the past.[37]

As the "New York game" swept the ball-playing fraternities in many antebellum American cities and towns, it also penetrated into more remote areas. When its advocates introduced the sport into small communities, they repeated familiar patterns of cultural interaction between rural and urban America. Folk versions of baseball originated in country villages, but the modern sport was rationalized and ultimately perfected in the emerging commercial and industrial cities of the mid-nineteenth century. Then it was re-exported into the hinterland, where it prospered. The *New York Times* sensed this process in action in an 1858 editorial: "We predict that [baseball] will spread from the city to the country, and revive there, where it was dying out, a love of the noble game."[38]

There are many instances of city players instructing farm boys in the latest "scientific" rules and techniques of the sport. For example, in November 1860 several members of the Athletics of Philadelphia journeyed to Mauch Chunk to play ball with some of that Pennsylvania town's young men. The Athletics and their hosts agreed to one contest of townball and one of New York–style baseball, thus introducing the more modern game into a rural area.[39] In 1866 an early surveyor of American sport credited the Athletics with having "done more to advance the popularity of the game, by visits to towns and villages where baseball was previously unknown, than almost any other club in the United States."[40] While the teaching of modern baseball proceeded, the sport never lost its special quality of being part pastoral country game and part scientific, rational urban amusement.

Like cricket, baseball benefited greatly from the publicity provided by the New York City weekly sporting periodicals. The *Clipper, Porter's Spirit,* and *Wilkes' Spirit* published editorials extolling the game and printed all the convention news as well as detailed stories and box scores on major and minor matches. The

Clipper presented a regular column that answered questions from its readers on all sporting topics, including many on baseball. From October 1857 to January 1858 *Porter's Spirit* ran a series of fourteen articles on the early history and current practice of baseball, and two years later the *Clipper* followed with a series on organizing a club and playing the game. Although these periodicals also printed material on townball and the "Massachusetts game," the New York City version got far more space. Even local daily newspapers began irregular coverage of baseball before the Civil War, giving the sport a crucial boost in numerous cities and towns across the land.[41]

Among all of the early sportswriters, none was a more tireless advocate of baseball than Henry Chadwick. Born in Exeter, England, in 1824, he moved to America with his family in 1837. He inherited both a love of journalism and a passion for outdoor recreation from his father, an editor. Chadwick was a member of the New York Cricket Club and Manhattan's National Base Ball Club during the 1850s, and he played and reported on both games during their infancy in the United States. A life-long resident of Brooklyn, he wrote first for the *Clipper* and later for the *Brooklyn Eagle,* the *New York Times,* the *Herald,* the *World,* the *Sun,* and the *Tribune.* Chadwick had a powerful influence on the development of baseball rules and devised scoring systems that helped reporters compile box scores, averages, and other statistics. Always a Victorian gentleman, he stressed the health, moral, and character-building advantages of the sport, repeatedly condemning rowdyism and gambling whenever they threatened to ruin baseball's reputation.[42]

A good example of the propaganda provided by sports journals and of Chadwick's personal role was the effort to stimulate interest in baseball in Richmond, Virginia. In 1848 Chadwick married a young lady from that city, and he and his wife regularly visited her relatives there. While in town he tried to organize both cricket and baseball clubs, with little success. In March 1861 the *Clipper* expressed surprise at the tardy development of these sports in a town with good fields and plenty of young men with ample leisure time, noting that "as organizations already so successfully commenced in Baltimore and Washington have initiated the institution in Southern cities, we hope Richmond will this season follow suit, by getting up a club of her own." The paper advised any interested parties to contact "H.C." in the hope that a nine might be formed by mid-April. A few weeks later, however, the firing on Fort Sumter and the ensuing Civil War spoiled plans to initiate baseball in a city that soon became the capital of the Confederacy.[43]

Individuals, clubs, and the press all gave baseball a big boost during the 1850s, but perhaps the key event in the sport's early modernization was the founding of its first centralized governing body—the National Association of Base Ball Players (NABBP). As Harold Seymour has pointed out, the creation of this organization was crucial in baseball's history, launching an era in which players met annually to refine the rules, resolve disputes, and control the sport's development.[44]

The idea of a baseball convention originated toward the close of the 1856 season in New York and Brooklyn, when several clubs considered the advantages of revising the Knickerbockers' rules and regulating interclub competition. As the senior organization, the Knickerbockers issued a call in December for a meeting that would "promote additional interest in baseball playing" and "regulate various matters necessary to the good government and continued respectability of this truely National Game."[45] In five gatherings between January 1857 and December 1860, delegates tried to establish their authority as the dominant force in American baseball. *Porter's Spirit* explained in 1858 that the goal was to "give this association of the Base Ball Clubs of Manhattan Island a similar standing which the Marylebone Club of London exercises over the game of cricket throughout the British Islands."[46] The delegates took their responsibility very seriously, following the parliamentary procedures of all formal deliberative bodies. They also exhibited the common nineteenth-century American fondness for oratorical display and legislative maneuvering, many times becoming bogged down in tedious debate over rules of order.[47] But the long hours paid off, for by the Civil War the NABBP was strong, growing, and known across the nation.

When the 1858 convention decided to perpetuate itself by drawing up a permanent constitution, bylaws, and rules of the game, self-designation as a *national* association indicated ambitious designs. Although only clubs from the New York City vicinity were represented, the aim was to rule the continent. The *Clipper* pointed out that "the convention seems to be rather sectional and selfish in its proceedings . . . there having been no invitations sent to clubs in other States." Furthermore, the association was "a mere local organization, bearing no *State* existence even—to say nothing of a *National* one." The paper urged delegates to invite baseball players from everywhere "to compete with them, and endeavor to make the game what it should be—a truely National one."[48]

The officers did work to increase membership, and the NABBP grew from 14 clubs in 1857 to 74 as of early 1861 (a total of 104 were admitted during these years, but about one-quarter disbanded or were absorbed into other clubs). While many of the member clubs failed to send delegates to the annual gatherings, the last two meetings before the Civil War did attract representatives from Boston, New Haven, Baltimore, Washington, D.C., and Detroit. Most encouraging was the attendance of five Philadelphia clubs in December 1860, which reflected that city's recent baseball mania. When the convention elected Col. Dewitt C. Moore of the Philadelphia Athletics to the post of first vice president, it acknowledged the importance of the sizable contingent from the City of Brotherly Love.[49] And while the NABBP was still dominated by New York and Brooklyn clubs, in just a few years it had considerably broadened its base and its influence, prompting the *Clipper* to state in 1860 that "this association is national in every respect, and is intended to include delegates from every club in the Union."[50]

Perhaps the most sensitive organizational problem faced at the first two annual meetings of the NABBP concerned whether or not to admit junior teams (composed of young men under the age of twenty-one) as full voting participants. This was a delicate issue because many older men wished to show the public that baseball was a "manly" game, not merely a child's pastime. The 1857 convention avoided the matter by ignoring the young clubs, but in 1858 the teenaged players were determined to be recognized. The adults were split on the question. Some of the men, like Dr. Daniel Adams of the Knickerbockers, argued to admit all junior teams that applied that year; others did not want to deliberate or play with "children" and were afraid that the numerous junior outfits would "over-rule those improvements that did not chime with their ideas of the game."[51] Many senior players doubted the youngsters' understanding of the sport and believed that they quarreled too much at matches. As a result of these objections, the 1858 convention permitted junior clubs to attend meetings but denied them voting privileges. *Porter's Spirit* suggested that the juniors form an organization of their own, which they did in 1860.[52]

Some of the adult and youthful followers of baseball interpreted the exclusion of the junior teams as undemocratic and unnecessarily restrictive. The *Clipper* considered it a mistake to pretend that "our younger friends were in no wise interested in the enjoyment and furtherance of the game."[53] A correspondent to *Porter's Spirit,* who signed his letter "Infant Ball Player," bitterly resented being denied "voice or vote" at future meetings. He rejected all of the arguments used against young athletes, stating that boys wanted "to keep up those points of the game which require the utmost physical exertion, and the exercise of skill and strength combined," and attacked "those 'pseudo' Senior Clubs, which . . . wish to make the game a means of showing off their figures in fancy dresses, and their wealth in fancy dinners." After denying that the juniors argued any more than the delegates themselves, the writer pointedly suggested that "the *boys* have a say in regard to this game, which they have *always* played, and which most of you have only just now taken out of their hands—unless you have no other way of showing the world that you are *not children,* except by refusing to have anything to do with boys." Another young player called for a challenge match between picked nines from the junior and senior clubs.[54]

In the long run, the most important work of the national conventions involved rule revisions. The 1857 meeting adopted virtually all of the Knickerbocker regulations but changed the method of deciding the outcome of matches from twenty-one runs (aces) to nine full innings. One year later the delegates approved a rule that permitted the umpire to call a strike if a batter repeatedly refused to swing at "good balls."[55] The most heated debate occurred over the rule that counted a batter out if a fielder caught the ball on the first bounce. Opponents of this rule wished to replace it with the "fly game" rule, which preserved all of the other modes of retiring a runner but mandated that a ball caught on the first bound was fair and in play. They argued that the bound rule made baseball less scientific and "manly."

Leading clubs like the Knickerbockers and the Excelsiors tried to demonstrate the superiority of the "fly game" with exhibition matches. *Porter's Spirit* stated the case plainly in 1858: "What is more annoying to an admirer of good fielding than to see a splendid hit to the centre field, such as would merit a home run, entirely nullified by the puny effort of waiting until the force of the ball is spent on the ground and then taking it on the bound, and yet as long as the present rule exists this will be done on every occasion, for there are few that will attempt the difficult catch when the easy one is at their command."[56] At first, the *Clipper* also supported this view, remarking that "for those who desire to witness the game played skillfully the fly game is the only one worth seeing."[57]

Proponents of the fly rule wished to see modern baseball made more challenging than the old boys' pastime from which it had sprung, while defenders of the bound rule argued that it was easier on the fielder's hands, that it had worked well in the past, and that most players were accustomed to it. Some players believed that the bound rule was superior to the fly rule (also used in cricket) because it forced baseball players to be better fielders than were cricketers. The *Clipper* reversed itself and endorsed this unusual position in November 1860, stressing that in baseball additional effort was necessary "to catch the ball on the bound when it cannot be taken on the fly." It quickly added: "Of course we entirely exclude . . . the custom of sacrificing the catch on the fly to the more simple effort on the bound, which no manly or skillful fielder will ever be guilty of."[58] For a time, tradition and conservatism prevailed as delegates repeatedly voted down the fly rule. That innovation finally passed in 1863, however, in the very different circumstances that prevailed during the Civil War.

One of the stated objectives of the NABBP was "the cultivation of kindly feelings among the different members of Base-Ball clubs." To promote good sportsmanship and friendly competition, the association passed several regulations concerning the eligibility of players for club matches. In particular, it required competitors to be regular members of the clubs they represented for at least thirty days prior to a contest, the purpose being to prohibit any club's use of talented outsiders to gain an advantage. According to the first vice president of the 1858 session, however, this regulation was "ambiguous and open to malpractice or evasion." He noted that clubs often permitted exceptions through the courtesy of both parties, and he argued for a strict policy of no substitutes for absent players. *Porter's Spirit* agreed that teams that "failed to bring their regular players on the ground, should be the losers, and no substitutions should be allowed, by consent or otherwise." That journal stressed the importance of club loyalty in baseball and considered it more creditable "for a club to have played a losing or an uphill game with the loss of a crack player of their own club, than to win with the borrowed aid of an outsider."[59] While cricketers remained more lenient in permitting nonmembers to play in matches, baseball players seemed to place more value on team unity and therefore tried to discourage the recruitment of "ringers."

In addition to prohibiting gambling by contestants and umpires, as well as interference by spectators, the 1859 convention also barred professionals by prohibiting any player who received compensation from competing in a match. This further distinguished baseball from cricket, for in the latter professionals played with amateurs. The banning of paid players was clearly an attempt to preserve baseball as a recreation rather than as a vocation, yet it was not universally popular among the followers of America's national pastime. The *Clipper* questioned whether outlawing professionals had "something of an aristocratic odor" and, as such, exhibited "a rather uncharitable disposition toward poor players." Comparing baseball to cricket, where "peer and peasant" sported together on the same level, *Porter's Spirit* pressed the point further: "If, from any circumstances, personal or pecuniary, a lover of the sport cannot afford a day to travel from his home to play . . . and his brother members of the club are able and willing to remunerate him for his time and expenses, why should they not be permitted to do so? It is a good democratic rule, and tends to level the artificial distinctions between wealth and poverty."[60]

Francis Pidgeon, a skilled craftsman and member of Brooklyn's Eckford club, argued that *Porter's Spirit* had misunderstood the true effects of professionalism. The delegates, he explained, had not banned it because of "snobbish inclinations"; rather, they had acted to protect the more humble clubs. "How would you like to see those you depended upon to uphold the name and fame of the club bought up like cattle," he asked, "or if not bought, would you like to see the bribe repeatedly offered to them, to desert their colors. These things have occurred, and it was thought best to nip them in the bud. . . . this rule was passed to protect ourselves against the influence of money, and give 'honest poverty' a fair chance, and in a struggle for supremacy between clubs to let skill, courage, and endurance decide who shall be the victors."[61] Undoubtedly gentlemen's clubs (like the Knickerbockers) abhorred the idea of playing for money; and men like Pidgeon realized that while professionalism might aid some indigent players, it would hurt many artisan nines.

A final factor that accelerated the rise of the "New York game" was the excitement generated by the unofficial city championship held in Brooklyn in 1860. While other states, cities, and towns held local tournaments, most baseball enthusiasts recognized Brooklyn as the sport's capital and that city's champion as the best in the nation. The three leading contestants in Brooklyn were the Excelsiors, the Atlantics, and the Eckfords. The three-game series that began in July between the Excelsiors and Atlantics attracted huge throngs estimated at 8,000–20,000 people, including hundreds of players from nearby New Jersey cities, Washington, D.C., Baltimore, Philadelphia, Boston, and Rochester, Buffalo, Troy, and Newburgh, New York.[62] The Excelsiors won the inaugural match in a romp, 23–4, while the second game, a thriller, was won by the Atlantics, 15–14. All awaited the deciding game in late August, but that contest ended abruptly when intense crowd heckling forced the Excelsiors' captain to remove his men from the field, disappointing many fans and prompting some negative reaction among the city's newspapers, including the *Brooklyn Daily Eagle*.[63] The Atlantics retained their city championship by default, then successfully defended it in a hard three-game series against the Eckfords later that fall.[64]

By 1860 the players and promoters of Philadelphia townball and the Massachusetts and New York varieties of baseball had succeeded in spreading the gospel of their games across most of the United States. All of the New York City sporting weeklies regularly proclaimed baseball to be "the national game of ball" before the Civil War. A geography of the sport before 1861 proves this judgment to be reasonably accurate. Most formally organized teams were located in cities, but a few also appeared in rural areas. Among the competing versions, the NABBP rules were well known, dominating in most of the larger communities. The hotbeds of baseball fever were in the New York City vicinity, the Hudson River Valley, central and upstate New York, and the Boston area; and during the 1850s the game also took root in numerous eastern, southern, and western localities.

In New England the "Massachusetts game" remained the sportsmen's favorite form of ball play, even though several clubs switched to the NABBP rules. In 1859 a Boston correspondent to the *Clipper* wrote that the "New York game" was "fast gaining ground in this State, and I should not be surprised if, in the course of a few years, it should become the only game played in Boston."[65] Although some thought that the Massachusetts version was more "scientific," it was obvious that the NABBP/New York style of play was winning converts. A report from the Bay State noted that fifty-nine clubs observed the Massachusetts rules while eighteen followed those of New York.[66] In 1860 two Massachusetts nines, the Bowdoins and the Tri-Mountains, played a spirited match in Boston using the New York rules. The Tri-Mountains' pitcher was none other than E. G. Saltzman, the transplanted Gothamite who had helped to pioneer the new rules in Boston. *Wilkes' Spirit* praised his missionary work and wondered: "When will some of our crack clubs make a flying visit to Boston, and by a handsome trial on Boston Common, with the Bowdoin or Tri-Mountain boys, help those clubs along who are working hard in Boston to demonstrate the superiority of our 'National Game', over the so-called 'Massachusetts Game.'"[67]

In the New York City vicinity the NABBP rules dominated, with only a few pockets of old-style townball remaining. Manhattan had dozens of clubs competing there and across the river in Hoboken, New Jersey. But the real center of baseball mania was Brooklyn, which fielded over one hundred junior and senior clubs before 1861.[68] In 1857 *Porter's Spirit* remarked: "Verily Brooklyn is fast earning the title of the 'City of Baseball Clubs,' as well as the 'City of Churches.' As numerous as are its church spires, pointing the way to heaven, the present prospect indicates that they may be soon outnumbered by the rapidly increasing ball clubs."[69] Over in New Jersey, at least 130 baseball clubs were active between

1855 and 1860, with Newark alone accounting for 36 junior and senior organizations and Jersey City adding another 42.[70]

The NABBP conquered the City of Brotherly Love in 1860, when the Olympic Ball Club dropped townball after nearly thirty years and adopted the New York rules of play. According to one of the club's chroniclers, this decision produced "an honorable retirement of most of their old members. . . . mutterings both loud and deep were freely heard at the innovation."[71] The first club in that city to play the New York style of baseball was the Penn Tigers (later the Winonas), during an intrasquad match in late 1858. The next year brought Philadelphia's first full season of interclub play, as about a dozen nines laid out diamonds and played a primitive form of baseball. According to the *Clipper,* they had "bases . . . a cubic foot in size" that base runners used as stools, and "any one taking a ball on the fly was entitled to a drink, and even bound catches were applauded."[72] Townball and the "Massachusetts game" still lingered in Pittsburgh and in such rural hamlets as Allegheny, Mauch Chunk, and Conneaut Lake.

In the South, the Brooklyn Excelsiors' tour had sparked the creation of several Baltimore clubs, while Washington, D.C., inaugurated the Potomac and National clubs in 1860. New Orleans experienced a boom in 1859 when seven teams were started, and two more followed the next year. These early New Orleans nines at first used the Massachusetts rules, but by 1860 they all had switched to the NABBP regulations.[73] In 1860 Kentucky boasted four clubs in Louisville and one in Newport, while Missouri had five in St. Louis and one in St. Joseph. Even Houston, Texas, reported a club in 1861.

The Midwest and West also shared in the excitement over baseball. Chicago had several clubs that played by the New York rules in 1860, while that style also governed play in Milwaukee in 1860 and Nininger City, Minnesota territory, in 1857. Detroit, Oberlin (Ohio), Cleveland, Davenport (Iowa), Fox Lake (Wisconsin), and St. Paul all reported clubs and matches to the New York sporting journals. On the Pacific Coast, California claimed at least five teams in San Francisco, Stockton, and Sacramento, and several tournaments played according to the NABBP regulations in the fall of 1860 created much interest in the new team sport in the Golden State.[74]

The question remains: Why did the "New York game" prevail over its rivals? One answer is simple: both spectators and players favored its rules. To a modern eye, the New York version seems more efficient and appealing, especially considering the symmetry of the diamond compared to the townball square. The containment of play by foul lines permitted spectators to crowd closer to the action and cut down the ground that fielders had to cover. Furthermore, the NABBP game was undoubtedly safer, simpler, and easier for adults to learn and master. Surely the older players must have preferred the force and tag rules for putouts, instead of the townball custom of throwing (or "burning") the ball at the runners.[75] James D'Wolf Lovett's preference for the "New York game" undoubtedly was shared by many: "The pitching, instead of swift throwing, looked easy to hit, and the pitcher stood off so far, and then there was no danger of getting plugged with the ball while running bases; and the ball was so lively and could be batted so far!"[76] Three outs to a side also seemed to be an improvement over the New England custom of "one-out, all-out," permitting more action, more base runners, and hence more tension and drama. Nine innings brought the game to a conclusion within three hours, while many Massachusetts matches failed to reach a deciding one hundred runs before nightfall. Yet the latter game also had its good points and excitement, such as overhand pitching and the fly rule, later adopted by the NABBP and its successors. Rule differences thus provide only part of the reason why the "New York game" won out over its rivals.

A better explanation may be found in the "urban imperialism" of the great city on the Hudson. During the middle decades of the nineteenth century, New York extended its economic influence throughout the west and south via its monumental transportation network of canals, railroads, and steamships. New York traders and bankers were active in attracting business toward their home city, and in doing so they established contacts with many strangers who came under their influence. At the same time the city was becoming a cultural center and a major threat to Boston as a leading literary and communication headquarters. Its sporting weeklies, as previously emphasized, also played a significant role in promoting New York baseball. Wherever New York businessmen and newspapers appeared, they carried with them their local sport.

Thus it was not surprising to find baseball thriving in those cities where New Yorkers were active: Baltimore, St. Louis, New Orleans, Chicago, Washington, D.C., and San Francisco. More significantly, in many of these cities sportsmen imitated the men from Manhattan and Brooklyn by naming their clubs after the famous Atlantic, Excelsior, Eagle, and Empire clubs. Even Boston and Philadelphia came under the New York baseball influence as they fell further behind in population and commercial power. Thus, just as New York was defeating its major trade rivals and strengthening its position as the largest and most powerful city in the United States, it was also exporting and promoting its native sport as the American national pastime— an entertaining product that it marketed extremely well. There were certainly many men in smaller communities who looked to the big city for leadership, even as they may have resented its dominance. In contrast, Philadelphia and Boston were not as influential in the hinterlands, and their styles of ball play were not as attractive and could not compete with the game from Gotham.[77]

Baseball boomed before the Civil War, with the key preconditions for its modernization and diffusion across America having been achieved by 1860. As men sought wholesome relief from their toil in oppressive factories, shops, and offices, they naturally turned to a familiar childhood game that was simple and inexpensive. Modern communication and transportation facilitated both interclub and intercity competition as well as the standardization of rules. Baseball drew upon and reinforced urban pride and boosterism, which were so powerful in nineteenth-century America, and benefited from the more liberal attitude toward recreation promulgated by such public opinion leaders as clergymen and newspaper editors. Perceived as a harmless, healthy, and refreshing activity, the game was far more morally acceptable than boxing, football, or the animal amusements of the premodern era. Furthermore, it was a team sport that also highlighted individual achievement. While it fostered group loyalty, it gave star players a chance to shine.

With all of these advantages, baseball also faced some difficulties as the antebellum era ended. Many still dismissed it as a fad or a child's pastime that no dignified gentleman should pursue. Others accepted baseball as a manly and appropriate adult sport but worried about its association with gambling, drinking, and crowd disorders. These links to the urban underworld clouded baseball's future just as the masses embraced it as their favorite sport. But before the game could cope with these problems, it first had to survive the disruptive effects of the great intersectional struggle. While it met that test, it saw its amateur era give way to one of commercialism and professionalism.

NOTES

1. Charles A. Peverelly, *The Book of American Pastimes* (New York, 1866), 338.
2. Quoted in Francis C. Richter, *The History and Records of Base Ball* (Philadelphia, 1914), 19.
3. Information in this and the preceding paragraph from Richter, *Records of Base Ball,* 20–25 (quotes on 22, 25).
4. Richter, *Records of Base Ball,* 27–30 (quotes on 27, 30).
5. Richter, *Records of Base Ball,* 30.
6. See Robert W. Henderson, "How Baseball Began," *New York Public Library Bulletin* 41 (April 1937), 287–91; "Baseball and Rounders," *New York Public Library Bulletin* 43 (April 1939), 303–14; "Baseball: Notes and Materials on Its Origins," 1940 Scrapbook, New York Public Library; *Ball, Bat, and Bishop* (New York, 1947), 132–96. See also Harold Seymour, "How Baseball Began," *New-York Historical Society Quarterly* 30 (October 1956): 369–85.
7. Henry Chadwick, ed., *Beadles's Dime Baseball Player* (New York, 1864), 5.
8. *Wilkes' Spirit* 11 (December 17, 1864): 244.
9. Peverelly, *American Pastimes,* 472–73; Scrapbook 8.19.20, Historical Society of Pennsylvania. A copy of the "Constitution and Field Rules of the Olympic Ball Club of Philadelphia, Instituted May, 1833" is in the Rosenbach Museum, Philadelphia.
10. *Wilkes' Spirit* 3 (March 2, 1861): 404.
11. *Clipper* 6 (June 19, 1858): 70; (July 10, 1858): 91, 7 (October 15, 1859): 204; (January 28, 1860): 322; 8 (July 14, 1860): 98; (August 4, 1860): 125; (August 11, 1860): 132; *Wilkes' Spirit* 1 (December 10, 1859): 214; *Philadelphia Sunday Dispatch,* October 21, 1866. For evidence that many Philadelphians migrated to Cincinnati and northern Kentucky, see James M. Bergquist, "Tracing the Origins of a Midwestern Culture: The Case of Central Indiana," *Indiana Magazine of History* 87 (March 1981): 20.

12. Albert G. Spalding, *America's National Game* (New York, 1911), 39.

13. *Porter's Spirit* 1 (December 27, 1856): 276–77.

14. James D'Wolf Lovett, *Old Boston Boys and the Games They Played* (Boston, 1907), 131.

15. *Clipper* 5 (October 10, 1857): 197; *Clipper* 6 (May 29, 1858): 44.

16. *Clipper* 6 (September 11, 1858): 162 ("Melville"); *Wilkes' Spirit* 1 (October 15, 1859): 84. For the 1859 and 1860 Massachusetts baseball conventions, see *Porter's Spirit* 4 (May 7, 1858): 148; *Wilkes' Spirit* 1 (March 17, 1860): 378.

17. Melvin L. Adelman, *A Sporting Time: New York City and the Rise of Modern Athletics, 1820–70* (Urbana, Ill., 1986), 122–23.

18. Adelman, *A Sporting Time,* 121–22; Harold Peterson, *The Man Who Invented Baseball* (New York, 1969, 1973), 53. According to Peterson, Cartwright was a bank teller in 1845 and his father was a marine surveyor and former sea captain.

19. Richter, *Records of Baseball,* 12–13.

20. For baseball clubs and matches that preceded the Knickerbockers and their first interclub games, see Melvin L. Adelman, "The First Baseball Game, the First Newspaper References to Baseball, and the New York Club: A Note on the Early History of Baseball," *Journal of Sport History* 7 (Winter 1980), 132–35.

21. Peverelly, *American Pastimes,* 339–77, 400–416.

22. These estimates are based on a close reading of the New York City weekly sporting journals and the daily newspapers published in New York, Brooklyn, Newark, and Jersey City.

23. *Clipper* 7 (May 28, 1859): 48; Spalding, *National Game,* 63.

24. Newspaper clipping from the *Cincinnati Inquirer,* undated, Henry Chadwick's scrapbooks, vol. 1, Albert G. Spalding Collection, New York Public Library; Harry Ellard, *Baseball in Cincinnati* (Cincinnati, 1907), 30–38.

25. Peterson, *Man Who Invented Baseball,* chaps. 6, 7.

26. *Clipper* 8 (November 17, 1860): 244.

27. Fred W. Lange, *History of Baseball in California and the Pacific Coast Leagues, 1847-1938* (Oakland, Calif., 1938), 6.

28. *Porter's Spirit* 4 (June 26, 1858): 260.

29. *Clipper* 6 (July 24, 1858): 106.

30. For examples of coverage of this series, see *Porter's Spirit* 4 (July 24, 1858): 332; (August 21, 1858): 388; 5 (September 18, 1858): 36; *New York Times,* July 21, August 18, September 11, 1858; *Brooklyn*

Daily Eagle, August 18, 1858; *Clipper* 6 (July 24, 1858): 110. This series may have stimulated the men of Newark and Bloomfield, New Jersey, to play an all-star match in October 1858. See *Porter's Spirit* 5 (October 23, 1858): 117.

31. *Porter's Spirit* 6 (August 6, 1859): 361.

32. *Brooklyn Daily Eagle,* September 3, March 12, May 10, 1860.

33. For example, the Hamiltons of Jersey City and the Adriatics of Newark began a series of home-and-home matches in 1858. For the opening encounter, see *Jersey City Daily Courier and Advertiser,* October 7, 1858.

34. *Clipper* 8 (June 23, 1860): 76; *Wilkes' Spirit* 3 (November 17, 1860): 164.

35. Spalding, *National Game,* 91.

36. *Clipper* 8 (October 6, 1860): 197.

37. *Clipper* 8 (October 6, 1860): 195; *Philadelphia Morning Pennsylvanian,* September 22, 24–25, 1860.

38. Quoted in *Clipper* 6 (September 18, 1858): 172.

39. *Clipper* 8 (November 24, 1860): 250.

40. Peverelly, *American Pastimes,* 486.

41. *Porter's Spirit* 2 (June 20, 1857): 244-45; 3 (October 24, 1857–January 23, 1858): passim; *Clipper* 7 (April 30, 1859): 10; (February 18, 1860): 349; (March 10, 1860): 372; (March 17, 1860): 380; (March 31, 1860): 396; (April 7, 1860): 404.

42. *New York Times,* April 21, 1908; *Brooklyn Daily Eagle,* April 20, 1908; *Dictionary of American Biography,* vol. 3 (New York, 1929), 587. For an early scoring system, see *Clipper* 8 (March 23, 1861): 388.

43. *Clipper* 8 (March 30, 1861): 394.

44. Harold Seymour, *Baseball: The Early Years* (New York, 1960), 37.

45. *Porter's Spirit* 1 (October 11, 1856): 93; (December 20, 1856): 257; *Spirit* 26 (January 3, 1857): 558; *Wilkes' Spirit* 3 (January 17, 1861): 308. Some baseball historians have maintained that these conventions rejected the attempts by the "aristocratic" Knickerbockers to control the destiny of baseball. But Adelman argues convincingly that the Knickerbockers did not try to dominate the proceedings and that there was no "palace revolt" against them. See *A Sporting Time,* 127–28.

46. *Porter's Spirit* 4 (April 3, 1858): 68.

47. *Porter's Spirit* 4 (March 13, 1858): 21; *Spirit* 30 (March 24, 1860): 53.

48. *Clipper* 5 (April 3, 1858): 396.

49. *Wilkes' Spirit* 2 (March 24, 1860): 37; 3 (December 22, 1860): 244; (January 5, 1861): 277; *Clipper* 7 (March 24, 1860): 387; 8 (December 22, 1860): 284.

50. *Clipper* 7 (March 3, 1860): 364.

51. *Spirit* 28 (March 20, 1858): 65; *Porter's Spirit* 3 (January 2, 1858): 277; *Clipper* 5 (May 16, 1857): 26.

52. *Porter's Spirit* 4 (March 20, 1858): 37; *Clipper* 5 (March 20, 1858): 379; *Wilkes' Spirit* 3 (March 2, 1861): 403–4.

53. *Clipper* 5 (April 3, 1858): 396.

54. *Porter's Spirit* 4 (March 20, 1858): 37; (March 27, 1858): 60.

55. *Clipper* 5 (May 2, 1857): 13; *Porter's Spirit* 4 (April 17, 1858): 100.

56. *Porter's Spirit* 4 (August 20, 1858): 388.

57. *Clipper* 6 (March 19, 1859): 378; 8 (June 30, 1860): 83. See also *Clipper* 7 (July 9, 1859): 95.

58. *Clipper* 8 (November 10, 1860): 234.

59. *Porter's Spirit* 4 (April 3, 1858): 69.

60. *Clipper* 6 (March 26, 1859): 386; *Porter's Spirit* 6 (March 19, 1859): 35.

61. *Porter's Spirit* 6 (March 26, 1859): 52.

62. *New York Sunday Mercury,* July 22, August 12, 26, 1860; *New York Times,* August 10, 1860.

63. *Brooklyn Daily Eagle,* August 24, 1860. For accounts of these games, see *New York Times,* July 20, August 10, 24, 1860; *Wilkes' Spirit* 2 (September 1, 1860): 404–5.

64. *Wilkes' Spirit* 3 (November 10, 1860): 149.

65. *Clipper* 7 (May 28, 1859): 48.

66. *Clipper* 6 (September 11, 1858): 162 ("Melville"); 7 (November 19, 1859): 244. In 1860, seventy-five clubs played by the rules of the Massachusetts Association of Base Ball Players, and half of them were members of that organization. See *Clipper* 7 (March 17, 1860): 378.

67. *Wilkes' Spirit* 2 (June 2, 1860): 202. New Englanders founded clubs in Manchester, New Hampshire (1860), Vermont (1860), and Connecticut (1860). Portland, Maine, boasted four clubs playing by the New York rules in 1859.

68. This estimate is based in part on information in *Clipper* 5 (December 26, 1857): 284; *Brooklyn Daily Eagle,* July and August 1859; *Porter's Spirit* 5 (October 16, 1858): 100.

69. *Porter's Spirit* 2 (June 20, 1857): 245.

70. These estimates are derived from the New York sporting journals and the Newark and Jersey City daily newspapers. In Newark, the Knickerbocker Antiquarians persisted in playing the "old-fashioned way" dur-

ing the late 1850s. See *Porter's Spirit* 3 (November 7, 1857): 149; (November 14, 1857): 165.

71. *Wilkes' Spirit* 3 (March 2, 1861): 404.

72. *Clipper* 7 (August 20, 1859): 141; 8 (May 20, 1865): 42; *Wilkes' Spirit* 1 (February 11, 1860): 365; *Spirit* 20 (February 20, 1869): 3; *Philadelphia Morning Pennsylvanian*, June 18, 23, September 24, 1860; *Philadelphia Sunday Mercury*, November 4, 1866.

73. Dale Somers, *The Rise of Sports in New Orleans, 1850–1900* (Baton Rouge, La., 1972), 49–50.

74. *Clipper* 8 (October 21, 1860): 215; (November 17, 1860): 244. See also "Baseball! The Story of Iowa's Early Innings," *Annals of Iowa* 22 (January 1941): 625–54; Cecil O. Monroe, "The Rise of Baseball in Minnesota," *Minnesota History* 19 (1938): 62–81; Carl Wittke, "Baseball in Its Adolescence," *The Ohio State Archeological and Historical Quarterly* 61 (April 1952): 111–27.

75. One account of the Knickerbockers' new tag rule attributes it to "one or two severe accidents" caused by the old practice. See *Wilkes' Spirit* 11 (December 17, 1864): 244.

76. Lovett, *Old Boston Boys*, 142.

77. See Robert G. Albion, *The Rise of the New York Port, 1815–1860* (New York, 1939).

CHAPTER

4

Civil War Interlude

IN the spring of 1861, baseball players and cricketers in dozens of American cities and towns prepared their minds, bodies, and grounds for another brilliant season of play. But the news from Fort Sumter, South Carolina, sent shock waves throughout the sporting world. The beginning of four terrible years of civil war had important short- and long-term repercussions for cricket and baseball. Both sports became features of military life, and athletic competitions took on new meanings in the context of war. Observers of American sporting life stressed the analogy between team sports and battle, urging the former as training for the latter. Thousands of players enlisted in regiments and competed on makeshift camp grounds as they awaited combat on battlefields. Meanwhile, on the homefront, civilians pursued their favorite pastimes. Baseball weathered the trial better than cricket and at war's end began a new phase of expansion.

The sporting press of the late 1850s and early 1860s frequently pointed out the parallels between America's first team sports and war. In wrapping up its review of the 1857 season, the *Clipper* remarked that the players "will be compelled to lay by their weapons of war, enter into winter quarters, there to discuss and lay plans for the proper conducting of next season's campaign."[1] Yet sportswriters were acutely aware of the crucial differences between play and mortal struggle. In 1858 the *Clipper* reported that after the Trenton club played the Lambertville eleven, "they had a collation served up on the field, and though at *war*, were the best of friends."[2] A Rochester reporter noted that "many of our first class players are now engaged in the 'grand match' against the rebellious 'side,' and already have made a 'score' which, in after years, they will be proud to look upon." Another remarked that "Cricket and Baseball clubs . . . are now enlisted in a different sort of exercise, the rifle or gun taking the place of the bat, while the play ball gives place to the leaden messenger of death." He continued: "Men who have heretofore made their mark in friendly strife for superiority in various games, are now beating off the rebels who would dismember this glorious 'Union of States.'"[3]

In March 1861 the *Clipper* hinted at the impending crisis: "God forbid that any balls but those of the Cricket and Baseball field may be caught either on the fly or bound, and we trust that no arms but those of the flesh may be used to impel them, or stumps, but those of the wickets, injured by them." A Union soldier encamped with his regiment at Culpepper Court House in Virginia reported in April 1864 that "if General Grant does not send them to have a match with Gen. Lee, they are willing to have another friendly match, but if he does, the blue coats think that the leaden balls will be much harder to stop than if thrown by friendly hands on the club grounds."[4] *Wilkes' Spirit* endorsed a proposal to hold a grand benefit cricket tournament to supply enlisted players "with bats and balls enough to enjoy themselves to their hearts' content, when there are no leaden or iron messengers of death flying about, to 'bowl them out,' or knock down their wickets of Life."[5]

Soldier-athletes believed that baseball and cricket were useful in preparing them for the more serious and deadly contests. The *Rochester Express* noted that with "the serious matter of war . . . upon our hands, . . . physical education and the development of muscle should be engendered" by indulgence in baseball. *Wilkes' Spirit* argued that cricket should be fostered in the United States as a national institution: "There can be no better preparatory school for the army than the cricket field. A quick eye and a ready hand, good stamina and a developed muscle, a generous emulation, an earnest desire to strain every nerve for the success of 'our side,' the discipline that yields obedience to a glance from the captain's eye, that never questions the umpire's decision—all essentials to the true cricketer—are qualifications and materials from which a good soldier is readily formed." The *Clipper* concurred, stating that "a body of cricketers would make good troops and would be physically equal to twice their number."[6]

Thousands of northern club members volunteered for service in the Union army, while a few enlisted in the Confederate cause.[7] The sportsmen who marched off to war took their love of play (and sometimes their bats and balls) with them. Military authorities permitted recreation for soldiers at appropriate times and places because it supplied diversion and proved useful. The United States Sanitary Commission recommended that to preserve the health of soldiers, "when practicable, amusements, sports, and gymnastic exercises should be favored amongst the men,"[8] and it listed cricket and baseball among the approved pastimes. Officers encouraged sport to relieve the boredom of camp life. Organized games also helped to motivate men during training, to foster group cohesion and loyalty, and to upgrade the physical condition of recruits. The *Clipper* praised the practice of athletic games in camp, noting the "beneficial effect they have on the spirits and health, and how they tend to alleviate the monotony of camp life. They also lead to a wholesome rivalry between companies and regiments, and augment the esprit du corps of the same, to an extent that to those who have not witnessed it would appear marvelous."[9] Ball play was even allowed in certain prison camps. For example, a prominent postwar southern baseball nine originated at Johnson's Island, where inmates learned the "New York game" while being held by Union forces.[10]

To enjoy their games, baseball players and cricketers improvised makeshift grounds, constructed rudimentary equipment, and arranged contests both in camp and perilously close to enemy positions. One baseball enthusiast sent the *Clipper* the score of a match played on the parade ground of the "Mozart Regiment, now in Secessia," in October 1861. He wanted to report the sports news to civilians on the homefront, "lest you might imagine that the 'sacred soil' yields only to the tramp of the soldier; that its hills echo only the booming gun, and the dying shriek." The scrub game, he wrote, totally "erased from their minds the all absorbing topic of the day."[11] Both the Massachusetts and New York versions of ball were played, and the men arranged pickup games within their own regiments or challenged rival units from their own or other states. Generally they sported within the relative security of their encampments, though sometimes they violated army regulations and competed outside the fortifications and beyond the line of pickets. George H. Putnam remembered a contest among Union troops in Texas that was aborted by a suprise enemy assault: "Suddenly there came a scattering fire of which the three fielders caught the brunt; the center field was hit and was captured, the left and right field managed to get into our lines." The northern soldiers repulsed the Confederate attack, "but we had lost not only our center field but . . . the only baseball in Alexandria."[12]

Cricket was not as prevalent in army camps as baseball, but its enthusiasts did play, even when they had to "make bats out of anything." Lt. William Moore of the 62nd New York Volunteers, an Englishman who visited New York City while on leave, took bats and balls back to his cricket club in the Army of the Potomac. One of the feature contests matched elevens chosen from New York's 32nd and Pennsylvania's 95th regiments, at White Oak Church, Virginia, in April 1863.[13]

While baseball enthusiasts enjoyed their favorite sport in army camps, the game suffered some understandable setbacks on the homefront. With so many sportsmen marching off to war, and with civilian anxieties focused on battlefield news, interest in playful contests naturally waned. Two months after the first shots at Fort Sumter, a *Clipper* editorial on the impact of the war on New York City life noted that the conflict "has knocked sports out of business, and thrown a damper on every little amusement we heretofore enjoyed so well." At summer's end in 1861 that journal described the dullness of New York's sporting life: "many of our . . . friends have enlisted in the defence of the Union, while those that remained . . . lacked the spirit to endulge in those recreations so rife among us in former seasons."[14] Proof of the disruptive effects of the war on baseball was the disbanding of many clubs, the reduction in the number of first-nine contests, and the drop in attendance at the annual conventions of the National Association of Base Ball Players.

Baseball nonetheless persisted and even progressed under trying conditions. The New York style of play gained momentum in New

England in 1862 when a tour by the Brooklyn Excelsiors excited Boston's sporting fraternity. In Philadelphia baseball overtook cricket in popularity during the early 1860s. Near the end of the ordeal the nation's capital experienced a baseball revival, thanks in part to resident New Yorkers who worked in the Treasury Department and played for the National and Union clubs on the grounds at the rear of the White House. In the South the conquest of New Orleans brought baseball back deep into Dixie, while in the West a contingent of "Rocky Mountain Boys" played the "New York game" in Denver in 1862.[15]

As before the war, the Middle Atlantic region was the center of baseball fever. Although fewer clubs and players competed in New York, New Jersey, and Pennsylvania, those states inaugurated the sport's first championship system as well as several intercity all-star contests and club tours. The early 1860s also ushered in an era of commercialism and professionalism,[16] while the NABBP continued to supervise interclub play and experiment with the rules of the sport. During the war the New York style of play continued to gain ground over its New England rival. The "Massachusetts game" still remained quite popular among army men, but on the homefront the NABBP rules predominated. *Wilkes' Spirit* grandly proclaimed in 1863 that "the National Association game has won for itself the almost unanimous approval of all who take any interest in the sport; and the clubs who adopt any other style of playing are every day, becoming 'small by degrees, and beautifully less.'"[17] New York–style baseball also increased its presence in Canada during these years. In 1864 the Young Canadians of Woodstock met the Brooklyn Atlantics for "the championship of the American continent," at the Rochester (N.Y.) State Fair. The Atlantics crushed the foreign challengers, yet the event sparked interest north of the border.[18]

After an initial setback baseball generated a surprising amount of enthusiasm during the war era. In its review of the 1861 season in the New York City vicinity, the *Clipper* reported that "the game has too strong a foothold in popularity to be frowned out of favor by the lowering brow of 'grim-visaged war,' and if any proof was needed that our national game is a fixed institution of the country, it would be found in the fact, that it has flourished through such a year of adverse circumstances as those that have marked the season of 1861."[19] The main events of that year were the championship contests between the Brooklyn Atlantics and the New York Mutuals, as well as a "Silver Ball" all-star game between select nines from New York City and Brooklyn, sponsored by the *Clipper* in October. The Brooklyn side won the latter match, with the delegation from the Atlantics carrying off the trophy for most runs scored. Despite efforts by rival newspapers to ruin the event through misleading publicity, about 8,000 persons attended.[20] The year 1862 witnessed great excitement over a championship series between the Atlantics and the Eckfords, the net proceeds going to the Brooklyn Sanitary Commission, earmarked for sick and wounded soldiers.[21]

The most striking evidence of baseball's capacity to flourish amid the adversity of war occurred in Philadelphia. The first invasion of Philadelphia players into the New York vicinity took place in 1862, as a select nine competed before about 15,000 spectators in a series of games against teams from Newark, New York, and Brooklyn. *Wilkes' Spirit* reported that the excitement of the Philadelphia challenges awakened in the New York area "the old *furore* for the game that marked the years 1857–8 and 9." The paper noted that the victory of the guests over a New York nine at Hoboken did more to advance the interest and popularity of the game in that city than five ordinary seasons' play would have done. The *Clipper* agreed, predicting that the contests would give "an immense impetus" to the sport in Philadelphia, "where it is rapidly taking the place of cricket." Select nines from Brooklyn and New York returned the visit later in the summer, generating excitement in their contests with the local Olympics, Adriatics, Athletics, and Keystones.[22] The following year the Philadelphia Athletics won two of six games against tough opponents and established themselves as contenders for baseball's championship.[23] By the end of the war, trips by Brooklyn, New York, and New Jersey clubs to the City of Brotherly Love were commonplace, with some benefit matches arranged for the United States Sanitary Commission.[24]

These tours succeeded despite the atmosphere of crisis that pervaded the entire region. In most cases the war did not detract from the excitement of the contests, and there is very little evidence that citizens disapproved of men who played ball rather than fought. Understandably, however, military news sometimes overshadowed baseball. When Brooklyn's crack Atlantics swept a series at Philadelphia in early August 1864, there was little interest or attendance. The *Clipper* explained that the local citizens "were absorbed in the important subject of resisting the rebel invasion of the State, and this and the preparations to respond to the Governor's call for 30,000 militia, materially interfered with the sensation their visit would otherwise have created." It added that most of the Philadelphia clubs could not play many of their best men because they had responded "to the call of duty."[25]

While baseball clubs kept the sport alive during the nation's ordeal, the NABBP struggled to survive and to govern the game's growth. The annual December conventions in New York City experienced a sharp drop in attendance as many clubs disbanded and others did not send delegates.[26] Local clubs dominated these meetings, which accomplished little during the first two years of the conflict. But in 1863 and 1864 the conventions addressed a series of significant issues, acting on important rule changes and on the eligibility of players to compete in recognized interclub matches. These sessions demonstrated the continuing vitality of baseball in the New York area and suggested the spirit of experimentation and the fluidity in rules that characterized early American baseball.

The 1863 meeting approved changes in pitching regulations that were designed to shift the balance of play toward batting and fielding. The primitive style of underhand slow pitching prevalent in the 1850s had given the advantage to the batter, but during the early 1860s the hurlers became more expert in swift (and often wild) deliveries. The NABBP acted to "transfer the interest of the game from the pitcher to the fielders" with new regulations that confined the pitcher to a small space, forced him to deliver "fair balls" to the batter (with the umpire empowered to declare a walk after three called balls), and required him to release the ball with both feet on the ground. (Umpires already had the authority to call strikes on a batter who refused to swing at good pitches.) The *Clipper* explained that these new rules were passed to produce slower but more accurate pitching, and it expected the result would be more scoring, better fielding, and more enjoyable games.[27] In 1863, after many years of debate and defeat, the fly rule was finally adopted, eliminating a putout from a ball caught on one bounce. This, too, was meant to encourage better fielding, but of course it also gave the offense added advantage.[28]

The Civil War had a far more damaging impact on American cricket than it did on baseball, mainly because cricket was simply not as popular as its rival, especially among players who were too young to serve in the military. Also, most of the Philadelphia leadership was removed from the cricket fields to the battlegrounds, dealing a particularly severe blow to the fate of the English game in America. While cricket did not disappear completely from the American sporting scene during the early 1860s, there were far fewer clubs, matches, and special all-star contests. To make matters worse, the annual cricket conventions commanded little respect and displayed much less vitality than the gatherings of the baseball crowd. The cricketers' version of a national organization deteriorated into confusion and inaction before passing into oblivion after 1862. At war's end the sport revived quickly in Philadelphia and in several other cities, but the nation's troubles had seriously retarded cricket's prospects for future vitality in the United States.

An early symbolic indication of the negative effects of the war on cricket in the New York City vicinity occurred in the spring of 1861, shortly after hostilities began at Fort Sumter. A large number of spectators appeared on the grounds of the East New York club, which was hosting the renowned Dragon Slayers of St. George. But they had not come to watch cricket. Instead, they had turned out "to witness the evolutions and drilling of the regiments of cavalry and infantry encamped at East New York." The troop movements "interfered considerably with the cricketers, who were at one time obliged to suspend play." The *Clipper* considered this match "an illustration of the 'pursuit of *cricket* under difficulties.'"[29] Brooklyn and adjacent Long Island fielded eight teams in 1862, but by the following year there were only three. In 1864 New York City had just three active clubs, with Newark and other nearby New Jersey towns (Orange, Paterson, and Trenton) adding perhaps another half dozen.[30] The *Clipper* lamented that in New York City and Brooklyn, with a million people and 20,000 British residents, cricket had "declined in popularity among young Americans, and it is now almost exclusively enjoyed by those old-country people who have time to devote a few hours a week to the game of the fatherland."[31]

The fate of American cricket did not rest with the sport's prospects in the New York City vicinity but rather with its fortunes in the City of Brotherly Love. There the news was discouraging. The Philadelphia Cricket Club's grounds committee report for 1861 complained that because of the outbreak of war it had been impossible to play any matches or even get the members out for practice. The officers had to wait until peace was restored to hire a professional. The club released its men from the payment of their annual dues during the time they were in the military.[32] In 1864 the *Clipper* reported: "The *locale* of American cricket, Philadelphia, has become occupied by the American National Game of Base Ball, nearly all the young American cricketers of Philadelphia having volunteered to defend the nation's stumps, at the expense even of their own." It noted with regret that Walter Newhall and "other brave young Philadelphia cricketers . . . have offered their lives as a sacrifice in defence of their country" and that "war and death have so depleted the ranks of the cricketing fraternity of the 'City of Brotherly Love,' that the game there has almost died out."[33] The Philadelphians, Young Americans, and a few lesser clubs played a reduced schedule during the war years, but clearly cricket in the city had suffered dramatically.

Outside of the Middle Atlantic region, cricket survived in curtailed form in Boston and neighboring Massachusetts factory towns, as well as in the South and West, especially New Orleans, Washington, D.C., Chicago, Cincinnati, Detroit, and San Francisco.[34] While the war forced suspension of the annual international challenges with Canada, there were a few regional battles that kept interest alive in the Northeast. The two highlights of each of the wartime summers were the annual matches between the New York Cricket Club and an all-Massachusetts eleven and those between the St. George and Boston clubs. Each year a Massachusetts cricketers' convention chose participants for the contest against the New Yorkers, an event that stimulated the sport in such pockets of cricket as Boston, Lowell, Dorchester, Shelbourne Falls, Fall River, and Charlestown.[35]

Considering the unfavorable conditions that plagued American cricket during this period, it is not surprising that the New York City conventions failed to promote or regulate the sport in the

United States. The 1861 session had been scheduled for Philadelphia for the first time, with high hopes for the inauguration of a new era. But these dreams were dashed by the news from Fort Sumter. Eleven clubs appeared to plan for special international and all-star matches that were never held. Their delegates also debated again the controversial proposal to bar players from competing for more than one organization. The measure was defeated in 1861, but the next year it passed amid considerable confusion and disorganization. Five clubs from New York City's Free Academy (later City College) attended the 1862 session and swung the balance toward prohibiting multiple memberships. But since the credentials of these clubs were questionable (they had no regular playing grounds), there was much dissatisfaction among the regulars. New York's prestigious St. George club did not bother to attend, and those clubs that did apparently did not take the proceedings very seriously. According to the *Clipper,* the meeting degenerated into "a farce." Most of the old clubs respected the English custom of permitting players to compete for several organizations, and therefore the ruling of the 1862 convention was moot. This abortive attempt to Americanize cricket ended the first effort to create a national association to govern the sport in the United States.[36]

During the Civil War both cricket and baseball were still in their adolesence in America, and both were profoundly affected by the four years of conflict. Cricket- and baseball-playing soldiers incorporated their games into army life, while they and their civilian counterparts pondered the analogies between team sports and the more serious and deadly contests of the battlefields. The war dealt baseball a temporary setback in some quarters, while in Philadelphia and other localities it thrived. Cricket suffered more severely from the turmoil of the era, especially in the City of Brotherly Love. When peace returned in April 1865, sportsmen eagerly awaited the spring season and a new beginning for both pastimes in the United States.

NOTES

1. *Clipper* 5 (October 24, 1857): 212.
2. *Clipper* 6 (August 26, 1858): 149.

3. *Clipper* 12 (April 23, 1864): 10; 9 (June 22, 1861): 68.
4. *Clipper* 8 (March 9, 1861): 372; 12 (May 7, 1864): 27.
5. *Wilkes' Spirit* 8 (May 30, 1863): 201.
6. Quoted in *Clipper* 12 (April 23, 1864): 10; *Wilkes' Spirit* 10 (August 27, 1864): 403; *Clipper* 9 (April 27, 1861): 10. Decades after 1865, several analysts noted the similarity between team sports and warfare and suggested that this partly explained the appeal of baseball and cricket. Chadwick and Spalding stressed the factors of force, strategy, and tactics common to both. More recently, Lamoreaux has argued that nineteenth-century baseball resembled eighteenth-century warfare in that both were hotly contested yet strictly controlled by rules of etiquette and limitations on the use of force. See Henry Chadwick, *How to Play Baseball* (New York, 1889); Albert G. Spalding, *America's National Game* (New York, 1911), 7, 9; David Lamoreaux, "Baseball in the Late Nineteenth Century: The Source of Its Appeal," *Journal of Popular Culture* 11 (1977): 597–613.
7. *Clipper* 9 (April 27, 1861): 10; (May 4, 1861): 20; 11 (July 4, 1863): 90; (August 8, 1863): 135; 12 (July 30, 1864): 123; *Wilkes' Spirit* 4 (May 31, 1861): 196; *Newark Daily Advertiser*, September 3, 26, 1862.
8. John R. Betts, "Home Front, Battle Field, and Sport during the Civil War," *Research Quarterly* 42 (May 1971): 127.
9. *Clipper* 11 (May 9, 1863): 31. See also Betts, "Home Front, Battle Field, and Sport," 113–32; David S. Crockett, "Sports and Recreational Practices of Union and Confederate Soldiers," *Research Quarterly* 32 (October 1961): 335–47; Lawrence W. Fielding, "Sport and the Terrible Swift Sword," *Research Quarterly* 48 (March 1977): 1–11; "War and the Trifles: Sport in the Shadows of Civil War Army Life," *Journal of Sport History* 4 (1977): 151–68.
10. *Clipper* 17 (July 17, 1864): 115.
11. *Clipper* 9 (October 26, 1861): 220.
12. Quoted in Betts, "Home Front, Battle Field, and Sport," 128–29. For other examples of baseball played in army camps, see *Newark Daily Advertiser*, November 21, 1861; June 6, 1863; *Clipper* 10 (July 12, 1862): 99; 11 (June 13, 1863): 68; (June 20, 1863): 74; 12 (May 7, 1864): 27; *Wilkes' Spirit* 10 (March 26, 1864): 52; (April 30, 1864): 132; (May 21, 1864): 180; (July 13, 1864): 292; Edward B. Bingham to Bell Bingham, April 24, 1863, Edward B. Bingham Papers, New Jersey Historical Society; Henry H. Blanchard to Horace Blanchard, May 1, 1864, catalog of James Lowe Company, Manuscripts, New Jersey Historical Society.
13. *Wilkes' Spirit* 5 (November 16, 1861): 164; 8 (May 9, 1863): 155; (May 30, 1863): 195; *Clipper* 11 (May 9, 1863): 31.
14. *Clipper* 9 (June 15, 1861): 66; (August 31, 1861): 154.

15. *Clipper* 9 (April 12, 1862): 411; 10 (June 21, 1862): 74; *Wilkes' Spirit* 11 (October 22, 1864): 116; (November 25, 1864): 204; Dale Somers, *The Rise of Sports in New Orleans, 1850–1900* (Baton Rouge, La., 1972), 74, 77–78.

16. For a full discussion of these issues, see Chapter 9.

17. *Wilkes' Spirit* 8 (March 7, 1863): 11; 11 (December 31, 1864): 277.

18. *Wilkes' Spirit* 9 (October 3, 1863): 67; 11 (September 10, 1864): 20; *Clipper* 12 (September 10, 1864): 172; (October 1, 1864): 195.

19. *Clipper* 9 (January 11, 1862): 308.

20. *Clipper* 9 (September 21, 1861): 179; (October 5, 1861): 194; (October 12, 1861): 202; (October 19, 1861): 210; (October 26, 1861): 223; (November 2, 1861): 226, 228; *Wilkes' Spirit* 5 (November 2, 1861): 133.

21. *Wilkes' Spirit* 6 (July 19, 1862): 308; (July 26, 1862): 333; (August 2, 1862): 340; 7 (September 27, 1862): 52.

22. *Wilkes' Spirit* 6 (June 14, 1862): 227; (August 30, 1862): 404; 7 (September 6, 1862): 4, 5; (November 1, 1862): 132; *Clipper* 10 (June 14, 1862): 66–68; (June 21, 1862): 74; (July 12, 1862): 99; (September 6, 1862): 163; (November 1, 1862): 227; (November 8, 1862): 237. For the Excelsiors' tour of New England, see *Wilkes' Spirit* 6 (July 5, 1862): 276; (July 19, 1862): 308. For the rise of baseball and the decline of cricket in wartime Philadelphia, see *Clipper* 13 (May 20, 1865): 42.

23. *Wilkes' Spirit* 8 (June 13, 1863): 243; (June 27, 1863): 259; *Clipper* 11 (June 13, 1863): 71; (June 27, 1863): 87; (July 4, 1863): 90.

24. *Wilkes' Spirit* 10 (May 28, 1864): 196; (June 4, 1864): 211; *Clipper* 12 (May 28, 1864): 51.

25. *Clipper* 12 (August 20, 1864): 151.

26. The number of clubs that attended these wartime meetings was thirty-four for 1861 and 1862, twenty-eight for 1863, and twenty-nine or thirty for 1864. See *Clipper* 9 (December 21, 1861): 283; 12 (December 24, 1864): 290; *Wilkes' Spirit* 5 (December 21, 1861): 245; 7 (December 20, 1862): 253; 9 (December 19, 1863): 243; 11 (December 24, 1864): 260.

27. *Clipper* 12 (May 7, 1864): 27. See also *Wilkes' Spirit* 9 (December 19, 1863): 243; 10 (May 21, 1864): 179–80.

28. *Clipper* 12 (November 5, 1864): 235; (November 19, 1864): 250; (December 24, 1864): 290; *Wilkes' Spirit* 11 (December 17, 1864): 244; (December 24, 1864): 260. The NABBP also moved to oversee interclub relations, regulate player eligibility for matches, and resolve disputes. See *Wilkes' Spirit* 9 (December 19, 1863): 243; 11 (December 24, 1864): 260; *Clipper* 12 (November 5, 1864): 235; (December 24, 1864): 290.

29. *Clipper* 9 (June 8, 1861): 63; *Wilkes' Spirit* 4 (June 15, 1861): 227.

30. *Clipper* 9 (March 29, 1862): 395; 11 (May 14, 1863): 46; 12 (September 3, 1864): 162–63; (September 24, 1864): 186; *Newark Daily Advertiser,* May 2, June 11, 1864.

31. *Clipper* 12 (April 30, 1864): 19.

32. Minute Book, Philadelphia Cricket Club, vol. 1, Historical Society of Pennsylvania.

33. *Clipper* 12 (April 30, 1864): 19. See also *Clipper* 11 (July 4, 1863): 90.

34. *Wilkes' Spirit* 6 (May 3, 1862): 141; (June 28, 1862): 269; (August 9, 1862): 355; 11 (October 1, 1864): 68; (October 8, 1864): 84; (December 17, 1864): 245; *Clipper* 11 (May 9, 1863): 31; (July 18, 1863): 111; (October 10, 1863): 204; 12 (April 16, 1864): 2; (June 18, 1864): 74; (August 13, 1864): 138; (October 8, 1864): 204; (October 15, 1864): 210; (November 5, 1864): 235; (November 19, 1864): 250; (November 26, 1864): 259.

35. *Clipper* 9 (August 24, 1861): 151; (September 7, 1861): 165; 10 (September 6, 1862): 167; 12 (July 16, 1864): 111; (July 23, 1864): 115; *Wilkes' Spirit* 6 (August 2, 1862): 340; (August 30, 1862): 404; 7 (September 13, 1862): 20; 8 (August 8, 1863): 356; (August 22, 1863): 388; 9 (September 19, 1863): 36; 10 (July 16, 1864): 308; (July 30, 1864): 340.

36. *Clipper* 9 (May 18, 1861): 36; 10 (May 24, 1862): 43; *Wilkes' Spirit* 4 (May 18, 1861): 165; 6 (May 17, 1862): 172.

CHAPTER

5

A National Game

THE creation of American team sports coincided with an intense wave of political and cultural nationalism that swept the country during the middle decades of the nineteenth century. In the domestic arena, the rise of sectionalism in the South threatened the life of the nation but also made northerners and westerners more conscious of their attachment to the Union. The influx of foreigners inflamed patriotic passions, as many citizens resented the arrival of thousands of Irish, Germans, English, and other Europeans. In foreign affairs, the United States defeated Mexico in a war that secured Texas; and it brought Utah, New Mexico, and California under the Stars and Stripes. A negotiated settlement with Great Britain over the Oregon boundary averted another war, though Anglo-American relations remained tense. As "Young America" became a popular slogan of the Democratic party, the United States expanded its trade and influence into Latin America and Asia. In their cultural lives, Americans strived for a literary and artistic independence from European (and especially British) influence that would match their political separation from the Old World. Cultural nationalism also appeared in the realm of sport, as Brother Jonathan challenged John Bull in horse racing, yachting, and boxing.[1]

Given this atmosphere of chauvinism, it is understandable why the idea of a national game appealed to the American imagination during this era. But in the 1850s it was not yet clear which sport would earn that distinction. Cricket had a strong head start over baseball in many cities and initially enjoyed more extensive newspaper coverage—especially from the New York City sporting press. In 1857 the *Clipper* reported that Britain's pastime was "rapidly making its way into popular favor as one of our national games," despite some prejudice against Englishmen.[2] A Philadelphia enthusiast proclaimed in 1859 that "there is no game that has attained in this country in so short a period such unlimited popularity, nor is there any so well calculated to retain its pre-eminence as Cricket. Ten years ago, there were but two or three clubs established here, and the game was but little understood outside of their immediate members. At present, the clubs can only be numbered by hundreds, and the interest which the mass of the people take in the game is evinced by the numbers that attend every good match, and the applause which brilliant batting and good fielding are sure to call forth."[3]

This prediction proved too optimistic, for by 1860 it was already clear that baseball had defeated cricket for the honor of being America's national game. References to "the national game of baseball" appeared frequently in the daily and sporting press throughout the late 1850s, even before the modern form actually achieved a truly national scope. In 1856 the *Clipper* noted that baseball "had its origin on this Continent, and is now thoroughly established as an American game, equal, to a certain extent, to the English game of Cricket." Four months later the paper announced that "the game of Base Ball is generally considered the National game amongst Americans; and right well does it deserve that appelation." *Porter's Spirit* reported on the growing popularity of "this noble American game, which all the seductions of the scientific game of Cricket have not been able to undermine." In the next issue it added: "This fine American game seems to be progressing in all parts of the United States with new spirit, while in New York and its neighborhood its revival seems to have been taken up almost as a matter of national pride." Commenting on the work of the first baseball convention in January 1857, the paper urged that baseball "ought to be looked upon in this country with the same national enthusiasm as Cricket and Football are regarded in the British Islands. . . . We recommend it because there should be some one game peculiar to the citizens of the United States. The Germans have brought hither their Turnverein Association. . . . and it certainly was quite time that some attempt was made to set up a game that could be termed a 'Native American Sport.'" In 1857 the *Clipper* conceded that baseball was still mostly confined to the New York area but was confident that it "will not be long ere it becomes one of our national pastimes." In 1860 the paper confirmed that baseball "may now be considered the National game of ball."[4]

The early association between baseball and American nationalism appears in several symbols that players adopted for their clubs. Many clubs selected such patriotic names as Young America, Columbia, Union, Independent, Eagle, American, Continental, Empire, National, Liberty, and Pioneer. Others honored such heroes as George Washington, Alexander Hamilton, James Madison, Thomas Jefferson, Andrew Jackson, and Benjamin Franklin. The nation's flag was also commonly used to consecrate baseball. For example, in 1859 in the small town of Danvers Centre, Massachusetts, a bevy of ladies presented the Stars and Stripes to the local Essex Base Ball Club. Their delegate praised the men for their healthy recreation, which she thought was far preferable to the frequenting of "the gilded saloon, or the table of chance."[5] Clearly, baseball had begun to acquire familiar connections with love of country, freedom, virtue, morality, the work ethic, and other traditional American values.

The respective fortunes of baseball and cricket in mid-nineteenth-century America provide data for intriguing case studies in comparative social history. Why do certain sports prosper in some countries but fail miserably in others? Baseball defeated its English rival to become the national game of the United States, yet by the turn of the century it had not generated much excitement in Europe, though it had taken root in the Caribbean and in parts of Asia. In contrast, after 1865 cricket became a distinctly second-rate sport in the United States but flourished in India, Australia, New Zealand, South Africa, and other British colonies. While the following discussion concerns only the fate of both games in the United States, it suggests some factors that might govern the prospects of other sports in various cultural and historical contexts.

Baseball boomed in America while cricket declined because of a variety of complicated, interrelated factors. The nature of American society and the special characteristics of each sport shaped their respective destinies, as did such external events as the outbreak of civil war. Local and regional influences also must be weighed, for New York City, Brooklyn, Newark, Philadelphia, and Boston, among others, differed in their sporting experiences. The most important forces affecting both pastimes in America during these years were: (1) the pre-1840 ball-playing tradition; (2) the availability of playing fields and other necessary equipment, as well as the expense of participation; (3) the nature and degree of sponsorship and promotion by advocates; (4) structural characteristics for players and spectators; (5) the degree of modernization and potential adaptability. A consideration of each of these topics helps to explain why baseball defeated cricket and also why cricket struggled to survive even as a minor sport in America.

The sports analysts of the Civil War era offered a simple but superficial explanation for baseball's triumph. They argued that Americans preferred it because it was indigenous and thus reflected their national character. The *New York Herald* called baseball "more suited to the genius of the people." Charles Peverelly wrote that "it is a game which is peculiarly suited to the American temperament and disposition. . . . the pastime suits the people, and the people suit the pastime."[6] Reporting on the lopsided baseball victory of an American nine over eleven cricketers in Syracuse (N.Y.), the *Jersey City Daily Courier and Advertiser* concluded, "Cricket is too solemn and deliberate a game for a Yankee, and Base Ball would seem too lively an exercise for Mr. Bull."[7] Henry Chadwick later declared that "every game or pastime of a nation possesses in part the peculiar characteristics of the people with whom it is a favorite, and probably, in no instance is this fact more strikingly illustrated than in the case of the English national game of cricket." He added: "We, fast people of America, call cricket slow and tedious; while the leisurely, take-your-time-my boy-people of England think our game of base ball too fast. Each game, however, just suits the people of the two nations."[8]

More recently, Melvin Adelman and Ian Tyrrell have shown the limitations of this "cultural nationalist" interpretation of the rise of baseball and the demise of cricket. While scholars still search for the essence of the American national character, it is clear that such a concept cannot adequately explain the relative popularity of particular sports in the United States. Both of these historians have presented sophisticated and helpful analyses, but their treatments leave room for further interpretation. In particular, Tyrrell's analysis is weak with regard to structural differences between the two sports, and Adelman does not place enough emphasis on the importance of anti-English feelings or on such practical considerations as availability of practice grounds, time constraints, and attempts by Americans to adapt cricket to conditions in this country.[9]

The colonial, Revolutionary, and early nineteenth-century American traditions of ball playing exerted a powerful influence on the competition between baseball and cricket after 1850. In Great Britain young men and adults commonly enjoyed ball games before mid-century, while in the United States the general public frowned upon such activity. It is true, however, that American children played primitive versions of baseball, and on special holidays grown men arranged townball contests, especially in New England. There is evidence that some American children played simplified forms of cricket ("wicket"), and a few formal cricket clubs for gentlemen existed in early Boston, New York, and other cities and towns. On the whole, the typical American child before 1840 was familiar with rounders, "old cat," or "base" but probably had little or no knowledge of either "wicket" or cricket.[10] The representative American adult male rarely played any ball sport. Yet obviously the greater popularity of baseball among American boys gave that game an important (but not insurmountable) advantage over cricket.

With the advent of the baseball and cricket manias of the 1850s, the availability of playing grounds became critical. In this area baseball enjoyed a vital edge: baseball diamonds did not have to be as well manicured as cricket surfaces, which were supposed to be rolled frequently to keep them level. (Since the bowler bounced the ball to the batsman in cricket, a smooth field was important to assist the former and to protect the latter.) Clubs in both sports had trouble acquiring or renting appropriate space in the exploding cities of mid-nineteenth-century America, but cricketers faced the greater difficulty. In 1856 *Porter's Spirit* noted the lack of public space for cricket in the United States and predicted that in New York City, "when we have our Central Park in order, there will be no lack of cricketers." Although the park commissioners approved the construction of baseball and cricket grounds, they delayed granting permission for their use. This prompted the *Clipper* to ask in 1863 whether the new facilities were "designed for use, or merely to excite the envy of every ball player who is in search of a good ground to practice his favorite game upon." The paper claimed that "it is only the want of suitable grounds for practice that limits the number of clubs" and suggested that permitting the New York Cricket Club to play in Central Park "would add materially to the summer attraction there, and to the prosperity of 'the noble game,' as there it would be brought more in contact with the people." It was not until 1865, however, that the commissioners allowed a practice game in Central Park, at which time the St. George club gave "the very fastidious gents . . . an opportunity of witnessing the effects of playing cricket on their carefully preserved field."[11]

According to an 1867 publication of the Germantown Cricket Club, "with the difficulty of procuring suitable grounds, and the expense required in the necessary preparation, Cricketers must expect for some time to hold, numerically, a secondary place to those of the Base-ball persuasion, when almost any piece of ground, with but little trouble can be made to serve their purpose."[12] James D'Wolf Lovett remembered that as a boy during the 1850s he joined the "Young Bostons" and was enthusiastic for cricket. But he found that Boston Common "was an impossible place for cricket, the hard baked ground making a good wicket or bowling crease out of the question." He explained that the senior Boston cricketers relocated in East Cambridge, "while the remaining clubs gradually disbanded. I with the others drifted into baseball."[13] The *Clipper* stressed the "trifling expense incurred in the preparation of a ground and the purchase of the materials of the game" as an advantage baseball held over cricket. Charles Peverelly also endorsed this view, describing baseball as "an economical recreation."[14] *Wilkes' Spirit* concurred: "The accessories being less costly than those of the turf, the aquatic course, or the cricket-field, it is an economic game, and within easy reach of the masses."[15]

In addition to prior traditions and practical considerations, the issue of nationality also affected the fortunes of both team sports in the United States. While nineteenth-century Americans associated cricket with Great Britain and baseball with the United States, they did not reject the former pastime simply because it was British. Anglo-Americans had imported British customs and recreations in colonial days, and after 1776 the new nation still shared much of the culture of the former ruling country, enjoying such English pastimes as hunting, fishing, horse racing, and boating. The special problem cricket faced in the United States was not simply one of origin but rather that the sport was controlled by an immigrant community that used it in part to preserve its own ethnic identity. The intense nativism of the 1850s did generate some anti-British sentiment in American cities, and there was certainly some hostility toward cricket because of it. But this liability could have been overcome through proper sponsorship and promotion.

The *Clipper* stated in 1857 that one obstacle facing cricket was "the assertion made by certain ignorant and prejudiced parties, that Cricket is only played by Englishmen." In 1861 it commented: "Three years ago it was a difficult matter to find any one member of the American ball playing community, in this vicinity, that could regard the English game of cricket with any favor. The practice of the game was confined almost exclusively to the British residents of this city. . . . we must endeavor to remove the prejudices that exist against a game that emanates from a foreign country, and . . . we must overcome the same prejudice that exists among the generality of cricketers against the American game of ball." The journal concluded by criticizing "the too great prevalence of that national feeling so characteristic of the foreign element of our community. . . . it sometimes degenerates into clannishness, and then it becomes decidedly objectionable."[16] *Porter's Spirit* noted that "animated and occasionally disagreeable debates" occurred between cricketers and baseball players when they compared the merits of their respective sports. It repeated a saying "that seems to be regarded by many English cricketers as a truism . . . that 'Americans cannot play cricket.'"[17]

To eliminate or reduce American antagonism toward cricket, Englishmen had to be willing to reach out to American youth and adult ball players. In New York City it appears that the St. George Cricket Club was not especially active in such missionary work. The *Clipper* was convinced that certain leading Dragon Slayers pursued an overly snobbish and exclusive policy. In 1860 that journal chided them for "having a great desire to obtain a controlling influence in all matters appertaining to cricket." With enclosed grounds and a full treasury, they did not "promote that cordiality of intercourse that should characterize the conduct of all thorough cricketers." In 1868 the *New York Times* maintained that "had our resident English cricketers observed a less exclusive and more liberal policy of action in the government of their clubs . . . we have not the least doubt that cricket would have gained much of the popularity its innate attraction is deserving of. But instead of this being done, an English exclusiveness has marked the government of the leading organizations, while no encouragement has been afforded young players."[18]

Henry Chadwick blamed the failure of Brooklyn's American Cricket Club on "international prejudice, the majority of cricketers refusing to sacrifice their national desire for supremacy in order that the game might be made popular in America." On the related issue of social class, the *Spirit* pointed out that English immigrant cricketers displayed an elitism that alienated many of the middle and lower ranks in the United States. That journal's publisher criticized "the imported snobbishness" exhibited and stated: "If Lord Dinglebury's son, with whom I played in the first eleven of the Nobshire Club, acted like one who felt himself superior to me, my first impulse is to show myself Sir Snob when I play in America." The Englishmen of the Newark clubs were more interested (and more successful) in converting American-born players; and in Philadelphia, the early takeover of the sport by upper-class residents reduced but did not eliminate the ethnic issue.[19]

One important factor that inhibited American acceptance of cricket was the Englishmen's tendency to monopolize play in both practice sessions and formal matches. This was frequently a problem in batting, for novices were usually retired quickly, while experts retained their turn for long periods. In baseball the beginner and the weaker batter had more chances to learn.[20] The British customs of multiple club memberships and permitting professionals to participate in challenges also deprived the native sportsmen of sufficient opportunity to learn cricket. Except in Philadelphia, older countrymen tended to dominate the action at all levels of recreation and serious competition. As an 1858 *New York Daily Times* editorial explained: "Yankees protested that when they fairly attempted a share of the honors of the field, they stood no chance; that the old cricketers, by fair means or foul, always conspired to seize the victory; even that they hired professional players to conduct the game for them when the odds were on Jonathan's side, and so it came to be believed that no man who did not drop his H's could possibly win honors at bowling or wicket-keeping."[21]

While ethnic loyalties and tensions certainly influenced the fortunes of both cricket and baseball in America, far more important were the structural characteristics of each sport. Within the cultural context of mid-nineteenth-century America, baseball had numerous features that made it more attractive than its English rival to both players and spectators. While today's sports fans appreciate the complexity of modern baseball, its early form was much simpler. Nineteenth-century observers believed that baseball was elementary in its rules and easy to learn, while they saw cricket as more "scientific" and more difficult to play well. According to *Porter's Spirit,* "There are many points in cricket which base-ball has not, and for real science it is preferable." Baseball had one advantage "in the simplicity of its rules, and the facility with which a thorough knowledge of the game is acquired." In further developing this theme, the journal explained that cricket was "a game of physical skill and mental cultivation, and requires . . . the union of great physical activity and courage, with considerable powers of the mind." New York's *Sunday Mercury* argued that "Base-ball is more popular than cricket, for the reason that it is more simple, more easily understood, more exciting, and quite as manly and noble, if properly played." The *Clipper* maintained that baseball "is capable of being played and learned in one fourth the time required in cricket."[22] Of course, many American-born players quickly learned the modern version of baseball because they already had some familiarity with primitive forms of the pastime from their childhoods. That was generally not the case with cricket.

Quite a few ball players preferred the American game because of time considerations and because its faster pace afforded them a greater chance to join in the action. As a form of recreation, on practice days there was little or no difference between the two sports; but for interclub and special competitions there was a striking contrast. Most baseball games played according to the New York rules lasted between two and three hours, while those governed by the Massachusetts regulations lasted several hours longer. Peverelly's 1866 observation seems valid for the NABBP game: "Baseball does not demand from its votaries too much time, or rather, too great a proportion of the day. In the long sunshiny days of summer, games are frequently commenced at four and even five o'clock in the afternoon, and completed some time before sunset. Consequently the great mass, who are in a subordinate capacity, can participate in this health-giving and noble pastime."[23] By comparison, the great majority of first-eleven and all-star cricket contests took at least one and often two full days to complete.

Nineteenth-century urban American sportsmen were extremely time-conscious. Even those who had ample leisure time available to them were reluctant to spend too much of it on sport. In 1844, for example, a cricketer complained to the president of the New York Cricket Club that the older English players were accustomed to starting a match in the morning and then "devouring a dinner in the middle of the day." But to conform to "New York habits and manners," this observer suggested that matches should begin at 1:00 P.M. and consist of one innings instead of two, with only a ten-minute intermission. Most players, he wrote, could arrange to participate in an afternoon match but did not wish to be absent from work for an entire day. He also criticized the time lost "in demolishing the dinner, (the eating of which in some measure incapacitates all the players for active exertion)."[24] In 1861 the *Clipper* bemoaned "the waste of time on cricket, as played in England and by Englishmen in America," and explained: "Time, in this country, is money. We have not in America any class of the community who have the leisure to practice the game as they do in England. Here we can only devote hours where they can spend days; hence, we have to economise in everything, even in exercises required for health."[25] James D'Wolf Lovett admired cricket as "a gentleman's game" but agreed that the length of time required for a full match was "a serious handicap for it in this country, and is at variance with the American temperament." He added: "The office boy can occasionally get a few hours off in the afternoon to see a baseball game, with the grandmother's funeral plea; but obviously this could not be worked two days running, for a cricket match." *Wilkes' Spirit* concluded that "the public prefer to see a game lively, active, boisterous even, which comes to a conclusion in a few hours, rather than one which drags along through two or three days, and which is always played as if time were indeed made for slaves, 'who had no rights which cricket players were bound to respect.'"[26]

Antebellum athletes were also eager to participate as much as possible within their allotted play time. Here the structure of baseball had a major advantage over cricket. In the former game a batter either reached base safely or was put out within a few minutes; three outs ended a half-inning and returned all players on a side to the field. But in cricket, batsmen could stand at their wicket for many minutes (or even hours), and all eleven men had to be retired before the teams switched positions. Thus it was common for a cricketer to be inactive for long periods—a situation that was rare in baseball. In 1858 a Philadelphia townball player attacked cricket as a dull sport with no action. With some exaggeration he argued that in cricket two men could stand at their wickets for a whole day without knocking a single ball solidly and that except for the bowler, wicket keeper, and long stop, the other fielders had nothing to do. Many Americans shared this perception.[27] At an 1856 baseball dinner a cricketer who was a recent convert to the new American pastime stated that "in baseball every one had a fair and equal chance to share in the game." Another guest quoted the late editor of the *Sunday Mercury*, Samuel Nicholls, "that where three had a fair chance to play cricket, twenty had a chance to play base ball."[28]

Thus, many sportsmen apparently preferred baseball because its games ended earlier than cricket matches and because it was "played quickly, spiritedly, and with the greatest enthusiasm," with "a wholesome change in the relative positions of the players." The captain of the English cricket team that toured the Northeast in 1872 argued along these same lines as he explained baseball's advantages over England's national game. He wrote that baseball "is of comparatively short duration; it has few pauses; it is constantly changing its aspect." "Cricket," he added, "has to contend against the business habits of Americans. They will not give the time necessary for the game. . . . Time is money there, and there is no denying that much of that valuable commodity is egregiously cut into ribbons at cricket."[29]

Baseball also proved to be more attractive to nineteenth-century American audiences. Huge throngs of several thousand spectators attended feature contests of the American pastime, while the English sport's premier events generally drew only hundreds at most. People preferred to watch baseball because each game was decided within a few hours, rather than within a few days, and because it appeared to offer more drama, excitement, and action. Contemporary sportswriters believed that Americans flocked to the ball park because they found the game faster and more stirring than cricket, which they dismissed as slow and tedious. Many of today's sports enthusiasts consider baseball to be slower and duller than hockey, basketball, or football, but in the Civil War era it seemed to offer abundant speed and action to its partisans.

Charles Peverelly claimed that baseball was more congenial to spectators because of the American temperament: "An American assemblage cannot be kept in one locality for the period of two or three hours, without being offered something above the ordinary run of excitement and attraction. They are too mercurial and impulsive a race not to get drowsy and dissatisfied with anything which permits their natural ardor to droop even for a brief space of time."[30] While his assertion that national character explained the appeal of baseball cannot be substantiated, it does seem that spectators favored baseball because of its brevity, pace, excitement, and also because they were more familiar with its rules and skills.

The sportswriters of the Civil War era preferred baseball partly because of its brevity but also because of its display of batting and especially fielding skills. In summarizing the results of an 1860 cricket contest, the *Clipper* explained why crowds flocked to first-class baseball matches while cricket grounds were comparatively deserted: "In the one case the spectators could enjoy a *quickly played* and exciting contest, marked by beautiful fielding, and in the other they had to wait hours, and visit the grounds two days, to see isolated instances of good play in fielding—skill in batting, except that shown by free hitting, not being appreciated by the generality of those who visit cricket and baseball grounds." One year later that periodical blamed cricket's lack of popularity on "the neglect of sure fielding," stating that "all can appreciate good fielding, but only cricketers can fully enter into the merits of superiority in batting and bowling. Fielding is the feature of Base Ball, hence its attraction to spectators."[31]

Jones Wister, a Philadelphia cricketer who wrote about team sports in the late nineteenth century, attributed the popularity of the American game to the "exhibition of base ball professionals," which "brought the play up to the highest standard." He also was convinced that the element of fielding was partly responsible for baseball's success. George Wright, who excelled in both sports, believed that cricket was "*the* game wherein a bat and ball are used," but he recognized that "the American people . . . condemn this as an 'old man's' game and not worthy of notice compared with our national game, base ball." He conceded that cricket "is not altogether a spectators' game."[32]

While baseball thus became America's favorite pastime because of its history as a child's recreation, its accessibility, its association with nationalism, and its structural attractiveness for both players and spectators, it also benefited greatly from its adaptability. During the mid-nineteenth century, baseball was still in the early stages of its transition from a folk recreation to a modern sport. The NABBP was free to experiment with its rules, especially in the areas of pitching and batting. By contrast, cricket was much farther along in its development. In 1850 it had time-honored rules and traditions, as well as a governing body in England (the Marylebone Club) that was indifferent to special American conditions. In sport, as in most other areas of culture, it is far easier to try innovations at the beginning than to impose major reforms during later periods. America's baseball officials of the Civil War era did not have to contend with the weight of history and tradition, as did those who wished to promote England's game in the United States.

Most historians have assumed that American cricketers did little or nothing to popularize and Americanize their sport in this country. Yet there is abundant evidence to demonstrate that many did a great deal to that end but met with very little long-term success. Contemporary analysts recommended two strategies to promote American cricket: first, they urged baseball players to try the English pastime; second, they suggested a series of changes in the rules and customs of the game to suit American tastes. Reformers launched a major drive on the eve of the Civil War, but that great conflict interrupted their efforts and retarded the progress of the sport in the United States. Later in the century American cricketers renewed their efforts but failed to revive the enthusiasm they had known briefly before the war.

In 1860 the *Clipper* started a crusade to promote the English sport by urging cricket clubs to enroll baseball players. It also advocated matches between baseball players and cricketers in their respective sports and applauded the recruitment by an East New York cricket club of two members of Brooklyn's Star Base Ball Club, calling these sportsmen "fair samples of the cricketing material existing in the numerous ball clubs of New York and Brooklyn, and which the cricket clubs would do well to enroll on their lists . . . if they are desirous of promoting the progress and popularity of the game." The *Clipper* proclaimed: "Introduce the American element, gentlemen, and rely upon it cricket will receive a marked impetus in its growth in this country, and especially in this vicinity." It argued that the best way to remove the prejudices of baseball players against cricket (and vice versa) was "by a proper fraternization among the respective admirers and players of the two games." Several years later, Henry Chadwick's *Ball Players' Chronicle* complained that New York's cricket clubs "isolate themselves too much from the base ball fraternity" and recommended more "social games" between followers of both sports to popularize cricket.[33]

During these years many baseball players did turn to cricket and cricketers also tried their hand at the American game. It is significant that several of the most prominent baseball players in New York City, Brooklyn, Newark, and Philadelphia joined cricket clubs,[34] in part as a result of the excitement caused by the 1859 visit of the All-England Eleven, which provided a showcase of cricket at its best. The *Clipper,* which pointedly noted the attendance of some of Brooklyn's leading baseball officials at the 1860 annual dinner of the St. George Cricket Club and at that year's cricket convention, was "gratified to notice this cordial feeling that is rapidly taking the place of the ridiculous jealousy and prejudice that has hitherto existed in reference to the peculiarities and respective merits of the two games."[35]

The boost that American baseball players gave to cricket became apparent in the fall of 1860, when many of them competed on both sides in an all-star match between Newark and Long Island elevens. According to the *Newark Daily Advertiser*, that contest drew "the largest collection of spectators ever seen on the East New York grounds."[36] The formation of Brooklyn's American Cricket Club, which enrolled many celebrated baseball players, was also a boon to cricket's popularity, as were the numerous friendly challenges between cricket and baseball clubs in both sports during this period. The latter became so common that the *Clipper* reported in 1864, "The admirers of the two national games of ball in this vicinity are rapidly getting rid of the prejudices each entertained against the other's favorite game."[37] It should be emphasized that this increasing harmony between clubs also encouraged cricketers to try baseball, and a few of them (including Harry and George Wright) became stars in their adopted sport.[38] But in the long run the friendlier relations between sportsmen helped baseball a good deal more than cricket.

The future of American cricket depended not merely on recruiting baseball players but also on changing the rules and customs of the sport so that American-born players and spectators would find it more appealing. Delegates to the annual New York City conventions, as well as the sporting press, suggested a variety of reforms to popularize the game in the United States. Some advocated the abolition of multiple club memberships and the ban on professionals in matches. These changes were proposed to give novices more opportunity to compete in first eleven-contests. Others addressed the more important and more vexing time problem by calling for one-day matches with strict limitations on all intermissions and breaks in the action.

In 1860 the Rochester and Buffalo clubs completed a two-innings regular cricket match in one day, at 6:15 P.M., prompting *Wilkes' Spirit* to report: "By commencing promptly at the hour named [10:00 A.M.], and avoiding the dilatoriness so often shown, ordinary matches can be played out, and the expense and loss of time incurred in a two days' match, much lessened. Besides this, the game, by being more lively, is rendered much more interesting to lookers-on, and one of the strongest arguments against its popularity, namely its 'slowness,' is removed."[39] One year later that journal announced the time rules for an upcoming one-day Long Island all-star match of Englishmen versus Americans. The game was scheduled to start at 10:00 A.M. sharp, with two minutes between batters, ten minutes between innings, and a half-hour lunch break.[40] In the Newark versus Long Island encounter mentioned previously, the baseball participants apparently sped up the pace, for the two-innings contest was over in about five hours—"the shortest regular game of cricket on record."[41]

After the Civil War some cricket lovers continued to try to reform the customs that seemed to inhibit the sport's progress in the United States. In 1867 Philadelphia's Olympian club proposed a forfeit rule for clubs that arrived late for matches and restrictions on expensive entertainments during or after games. Its organizational efforts resulted in the American Cricketers' Convention, though that body soon passed into oblivion. The following year *Wilkes' Spirit* suggested some changes that might promote the sport in America. It recommended shorter games, closer affiliations between cricket and baseball clubs, special events including more international matches, better relations with the press, and more encouragement for younger players.[42] In 1868 Henry Chadwick proposed that cricketers stop "unnecessary and tedious delays by playing the game in strict accordance with the English *rules,* not the English custom"; that they encourage young cricketers and not play old men exclusively; and that they make interclub contests "real trials of skill between club elevens, and not mere games rendered devoid of club interest from the fact of members of half a dozen clubs taking part in them." Two years later in Philadelphia, someone invented a game called "American cricket," featuring a triangular field with one wicket and two bases. It was an attempt to combine the best aspects of cricket and baseball, but it failed to generate a following.[43]

In the final analysis, initial attempts to promote an American style of cricket failed because of resistance by Englishmen. After the Civil War, the native lovers of the sport preferred to emulate the British rather than to create a new version of cricket that might win over the American masses. In the antebellum era, the British who controlled the sport everywhere except in Philadelphia did not want to tamper with the game they had learned from their fathers and grandfathers. Any radical innovations were simply "not cricket." The upper-class "Proper" Philadelphians who patronized the sport did not wish to democratize cricket and believed that it was superior to baseball. They preferred their game, with its leisurely pace and the great skill it required, because it was played by amateur gentlemen who prided themselves on their love of pure sport, untainted by money. Jones Wister expressed this philosophy in 1893, noting that he preferred the English pastime because it seemed to be morally superior to the American sport. For Wister it was not rule changes but rather "good fielding, good bowling, and . . . good wicket keeping" that would popularize cricket in America.[44]

Baseball became America's national game in the nineteenth century because it was well suited to the American culture of that era of transition into a modern society. It built upon familiar traditions and was inexpensive and simple to play. Playing fields, bats, and balls were readily available in most locations, and novices could have fun even if they were not competent players. The sport's enthusiasts promoted it effectively through the press and through such social institutions as neighborhood clubs, volunteer fire companies, and factories (see Chapters 6 and 7). Contests could be completed within a few hours and generated excitement and spectacles that entertained people who could afford only minimal time away from responsibilities at work or at home. Baseball also proved to be quite adaptable to the needs of its participants, through rule changes in pitching and fielding.

Cricket was attractive to thousands of sportsmen, but it suffered from serious disadvantages in its competition with baseball. It required more care for its grounds and was more expensive to play. Its association with the British alienated some, and its subtleties and skill requirements were quite challenging to the uninitiated. Spectators who were unfamiliar with the sport disliked the length of the matches and the slow pace. Americans who tried to adapt the game to their own sporting tastes discovered that its English adherents preferred to retain old customs. The tide of modernization carried baseball players along in its surge toward a time-conscious society that prized action and speed, but cricketers resisted the momentum of the age. Yet the success of the sport in Philadelphia down to the early twentieth century proves that under the right circumstances the English game could thrive in the United States. An elite subculture of Philadelphians embraced cricket, partly because they admired the British who had taught them the pastime and partly because they had played the game as youngsters and had learned to love it. They would pass the sport down from fathers to sons, until a future generation failed to keep the faith.

NOTES

1. See Albert K. Weinberg, *Manifest Destiny* (Baltimore, 1935); John Higham, *Strangers in the Land* (New York, 1965); Benjamin T. Spencer, *The Quest for Nationality: An American Literary Campaign* (Syracuse, N.Y., 1957).

2. *Clipper* 5 (May 16, 1857): 26.

3. *Clipper* 7 (July 2, 1859): 84.

4. *Clipper* 4 (August 16, 1856): 132; (December 13, 1856): 268; *Porter's Spirit* 1 (September 6, 1856):13; (September 13, 1856): 28; (January 31, 1857): 357; *Clipper* 5 (December 5, 1857): 259; 7 (February 18, 1860): 349. See also *Brooklyn Daily Eagle,* August 3, 1859.

5. *Clipper* 7 (August 20, 1859): 141.

6. *New York Herald,* October 16, 1859; Charles Peverelly, *The Book of American Pastimes* (New York, 1866), 337–38.

7. *Jersey City Daily Courier and Advertiser,* July 2, 1859.

8. *American Chronicle of Sports and Pastimes* 1 (February 13, 1868): 52 (hereafter cited as *American Chronicle*). The idea that baseball mirrored American tastes, while cricket reflected English habits, persisted into the next century. See Albert G. Spalding, *America's National Game* (New York, 1911), 4–6.

9. Ian Tyrrell, "The Emergence of Modern American Baseball c. 1850–80," in Richard Cashman and Michael McKernan, eds., *Sport in History* (St. Lucia, Queensland, 1979), 205–26; Melvin L. Adelman, *A Sporting Time: New York City and the Rise of Modern Athletics, 1820–70* (Urbana, Ill., 1986), 91–93, 109–10, 111, 112, 134, 137.

10. The relatively low rate of participation of American children in cricket requires further explanation by scholars of American pastimes in the colonial and early national periods.

11. *Porter's Spirit* 1 (December 20, 1856): 261; *Clipper* 11 (May 16, 1863): 46; 12 (January 30, 1864): 330; 13 (May 13, 1865): 34.

12. *Roll of Members and Constitution of the Germantown Cricket Club* (Philadelphia, 1867), 7.

13. James D'Wolf Lovett, *Old Boston Boys and the Games They Played* (Boston, 1907), 75–76.

14. *Clipper* 8 (April 28, 1860): 12; Peverelly, *American Pastimes*, 338.

15. *Wilkes' Spirit* 16 (May 4, 1867): 150.

16. *Clipper* 5 (May 16, 1857): 26; 9 (September 7, 1861): 164.

17. *Porter's Spirit* 3 (January 23, 1858): 325.

18. *Clipper* 8 (May 19, 1860): 37; *New York Times*, September 13, 1868.

19. *Ball Players' Chronicle*, September 26, 1867; *Wilkes' Spirit* 22 (July 16, 1870): 343; *American Chronicle* 1 (July 16, 1868): 250.

20. *Porter's Spirit* 3 (January 23, 1858): 325.

21. Quoted in *Clipper* 6 (September 18, 1858): 172.

22. *Porter's Spirit* 3 (January 23, 1858): 325; 4 (April 3, 1858): 77; (August 21, 1858): 389; *Philadelphia Sunday Mercury*, August 8, 1858; *Clipper* 8 (February 18, 1860): 349.

23. Peverelly, *American Pastimes*, 338.

24. *Spirit* 14 (August 3, 1844): 265.

25. *Clipper* 9 (September 7, 1861): 164.

26. Lovett, *Old Boston Boys*, 77; *Wilkes' Spirit* 19 (September 12, 1868): 53. See also *Wilkes' Spirit* 22 (July 16, 1870): 343.

27. *Clipper* 6 (August 14, 1858): 132.

28. *Porter's Spirit* 1 (November 8, 1856): 165.

29. *Wilkes' Spirit* 16 (May 4, 1867): 150; Capt. R. A. Fitzgerald, *Wickets in the West: Or, The Twelve in America* (London, 1873), 291–93.

30. Peverelly, *American Pastimes*, 337–38.

31. *Clipper* 8 (August 11, 1860): 131; 9 (August 24, 1861): 151.

32. Jones Wister, *A 'Bawl' for American Cricket, Dedicated to American Youth* (Philadelphia, 1893), 9–10; George Wright, *Cricket Guide* (n.p., 1894), 4–5.

33. *Clipper* 8 (April 28, 1860): 12; (May 5, 1860): 19; 9 (September 7, 1861): 164; *Ball Players' Chronicle*, August 22, 1867.

34. *Clipper* 8 (April 28, 1860): 12; (September 8, 1860): 165; (October 6, 1860): 199.

35. *Clipper* 7 (March 31, 1860): 395; 8 (May 19, 1860): 37.

36. *Newark Daily Advertiser*, September 6, 1860.

37. *Clipper* 12 (November 5, 1864): 235–36; (November 12, 1864): 242. For other examples see *Porter's Spirit* 6 (August 6, 1859): 357; *Clipper* 14 (June 23, 1866): 83; 16 (May 2, 1868): 26; 17 (June 26, 1869): 93; *Wilkes' Spirit* 2 (July 14, 1860): 298; 4 (August 10, 1861): 356–57; 9 (November 7, 1863): 147; 11 (October 29, 1864): 138; 14

(August 11, 1866): 381; 15 (November 17, 1866): 188; 17 (August 24, 1867): 7; *Spirit* 23 (September 24, 1870): 85; *Philadelphia Sunday Mercury,* June 6, 20, 1869.

38. *Porter's Spirit* 4 (July 17, 1858): 309; 5 (November 20, 1858): 181; *Clipper* 8 (November 24, 1860): 250.

39. *Wilkes' Spirit* 2 (July 23, 1860): 332.

40. *Wilkes' Spirit* 4 (August 24, 1861): 389.

41. *Newark Daily Advertiser,* September 6, 1860. See also *Spirit* 30 (September 15, 1860): 386.

42. *Clipper* 15 (April 27, 1867): 20; *Wilkes' Spirit* 16 (June 29, 1867): 327.

43. *Ball Players' Chronicle,* June 20, 1867; *Spirit* 19 (September 12, 1868): 50; *American Chronicle* 1 (July 16, 1868): 250; (June 18, 1868): 202; *Spirit* 23 (November 26, 1870): 240; *Clipper* 18 (December 3, 1870): 277.

44. Wister, *'Bawl' for American Cricket,* 11–12.

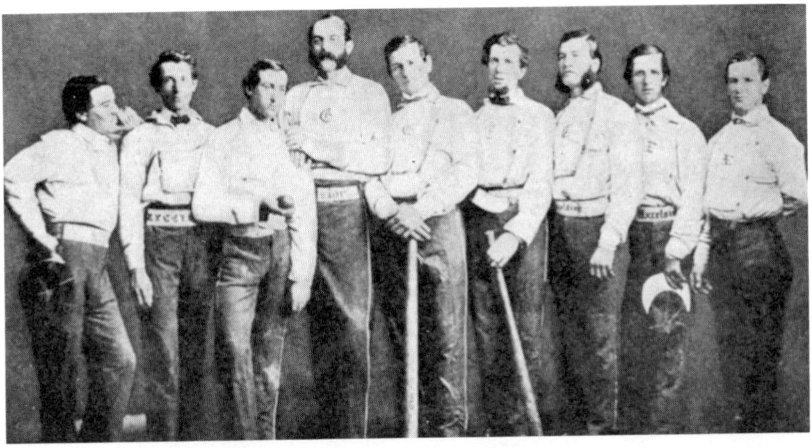

ATLANTICS OF BROOKLYN The dominant baseball club of the early and mid-1860s, the Atlantics enrolled many butchers and others from the food preparation trades and had a large working-class following. In June 1870 they snapped the Cincinnati Red Stockings' long winning streak.

EXCELSIORS OF BROOKLYN The first baseball club to promote the sport through tours, the Excelsiors were predominantly white-collar professionals. In 1860 they recruited the first professional player, James Creighton (third from left), but during and after the Civil War they stopped hiring players and dropped out of championship competition. Creighton, baseball's first star pitcher, tragically and ironically died in 1862 from injuries sustained while batting for the St. George Cricket Club in a match against the Willow Club of Brooklyn.

Forest Citys of Rockford, Illinois One of the leading clubs of the Midwest during the late 1860s, the Forest Citys engaged in a spirited rivalry with nines from Chicago, Cincinnati, St. Louis, and smaller towns throughout the region. During the 1870s Albert G. Spalding (third from right) became a star professional with the Boston Red Stockings and captain and manager of the Chicago White Stockings.

Cincinnati Red Stockings America's first all-salaried team, the Red Stockings were undefeated in 1869. Harry Wright (center, bottom row) and his brother George (second from left, top row) were also skilled cricketers. The Wrights and at least four of their teammates were from New York City or New Jersey; only one of the Red Stockings was from Ohio.

MUTUALS OF NEW YORK CITY Closely affiliated with the political machine of William M. "Boss" Tweed, the Mutuals were the archrivals of the Atlantics during the 1860s. They played their home games at the Elysian Fields of Hoboken, N.J., until the Stevens family banned championship match games there because of crowd disorders, gambling, and suspicion of "fixed" games. The Mutuals moved to Brooklyn's Union Grounds in 1867.

HAYMAKERS OF TROY, NEW YORK Originally from the village of Lansingburg, the Haymakers were one of the first baseball clubs from a small town to succeed against nines from the great metropolitan areas.

CRICKET AND BASEBALL Compare this *Harper's Weekly* depiction of the international cricket match (top) played at Hoboken, N.J., in October 1859 between the All-England Eleven and twenty-two players from the United States

with one of a baseball match (bottom) at Hoboken's Elysian Fields. Note the different configuration of players in each sport and also the baseball spectators seated in carriages close to the action. (Collections of the New Jersey Historical Society)

Young America Cricket Club, 1864 Founded by the younger brothers of the members of the Germantown Cricket Club, the Young America club was the premier cricket club in the United States during the Civil War. Most of its players were born into the upper levels of Philadelphia society. (C. C. Morris Cricket Library Association)

New York Cricket Club, 1865 Predominantly composed of Englishmen, the New York Cricket Club enrolled several New York City journalists, writers, and artists. The bitter rival of the St. George Cricket Club of New York City, it is pictured here at a match with the Philadelphia Cricket Club. (C. C. Morris Cricket Library Association)

THE ALL-ENGLAND CRICKET TEAM, 1859 George Parr's all-England eleven (plus one substitute) on board ship at Liverpool, England, on the morning of the group's departure for North America, September 7, 1859. Parr is standing in the middle of the back row. This cricket team was the first English all-star eleven to compete outside of Great Britain. (C. C. Morris Cricket Library Association)

CHAPTER

6

Players

In early January 1857, Frank Pidgeon, one of the founders of the Eckford Base Ball Club of Brooklyn, recalled the excitement of his team's inaugural match against the Unions of Morrisania (a section of the Bronx). He wrote: "We pulled off our coats, and rolled up our sleeves, we stood up to the rack, but were very nervous—first appearance on any stage!" His team's first and second batters made outs, but the third man up "gave the ball a regular crusher" and reached third base as "one desperate yell burst from eight throats." The next hitter drove him home. "Glory! one run. Ah, how proud the Eckford Club were of that run. Some ran to the Umpire's book, to see how it looked on paper." Thousands of antebellum baseball players shared Pidgeon's enthusiasm. A contemporary chronicler of early New York City sport quoted a local sportsman who swore that "when he died, he desired to be buried beneath first-base." The writer added: "Will any doubt, then, that the game has such powers of fascination, and that its admirers always crowd around every match, where they can watch the progress of a game?"[1]

During the middle decades of the nineteenth century many boys and men joined Pidgeon as ardent contestants in the new team sports. Native and foreigner, young and old, white and black, craftsman and clerk, merchant and manager, affluent and humble, all took part in the action. Before identifying those who created modern American baseball and cricket, however, it is important to understand why and how they played. What made team sports so attractive to both players and spectators? What was the participants' manner and style of exercise in both informal and organized competition?

In recent years theoreticians of leisure have debated whether people seek recreation as a relief from their labor or whether they choose (perhaps unconsciously) to replicate their toil in their amusements. While such questions may be asked of nineteenth-century sports, it is risky to probe the hearts and minds of athletes who have long since left both the workplaces and the playgrounds of life. They may haved flocked to a game that was very different from their labor, even as they brought to their play much of the culture of their vocation. A related issue concerns the transition of both work and team sports from premodern to modern forms. Mid-nineteenth-century Americans could select from a full range of sporting activities that extended from one extreme of spontaneous play to its opposite—deeply serious competition. Athletes who were learning the new rules of urban industrial society could choose to idle away their free time in traditional forms of leisure, such as horseback riding and swimming in the summer, ice skating and sledding in the winter; or they could seek more structured forms of amusement. In reviewing the behavior of cricketers and baseball players, one must recall that the new team sports offered their followers various levels of organization and degrees of seriousness of participation.[2]

At the grass-roots level of early American team sports were neighborhood street games and factory, shop, and office contests. Many boys honed their sports skills on open lots, streets, and fields in cities, towns, and villages. According to the *Newark Daily Advertiser,* youngsters in that city "seem to have become possessed with the identical ball mania now so prevalent among their older brothers, those 'children of a large growth.' Instead, however, of organizing themselves into clubs . . . these urchins seem content to take their stand upon the sidewalks and 'play catch'—very much to the annoyance of all pedestrians, and especially to the disquietude and alarm of ladies."[3] The paper noted that women were "being hit 'on their bonnets'" or smacked on their noses and that juvenile ball play also ruined gardens and smashed windows.[4]

In New York City and Brooklyn the boys were even bolder than in Newark. *Wilkes' Spirit* proclaimed: "Base-ball is everybody's game, and everybody plays it—. . . from the white-cravated parson, through every profession and grade down to the dirty-faced urchin." Juvenile street play was annoying citizen residents, as "impromptu 'nines'" converted "any old clout" into a ball and commenced play. The paper added: "Wo to the man or woman who ventures through that thoroughfare. To catch this wet and muddy rag bundle 'full swipe in the face,' aggravated by the congratulations of the *gamin* on your giving such evidence of shortstop ability, is no infrequent occurrence. Remonstrance on the part of the injured shows bad taste."[5] The *New York Times* marveled at a group of boys who played in the middle of busy Nassau Street. These fellows had fun bothering the drivers, while catching the ball "at the imminent risk of being crushed to atoms."[6] Street play became enough of a nuisance in 1871 to prompt Brooklyn's chief of police to order his men to enforce a city ordinance against kite flying and ball playing on public thoroughfares. At least one officer also broke up games on open lots, but the chief rejected his action, stating that no policeman had a right to interfere with boys playing baseball in vacant lots, unless they were guilty of disorderly conduct, willful trespass, or playing on Sundays.[7]

Many enthusiasts of early forms of "folk-ball" ignored local ordinances banning sports on the Sabbath. A Jersey City newspaper complained in 1855 of New York and Hoboken boys playing baseball on the outskirts of the city on Sunday. The *Newark Evening Journal* reported that the inhabitants of the Sixth Ward were frequently disturbed on Sundays by people pitching pennies and playing ball. Two officers arrested several members of a noisy party playing cricket, then released them with a reprimand from the justice of the peace.[8] During the late 1860s the Newark police were still arresting youths for playing on the Sabbath, and they sometimes broke up games on public streets if citizens complained.[9]

Sunday sports were popular for those who had little or no other leisure time, but factory workers, shop artisans, and white-collar employees sometimes played pickup games on weekdays, either during lunch breaks or after work. In 1860 the *Newark Daily Advertiser* remarked: "The streets in the vicinity of our factories are now full at noon and evening of apprentices and others engaged in the simpler games of ball, thus counteracting the injurious effects of the sedentary pursuits in which some of them are engaged."[10] After the Civil War the *Clipper* alerted "any one desirous of witnessing champion ball tossing" to go to Spruce Street at noon, when "the printer boys pass their leisure hour after twelve o'clock in passing the ball round."[11]

The sporting press and daily newspapers of this era are filled with accounts of work teams at play in both baseball and cricket. Firemen, pressmen, compositors, news agents, postal employees, harness makers, minstrel troops, engravers, Treasury Department plate printers, jewelers, sawyers, iron workers, grocers, hat finishers, plumbers, and many other groups challenged rivals to a friendly test of skill on the diamond or cricket field. For example, the printers of a Manchester, New Hampshire, newspaper challenged the other typesetters in town to a "friendly" game of baseball on a fast day in April 1858. The prize was an oyster supper, and each party used "such ball and bats as they may choose."[12] In 1865 New York City's Central Park commissioners, who were reluctant to allow anyone to use the new baseball grounds, received "some twenty or thirty applications from the employees of several manufacturing establishments."[13]

When workers challenged their counterparts in other businesses to a game of ball, the matches were usually contested in a spirit of friendliness. But there were some exceptional encounters for championship honors that became quite serious affairs. When the heavyweight saloon keepers of Newark's Fourth Ward defeated their beefy opponents of the First Ward in 1867, "much merriment was created by the field movements of the players," especially the two men who approached 300 pounds each. Newspaper games were popular and usually featured "good feeling manifested by the contesting nines towards each other, all the ill-natured rivalry of the opposing journals being confined to the editorial department."[14] "Muffin matches" between inept players were arranged to provide fun for competitors and spectators, as in 1866, when two downtown New York merchants fielded nines that were picked "for their non-acquaintance with the national pastime, the choice being to get the most inexperienced it was possible to get."[15] Matters became more intense when company nines played for the championship of their trade. In Newark, employees of the Traders'

Express Company claimed that they lost a July 4, 1870, match to the New Jersey Express Company because their opponents had "the assistance of some outside parties." They refused to continue the game unless the strangers were withdrawn, challenging their adversaries to play only "legitimate employees."[16]

While some employers were skeptical about their workers playing these new games, many others endorsed the athletic craze that was sweeping America.[17] A few of the more enlightened bosses gave working-class cricketers time off from their toil to play. In 1859 the employees of Philadelphia's Landberger and Company competed against men from Germantown's Spencer and Company. The *Clipper* was pleased to publicize this match, for earlier in the year a Philadelphia bank had barred its men from joining any athletic clubs. The New York journal hoped "to record many such friendly encounters between the wealth-producing classes of our country, which may be taken as a sure index of its and their prosperity." It praised the company owners for having "the good judgment to perceive that 'all work and no play' is not the most liberal or humane maxim on which to conduct a business" and emphasized that providing leisure time for wholesome recreation would serve the employers' interests: "They will secure the esteem and good wishes of their workmen to such an extent as will ultimately redound to their honor and success." Manhattanite Henry Sharp, president of the New York Cricket Club and a house and church decorator, sponsored a series of cricket outings at Hoboken, New Jersey, for his workers. In 1860 *Wilkes' Spirit* lauded Sharp for setting "a noble example to the employers of New York, in thus affording those engaged in his service a day's relaxation from the regular toils and cares of labor, for the purpose of enjoying in the green fields and pure air of the country a day of healthful recreation and social amusement." The paper added that his generosity "cements the kindly feeling which ought ever to exist between the employer and employed, and is productive of mutual advantage."[18]

American sportsmen of the mid-nineteenth century who joined regularly organized ball clubs had many motives for playing, and they brought to their favorite pastime their own habits and values. The culture of the emerging cities, factories, shops, and offices stressed individual achievement, but within the context of small or large organizations. It emphasized specialized skills, personal discipline, respect for rules and authority, and harmony among all members of society. Success on the playing field demanded many of the same qualities, yet there was also an inevitable tension between the spirit of idle play and the work ethic. To appreciate the appeal of both cricket and baseball in this transitional era, then, one must understand both the sportsmen's motives and their personal behavior and style of play.

The few extant personal accounts by antebellum ball players and spectators suggest that in sport they sought escape and diversion from their everyday occupations, as well as physical exercise and pyschological refreshment. They thrived on the excitement generated and the camaraderie; they frolicked for the fun of being young again. Frank Pidgeon remarked: "We had some merry times among ourselves; we would forget business and everything else, on Tuesday afternoons, go out into the green fields, don our ball suits, and go at it with a perfect rush. At such times, we were boys again. Such sport as this brightens a man up, and improves him, both in mind and body."[19]

Charles King Newcomb, a Philadelphia man of letters who loved to watch baseball, believed that the sport afforded workers a welcome escape from their toil, a fine mixture of play and work, and a return to their youth. In his journals he wrote that laborers "leave the shade & quiet of a shop for the sun & fury of a ball-ground; they stand, & they exercise for hours, at a strict laborious game; they attest that they mean to be men, & not machines." He added: "Athletic games carry men back to their days of childhood. There is, indeed, morally a home-base in all of them, as there is, literally, one in base-ball." Newcomb especially praised "off-hand & unprofessional games" as a "blessing" to young men, because of their "blending of glee & order, of innocence & health," as well as their relative freedom "from the concentration, strain, & over-eagerness of most more ambitious & contentious games." He preferred informal contests, in which "merriment & exhilaration" prevailed over "rivalry and anxiety," that combined play with work, "whilst games played under other motives and circumstances have more of work than of play about them."[20]

Once bitten by the cricket bug, enthusiasts devoted countless hours to its pleasures and pain. As one of them explained:

> To the uninitiated, particularly foreigners, cricket appears very tame and stupid: they cannot conceive what amusement there can be in standing up with a log of wood in your hand and devoting all your energies in preventing a ball from hitting three pieces of stick which are placed in the ground. But such men know nothing of the quickness of eye and hand, the bodily strength and activity which are required; and to one not skilled in the game, it must appear wonderful that a good bat is not only able to stop, but even to hit a ball delivered with immense velocity . . . at such an instant of time that the ball shall fly off at any particular angle which he pleases.[21]

An admirer of Philadelphia cricket testified that if a spectator did not leave the ground "impressed with the beauty and utility of the game, why then—you were not cut out for a cricketer." Many who became passionate for this game carried their love of cricket to their graves. Thomas Dodsworth, speaking at the twenty-first anniversary dinner of the St. George club, proposed his own epitaph: "Bowled out by death, here lies old Doddy, / A cricketer both soul and body, / Who hoped he'd cricket find in Heaven, / That he might join some good eleven."[22]

Novices sometimes failed to appreciate the appeal of these amusements. In 1846 a Philadelphian recommended that "any young gentleman who may be desirous of acquiring a knowledge of the art of *Cricketing* engage a friend to tie him fast to a fence-rail, and then pitch half-bricks at his head for one hour or two; after which, the friend should break a stout hickory club over his sconce, if possible. The 'learner' should then be released—to run a mile or two, at top speed, and if by chance he *returns*, after this last feat he promises fairly, with continued practice, to become 'one of 'em!'" Twenty years later a Newark resident confessed that he had tried to learn baseball but had quit because of a series of mishaps and injuries. A Chicagoan recalled his misadventures as a baseball novice: "I was covered with dust; my hands bled; my face glowed like coal. . . . I was in pain all over. . . . I could not walk. I could not lift my arms. I was stiff all over. . . . I cursed two days, the day I was born and the day I played base ball." He concluded that the sport was "an excellent game to be played when the snow is ten feet deep."[23]

While these sportsmen shunned the new pastimes, many others flocked to ball fields to refresh their bodies and minds and to enjoy the company of close friends. During competition they were expected to observe certain rules of proper personal conduct and to behave in a manly, respectable way. Promoters of both ball sports propounded a code of sportsmanship they hoped all participants would observe. According to the *Clipper,* a "Model Ball Player" was supposed to be punctual, obey his captain, the officals, and all the rules, comport himself like a gentleman, and abstain from profanity and obscenity. He was supposed to keep his temper under control, never censuring "errors in play made either by a brother member or an opponent." He should play for pleasure alone and accept victory or defeat with equal grace and good sportsmanship. He should never gamble and should always display "a courtesy of demeanor, liberality of action, and thorough good nature." His highest aim should be to make each contest "as much a trial as to which party excels in what may be called the moral attributes of the game, as it is one that decides any question of physical superiority."[24]

The evidence suggests that most of the ball players followed these guidelines, but since the athletes were only human, there were breeches of sporting etiquette from time to time. *Porter's Spirit* reported a few instances of foul language used by early baseball players, along with "the indulgence of a prurient taste for indecent anecdotes and songs" at postgame parties.[25] When the "New York game" replaced townball in Philadelphia during the 1860s, proper player conduct became an issue in the promotion of the new sport. Critics of that city's Olympics scolded the club for allowing a few men to argue with umpires, act wildly on the base paths, and carry liquor onto the grounds.[26]

Amateur sportsmen generally avoided arguments with umpires, but they often tried to influence the latter's judgments with side remarks.[27] They also did not always accept defeat gracefully, and sometimes they wagered on their own games.[28] Junior players sometimes engaged in wild antics inappropriate for fair play, especially when darkness approached during a close contest. In an

1861 junior all-star match between the best young players of New York and Brooklyn, the former were leading by two runs in the top of the eighth inning when the Brooklynites stopped trying to retire the side. The reason was obvious: since Brooklyn had led by one run after seven innings, it would win the game if the eighth inning could not be completed. After an interruption caused by spectators who swarmed onto the field, the umpire ordered play to resume. But "overpitching, miscatching, wild throwing, and missing the ball in the field was now the order of the play on the part of Brooklyn, and striking out and walking to bases, that of the New York side." The umpire finally called the game and declared Brooklyn the winner, but the match was clearly discreditable to the players and the crowd.[29]

Many sportsmen resisted turning their practice games and sessions into serious work, thus exibiting distinctly premodern patterns of ball play. For example, in the late autumn of 1861, members of several Brooklyn clubs arranged a "Donkey Match," whereby "the side making the *least* number of runs won the game, and the players having the least runs and most outs won the ball." The novel character of the game was a source of amusement to all.[30] In February 1866 Philadelphia's Enterprise and Crystal clubs played a very early season "scrub match" that neither side "manifested any desire to win." One participant observed: "Had it been a regular match, it is very certain that the pitcher of the Enterprise, who was playing first base, would not have so far forgotten his duty as to be some two hundred yards from his base, buying apples, while there was a man at the bat; nor would the fielders have been found lying upon the ground and allowing balls to pass over them, without making an effort to stop them."[31] In Washington, D.C., in 1867, two nines donned outrageous costumes and performed a burlesque version of baseball. One side, called the "Royal Japs," dressed themselves in red, yellow, and purple gowns and fans, with glove-boxes on their heads. Their rivals, the "Never Dismounts," appeared in black pantaloons, white linen coats, and broad-brimmed Panama hats.[32] The skating craze of this era also combined with the baseball boom to create a new fad—baseball on ice! Stallwart athletes braved bitter temperatures to play in the dead of winter.[33] According to *Wilkes' Spirit*, "the *furore* for base-ball playing rises superior to all obstacles. When players cannot run the bases on the greensward . . . they boldly mount their skates and take possession of an ice-field."[34]

In addition to these frolics, there is evidence that superior players did not always apply the most rational or scientific principles to their sport. The *Clipper* criticized the Brooklyn Atlantics for not practicing with each man in his regular position and suggested a more sophisticated approach:

> The only way to improve the play of a nine by practice, is, to play every first-nine player in his regular position on all occasions, and always to place first-nine players on one side, even if there be but three or four on the ground each practice-day. Any other style of practice weakens rather than strengthens their play, and, as practice, is useless. If fun and exercise are the only objects, the ordinary style of making up sides on practice days is well enough; but if excellence as a nine is desired, why, then, the only plan is, to practice the nine as a whole, with each man in his regular position. We do not care what the individual ability of the players may be, unless this plan is adopted, no nine will ever achieve the degree of excellence they otherwise would.[35]

Yet the Atlantics were the dominant team of their era, emphasizing "fun and exercise" as much as "excellence."

As baseball evolved after the 1860s it also became more organized, specialized, and scientific. Commenting on an early season match in 1867, the *Clipper* criticized both teams' pitchers for their ignorance of the revised rules and latest styles of pitching. The paper stated that both hurlers "seem to have forgotten that this is 1867, not 1860, and that pitching has got to be a science and a first class man in the position is one who can use his head as well as his hands, his judgment as well as his physical strength. . . . sending in balls just as swift as you can, without any other object in view than mere speed, and without regard to what the cost of your delivery may be in passed and called balls, is a style of pitching which has become obsolete in first class nines." Later the *Clipper* amplified its point: "Our national game has ceased to be a 'boy's game' in any shape or form, but has become a game requiring not only the physical skill of a practical athlete, but also the mental ability to properly control and direct the hands trained to act." It was no longer possible for a party of country lads to "come together and make up a ball playing party competent to hold their own pretty well in the field against the most experienced players of the cities." First-class nines that played baseball "to its highest point of excellence" required men with courage, strength, activity, and endurance"; also needed were men "with heads and active brains; men with quick powers of observation, of nerve, or presence of mind, men ready to act promptly and wisely on the spur of the moment, with no time for calculation, as able generals do in the life and death events of the battlefields."[36]

While the vast majority of athletes tried to leave their work behind them when they competed, a few were paid to play. All antebellum American baseball players were supposed to be amateurs, but a few probably accepted some compensation to join clubs that competed for championship honors. In cricket, there were a few professionals in the United States before 1860—*Porter's Spirit* estimated their number at eleven in 1859—all Englishmen and most of them hired by organizations in New York City, Brooklyn, and Philadelphia. They were paid to instruct club members, keep the grounds in good condition, and compete in interclub matches. Since their wages were low, they normally also worked at some other trade, and they were supported as well by some of their affluent teammates. Many professionals earned extra income from special benefit matches held in their behalf at the end of a season. Although some cricket clubs refused to play against an eleven that included professionals, the English practice of employing experts was accepted by most American cricketers. A few special contests between amateurs and professionals were modeled after the popular English event of the "Gentlemen versus the Players." While baseball did not develop the same system of professionalism as cricket, it did reflect the influence of the English game when it accepted payment of players after the Civil War.[37]

Professionalism, commercialism, and scientific play eventually subordinated the element of fun in favor of the spirit of work. Ball sports took on more of the trappings of big business and both mirrored and reinforced many of the tendencies of modern American life. Yet the amateur sportsmen of the Civil War era competed more for the love of play and retained more of the premodern ways of early American "folk-ball." They found temporary refuge from their sober responsibilities as husbands, fathers, providers, and workers on cricket grounds and baseball fields.

The thousands of players who enjoyed informal recreations remain anonymous, for there is no way to identify them or to generalize about demographic characteristics. It is possible, however, to gather personal information about those who joined clubs and whose names appeared in newspapers. Demographic data in sporting and daily publications, city directories, and federal censuses reveal patterns of ethnicity, race, age, occupation, wealth, and neighborhoods. It is also instructive to compare cricketers with baseball players. The following discussion is based on data presented in the tables in this chapter.[38]

Both cricket and baseball surged in popularity during a period of substantial immigration from Europe (see Tables 1 and 2). As might be expected, the overwhelming majority of men who played the American national pastime were native-born. For example, 84 percent of New Jersey's baseball players were Americans; since Newark's native population was about five-eighths and Jersey City's was about two-fifths of their respective totals in 1860, it is clear that immigrants were underrepresented in early New Jersey baseball. The British (including England, Scotland, and Wales) and Irish each contributed only about 7 percent of the state's baseball population. There is some evidence that in Orange and Jersey City, Irish boys and young men were beginning to play the sport before 1861. Box scores for those towns and for Brooklyn show many Irish names.[39] Very few of the large number of German newcomers played either baseball or cricket in New Jersey before the Civil War. And in Philadelphia the domination of baseball by natives was virtually complete—ninety-nine percent.

Cricket provides more interesting and complex ethnic patterns, for England's national game did attract significant numbers of Americans in certain localities, especially Newark and Philadelphia. Englishmen controlled New York City cricket, although Albany, Yonkers, and Long Island (including Brooklyn) fielded an impressive number of native players. This is apparent from the increasing frequency of special contests that matched Englishmen against Americans.[40] In Newark, natives and "old countrymen"

TABLE 1. Birthplace and Age of New Jersey Sportsmen, 1855–60

	Newark Baseball	Jersey City[1] Baseball	Orange Baseball	Total Baseball	Newark Cricket	Total Sportsmen
BIRTHPLACE (%)						
United States	89.0	81.6	78.3	84.2	45.3	75.5
Great Britain	6.6	7.9	0.0	6.6	45.3	15.4
Ireland	3.3	6.1	21.7	6.6	7.8	6.6
Other European	1.1	4.4	0.0	2.6	1.6	2.4
N	91	114	23	228	64	70
AGE (%)						
21 and under	24.1	40.7	60.9	36.3	11.9	31.5
22–29	32.2	31.0	39.1	32.3	30.5	31.2
30–39	24.2	17.7	0.0	18.4	28.8	20.8
40 and over	19.5	10.6	0.0	13.0	28.8	16.5
Mean (years)	30.2	25.8	21.0	27.0	33.6	28.4
Median (years)	28.2	24.0	20.0	24.0	30.4	26.1
N	87	113	23	223	59	279

[1]Includes data from adjacent Hoboken and Hudson City.

each contributed 45 percent of the total club members before 1861. In August 1854 the Newark Cricket Club organized the first all-American match ever played in the United States, splitting a home-and-home series with the New York Cricket Club.[41] Daniel W. Baker, an American-born jeweler and former president of the Newark club, was elected secretary of the New York City cricket convention in 1858.[42]

Philadelphia (including its environs) was far and away the capital of American cricket both before the Civil War and for the rest of the nineteenth century, with 85 percent of its cricketers born in the United States. The sport became much more popular among Americans in Philadelphia than in other cities because of the willingness of that city's British residents to promote their pastime and because of the greater receptiveness of middle- and upper-class residents. In 1858 the *Clipper* estimated that the City of Brotherly

TABLE 2. Birthplace, Age, and Occupation of Philadelphia Sportsmen, 1855–70

	All Players	All Baseball	White Baseball	Black Baseball	All Cricket
BIRTHPLACE (%)					
England	6.6	0.0	0.0	0.0	10.9
Ireland	1.9	1.2	2.3	0.0	2.3
Europe and elsewhere	1.0	0.0	0.0	0.0	1.5
United States					
Pennsylvania	77.7	73.2	79.5	66.7	80.6
Other	12.8	25.6	18.2	33.3	4.7
Total	90.5	98.8	97.7	100.0	85.3
N	211	86	44	42	129
AGE (%)					
21 and under	30.8	27.9	29.5	26.2	33.3
22–29	30.8	34.9	36.4	33.3	27.2
30–39	22.7	29.1	25.0	33.4	19.3
40–49	12.4	7.0	9.1	4.7	15.5
50 and over	3.3	1.1	0.0	2.4	4.7
Mean (years)	28.2	27.6	26.9	28.3	28.5
Median (years)	26.0	26.0	25.0	26.0	26.0
N	211	86	44	42	129
OCCUPATION (%)					
Student	0.3	0.8	1.2	0.0	0.6
Unskilled	3.1	5.4	1.2	13.6	1.2
Semiskilled	4.8	7.0	3.5	13.7	3.0
Skilled	20.2	24.8	23.5	27.2	16.5
Low white-collar					
Petty proprietors	8.6	7.7	7.1	9.2	8.9
Clerical	25.7	32.6	32.9	31.8	21.3
Total	34.3	40.3	40.0	41.0	30.2
High white-collar					
Merchants and managers	18.8	18.6	25.9	4.5	18.9
Professionals	18.5	3.1	4.7	0.0	29.6
Total	37.3	21.7	30.6	4.5	48.5
N	292	129	85	44	169

Love had more native players than any other ten cities of the Union, and later that year eleven of those players proved their superiority over local Englishmen with a decisive victory.[43]

The *New York Times* stated in July 1860 that cricket in Philadelphia was "as popular with Americans as Base Ball is in New York; and no other reason than Americans have controlled it." According to the *Times,* native sportsmen deserved the credit for the Philadelphia cricket boom, while the Englishmen who dominated the sport in Manhattan had "almost utterly squelched the rising spirit of cricket amongst Americans in New York, and driven it into base-ball, as a means of out-door exercise and recreation."[44] The man who was probably most responsible for promoting the English national pastime among Philadelphians was William Rotch Wister, known successively among the local cricketing fraternity as the "father" and then the "grandfather" of cricket. An 1846 graduate of the University of Pennsylvania, Wister was one of the founders of the Philadelphia Cricket Club, which was organized in his office in 1854. An authority on Philadelphia cricket described Wister as "genial, sparkling, lovable"—a "gusty, chirruping captain who urged on his men with cries of encouragement, side remarks, quips, and cracks."[45]

Race was a far greater factor than nationality in determining social status in mid-nineteenth-century America. There is no evidence that blacks of this era participated in organized cricket, but there is abundant proof that they played baseball. Newspapers report contests among all-black nines during the Civil War, and it is likely that northern blacks competed informally during the 1850s. In 1862 the *Brooklyn Daily Eagle* began an account of a local game between the Unknowns and the Monitors with the headline: "A New Sensation in Baseball Circles—Sambo as a Ball-player and Dinah as an Emulator." The *Newark Daily Advertiser* reported that "considerable excitement was created among the colored 'boys' of this city . . . by a base ball match between the Hamilton Club of this city and the Hensen Club of Jamaica, L.I., both composed of the descendants of Ham."[46]

A few leaders of the black community questioned the appropriateness of organized recreation during the years of trial for free northern blacks and recently emancipated slaves. In 1869 William Still, a coal dealer, scolded Philadelphia's Pythians after he received a bill for dues owed to that premier black ball club: "Our kin in the South famishing for knowledge, have claims so great and pressing that I feel bound to give of any means in this direction to the extent of my abilities, in preference to giving for frivolous amusements." The club secretary, Jacob C. White, Jr., claimed that Still had in fact agreed to become a contributing member, refused to comment on Still's priorities, and again requested that Still pay his debt.[47]

During this period most northern blacks were impoverished, but a few of the more privileged could afford the time and expense of baseball. Philadelphia's black ball players ranked near the top of that city's black social structure. A comparison of their demographic characteristics with those of Philadelphia's white baseball fraternity reveals similarities in nationality and age but striking differences in occupation, property, and residence (see Tables 2, 3, and 4). The city's black baseball players were all born in the United States, although more of them had come from southern states than their white counterparts, and were slightly older (the mean age being twenty-eight). Many more black players were unskilled and semiskilled workers, and few of them held high white-collar jobs; about two-thirds of both black and white groups held skilled and low white-collar jobs. This suggests that early baseball was popular among artisans, petty proprietors, and clerks of both races in Philadelphia. The statistics on real and personal estate show that black ball players were more prosperous than the black community as a whole,[48] but they were significantly less affluent than white athletes. Blacks resided in most sections of the city but were concentrated near the waterfront in Wards One through Four and especially in the historically black neighborhoods of Ward Seven.

Two mulatto baseball players became leaders of Philadelphia's black community during the Reconstruction era. Jacob C. White, Jr., secretary of the Pythian Base Ball Club, became principal of the largest and most advanced black public school in the city. While he joined several civic and civil rights organizations, he was a moderate on race questions, steadily pursuing a policy of accommodation with whites.[49] Octavius V. Catto, who was more dynamic and militant, lived a short but active life as a star baseball player, teacher, and civil rights advocate. He joined the Pennsyl-

TABLE 3. Wealth of Philadelphia Sportsmen, 1855–70

	All Players	All Baseball	White Baseball	Black Baseball	All Cricket
REAL ESTATE (%)					
None	70.2	77.5	77.6	77.3	64.4
$5,000 and under	7.5	7.8	3.5	15.9	7.1
$5,000–10,000	6.8	9.3	14.2	0.0	5.3
$10,000–50,000	11.7	5.4	4.7	6.8	16.6
Over $50,000	3.8	0.0	0.0	0.0	6.5
Mean ($)	8,840	2,452	2,732	1,911	13,610
Median ($)	0	0	0	0	0
PERSONAL ESTATE (%)					
None	58.2	66.7	71.8	56.8	50.9
$500 and under	26.7	11.6	5.9	22.7	5.3
$500–1,000	5.8	8.5	11.8	2.3	10.1
$1,000–5,000	6.9	8.5	3.5	2.3	7.7
$5,000–10,000	1.4	3.1	3.5	2.3	14.8
Over $10,000	1.0	1.6	1.1	2.3	14.8
Mean ($)	5,596	940	930	959	9,030
Median ($)	0	0	0	0	0
N[1]	292	129	85	44	169

[1]Includes all men whose occupations were identified. If no property holdings were listed for a player found in the census, a value of zero was assigned in computing the means and medians. But since some of these men undoubtedly did hold some real or personal property, these means and medians are somewhat lower than the actual amounts. In cases where only a player's parents' property holdings were listed, that value was used.

vania Equal Rights League, worked for the desegregation of Philadelphia street cars, and became a confirmed Republican dedicated to gaining the right to vote for all blacks. Admitted to the city's prestigious Franklin Institute, he had just launched himself into national prominence when an assassin's bullet cut short his life in October 1871. His untimely passing was mourned by both races, and his funeral was one of the largest ever held for a black man in Philadelphia. His death deprived the city of a black sports hero and civil rights leader and severely damaged the cause of racial equality in the City of Brotherly Love.[50]

TABLE 4. Residence and Place of Work of Philadelphia Sportsmen by Ward, 1855–70

	All Players	All Baseball	White Baseball	Black Baseball	All Cricket
RESIDENCE (%)					
Ward 5	5.7	5.1	3.6	8.4	6.0
Ward 6	2.0	1.6	2.5	0.0	2.2
Ward 7	12.2	11.8	1.2	36.1	12.5
Ward 8	14.5	5.1	1.2	13.9	20.3
Ward 9	4.1	2.5	3.6	0.0	4.9
Ward 10	8.8	10.1	13.2	2.8	8.2
Ward 22	16.8	5.8	8.5	0.0	23.5
N	296	119	83	36	183
PLACE OF WORK (%)					
Wards 1–4	2.4	2.0	2.0	—	2.6
Ward 5	43.7	39.2	39.2	—	45.3
Ward 6	29.1	45.1	45.1	—	23.0
Wards 7–22	24.8	13.7	13.7	—	29.1
N	165	51	51	0	117

In most if not all cities and towns baseball players ranged from young boys to men well into middle age. Originally a child's game, the sport was embraced by many adults in their twenties and thirties, and it was not uncommon to see active participants in their forties and even fifties. In 1865 the *Newark Daily Advertiser* suggested that "there is not an urchin in Newark" who did not belong to a club that emulated the senior nines. It praised "that little republic of base ball," where "the child of wealth is seen playing with the youthful ragamuffins from some neighboring alley, and the magic ball passes swiftly from the pretty hand of the patrician boy to the soiled fist of the little plebeian."[51] The veterans of Newark's Knickerbocker Base Ball Club continued to play the old style of ball that they enjoyed forty years earlier, while the hometown Eurekas defeated the New York Empires in "an exhibition by the supernumerary and superannuated of both organizations."[52] The average baseball player was about twenty-seven years old in both New Jersey and Philadelphia, but this figure would be lower if more of the boys and juniors could be identified and included in the sample.[53]

In cricket, the age structure (like the ethnicity trends) differed in several cities. Despite token efforts by the leading New York and Brooklyn clubs to recruit junior members, older men dominated the sport in those cities. There were more young cricketers in Newark than across the Hudson or East rivers, but even there the average club member was about six years older than his baseball counterpart (mean age = 33.6 years; median = 30.4 years). Nearly 60 percent of Newark's cricketing fraternity was over thirty, with half of those over forty. By contrast, only about 44 percent of Newark's baseball players were over thirty. This may have been because cricket was not well known among American boys and was more difficult than baseball for adults to learn. Of course, the high percentage of English immigrants playing cricket also affected the sport's age structure.

In its age patterns, as in its nationality trends, the Philadelphia cricket community differed sharply from its counterparts in New York, Brooklyn, and Newark. With a mean age of 28.5, Philadelphia cricketers were slightly older than that city's baseball players, but they were significantly younger than their fellow cricketers in other cities (60 percent were under thirty). In 1859 the *Clipper* reported that "every boy in Philadelphia, who plays ball at all, knows cricket thoroughly." When seventeen native Philadelphians (plus one player from Amsterdam, New York) defeated eleven Englishmen in an all-star match in 1860, the average age of the Philadelphians was only twenty. Several of the players were high school students at the Free Academy, where about 300 out of that institution's 500 pupils played cricket.[54] The City of Brotherly Love produced two young stars—Walter S. and George M. Newhall, scions of one of the city's famous cricketing families, second only to the Wisters. Walter was perhaps the best American batsman of his day, already a star at the age of eighteen, but his tragic drowning in 1863 while returning home on furlough from the Union army cut short his brilliant cricket career. George created a sensation at the age of thirteen when he bowled in front of about 6,000 spectators in an all-star match of Americans versus Englishmen. He lived to play a prominent role in promoting Philadelphia cricket after the war.[55]

An analysis of the social class of these pioneer American sportsmen requires a consideration of their occupation, wealth, neighborhood residence, and place of work. (There are, of course, other factors that affect social class, such as religion, education, and family and personal relationships, but they are not included in this study.) Most social historians have concentrated on occupation in evaluating an individual's social class, using the following six categories: high white-collar, low white-collar, skilled, semiskilled, unskilled, and student. The following discussion uses this scheme but also refers to data on real and personal property as well as residence and place of work, concentrating on New York, Newark, and Philadelphia.

Most of the first baseball players were skilled craftsmen, clerks, petty proprietors, or managers. The extensive participation of artisans in the national pastime may be explained in part by the group's declining status during the middle decades of the nineteenth century. One may speculate that these men turned to baseball to provide themselves with recreation and a means of asserting their prowess at a time when their prospects for advancement in their vocations were deteriorating. Melvin Adelman found that between 1850 and 1855, 87 percent of New York City's players and 56 percent of Brooklyn's participants were white-collar workers. However, during the second half of that decade the proportion of New York ball players who were skilled craftsmen rose from about 13 percent to about 33 percent, while in Brooklyn the percentage of artisans fell slightly from 44 to 37. By the eve of the Civil War, a combined total of roughly 64 percent of the players in the two leading centers of amateur baseball were white-collar workers. Although very few unskilled or semiskilled men played baseball in New York and Brooklyn before the Civil War, the sport did attract a wide following among skilled workers, office employees, and small shopkeepers. Artisans in particular were becoming increasingly important to the game, especially as frequent participants in interclub contests.[56]

In four New Jersey cities and towns (Newark, Jersey City, Hoboken, and Orange) the low and high white-collar groups combined for 45 percent of the total number of baseball players, which is significantly lower than in the neighboring cities (see Table 5). About 36 percent of the players were artisans—roughly the same as in New York and Brooklyn. Some of the difference may be accounted for by the percentage of students who played the game, but New Jersey baseball also attracted some players from the lowest

TABLE 5. Occupation of New Jersey Sportsmen, 1855–60

	Newark Baseball	Jersey City[1] Baseball	Orange Baseball	Total Baseball	Newark Cricket	Total Sportsmen
STUDENT (%)	6.5	13.1	8.7	10.1	1.4	8.2
UNSKILLED (%)	0.9	6.9	4.3	4.3	4.2	4.1
SEMISKILLED (%)	5.6	3.4	0.0	4.0	2.8	3.8
SKILLED (%)						
Building	7.4	7.6	13.0	8.0	4.2	7.3
Metal	9.3	6.2	4.3	7.2	43.7	14.7
Leather	4.6	1.4	8.7	3.3	2.8	3.2
Wood	7.4	9.7	0.0	2.5	5.6	2.9
Cloth	6.5	1.4	47.8	7.2	15.5	9.1
Other	2.8	2.8	0.0	8.0	5.6	7.3
Total	38.0	29.1	73.8	36.2	77.4	44.5
LOW WHITE-COLLAR (%)						
Petty Proprietors	7.4	8.3	0.0	7.2	1.4	6.2
Clerical	17.6	22.8	13.0	19.9	4.2	16.7
Total	25.0	31.1	13.0	27.1	5.6	22.9
HIGH WHITE-COLLAR (%)						
Merchants and Manufacturers	17.6	13.8	0.0	14.1	4.2	12.3
Professionals	6.5	2.8	0.0	4.0	4.2	4.1
Total	24.1	16.6	0.0	18.1	8.4	16.4
N	108	145	23	276	71	341

[1]Includes data from adjacent Hoboken and Hudson City.

rungs of the labor force. These men were decidedly in the minority, for the bulk of New Jersey's baseball fraternity were mechanics or clerks, along with a significant number of wealthy merchants, contractors, professionals, and other elites.[57] In Newark, both cricketers and baseball players were more likely to own property and were more prosperous than the townspeople in general.[58] That city's baseball players were predominantly prosperous white-collar workers (along with some well-to-do artisans) who resided on the more fashionable steets of the central business district and the adjacent wards of the town's "Old Core"[59] (see Tables 6 and 7).

TABLE 6. Wealth of New Jersey Sportsmen, 1855–60

	Newark Baseball	Jersey City[1] Baseball	Orange Baseball	Total Baseball	Newark Cricket	Total Sportsmen
REAL ESTATE (%)						
None	47.7	64.6	43.5	55.9	64.4	57.2
$5,000 and under	25.6	16.0	34.7	21.6	23.7	22.4
Over $5,000	26.7	19.5	21.7	22.6	11.9	20.5
Mean ($)	7,411	4,198	2,561	5,273	2,110	4,659
Median ($)	650	0	1,200	0	0	0
PERSONAL ESTATE (%)						
None	27.9	38.1	21.7	32.4	44.1	34.9
$500 and under	30.2	29.2	65.2	33.3	32.2	32.7
Over $500	41.8	32.8	12.9	34.3	23.8	32.4
Mean ($)	2,853	3,896	2,479	3,345	1,310	2,948
Median ($)	350	300	100	325	100	200
N	86	113	23	222	59	278

[1]Includes data from adjacent Hoboken and Hudson City.

These groups also dominated baseball in Philadelphia, where 62 percent of the players held white-collar jobs, one-quarter were craftsmen, and one-eighth were unskilled or semiskilled workers (see Table 2). Athletes were slightly more affluent than native white Philadelphians,[60] and their homes were fairly evenly distributed throughout the city, with some concentration in Wards Seven, Ten, and Fourteen, though 84 percent worked in Ward Four. Because their occupations brought them together in a small area, many were probably at least acquaintances, if not friends. In Philadelphia, Newark, and probably many other towns, the proximity of players' jobs and businesses may have contributed to their sporting lives by increasing personal contacts (see Tables 3 and 4).

Early baseball attracted many players who were successful businessmen or professionals during and after their playing days. For example, William Cauldwell of the Morrisania (Bronx) Unions owned the *New York Sunday Mercury*. Seamen Lichtenstein of the New York Gothams lived a true rags-to-riches life. Born into poverty in 1825 and orphaned as a young boy, he founded what became one of the largest produce houses in the United States. Lichtenstein served as the Gothams' treasurer from 1857 to 1859 and also owned and raced horses in his later years with such luminaries as William H. Vanderbilt.[61] Although New York's Knickerbocker Base Ball Club was not as exclusive or as fashionable as that city's leading athletic and social clubs, it did enroll several men who distinguished themselves in business. James Fowler Wenman, a first-nine shortstop during the 1850s, came from a prominent Irish family. During his playing days he traded in cotton, and in 1861 he organized the Board of New York Cotton Brokers; over the next several decades he prospered as a president, vice president, and manager of the New York Cotton Exchange. Wenman kept up his interest in recreation by serving as a Central Park commissioner during the 1870s.[62]

Joining these managers and professionals on the ball fields were numerous petty proprietors and skilled craftsmen who were acquiring property and status in America's cities and towns during the Civil War era. Among them was Hampton A. Coursen of the Jersey City Hamiltons, born in Sussex County, New Jersey, in 1826. Like many antebellum ball players, he was a member of a volunteer fire department; he also became senior member of a wholesale liquor firm and a director of the Hudson County Bank of Jersey City and the North River Insurance Company of New

TABLE 7. Residence of Newark Sportsmen, 1855–60

	Newark Cricket	Newark Baseball
CENTRAL BUSINESS DISTRICT (%)		
Ward 4	18.1	7.0
"OLD CORE" (%)		
Wards 1–3, 9	36.2	68.7
"INNER RING" (%)		
Wards 5–7	31.9	19.2
"OUTER RING" (%)		
Wards 10–11	13.9	5.1
N	72	115

York. Rochus Heinisch, an active player and umpire for the Newark Base Ball Club during the 1850s, was born in 1801 in Austria, where he learned the cutlery trade. He moved to Newark around 1834 and began a successful career as a manufacturer of patent shears and razors; he was also a member of the city council. His death in 1874 at the age of seventy-three deprived Newark of a respected businessman, sportsman, and civic leader.[63]

One should not forget the early baseball players who lived out their lives as middle-class mechanics or semiskilled or unskilled workers. They were little known outside their immediate neighborhoods and families, but they deserve to be noticed today, for they were the rank and file that created team sports in the United States.[64] These men included baseball-playing Irish laborers and hatters, policemen, and other common people who joined the sports boom of the 1850s and who have long been forgotten.

Although working-class English immigrants played a major role in popularizing their country's national sport in America during the 1830s and 1840s, by 1860 most of the cricketers in New York, Brooklyn, and Boston were professionals and merchants. In Philadelphia only one-sixth of the cricketers were artisans; nearly 80 percent were white-collar workers, including a large contingent of lawyers, doctors, merchants, and other managers and professionals. The sportsmen from the City of Brotherly Love were more affluent than their counterparts from Newark in both sports. Cricketers were at the top of Philadelphia's social scale (see Tables 2, 3, and 4). They owned about five times as much real estate and nearly ten times as much personal property as the Philadelphia baseball fraternity. With a combined average wealth of over $22,000, these men constituted a truly elite class.[65] About one-third of them lived in the fashionable area near Rittenhouse Square, in Wards Seven and Eight; another one-quarter resided in Germantown, a hotbed of cricket on the outskirts of the city. Sixty-eight percent of Philadelphia's cricketers worked in the city's central business district (Wards Five and Six), while Germantown residents tended to work closer to their homes in Ward Twenty-two.

Newark, one of several factory towns whose craftsmen patronized the English sport, differed sharply from Philadelphia in the occupation, wealth, and neighborhood residence patterns of its cricketers (see Tables 5, 6, and 7). More than three-fourths of the city's cricket players were skilled artisans, and nearly 85 percent were from the working class. (Metal workers, mostly jewelers and blacksmiths, accounted for 44 percent, while cloth workers, mostly hatters and tailors, contributed another 16 percent.) It is striking that whereas nearly one-half of Newark's baseball fraternity held white-collar jobs, only 14 percent of its cricketers did. Newark's baseball players were also wealthier. A higher percentage of cricketers reported no real estate, while one-quarter of each group claimed $5,000 or less in property, and a much higher proportion of baseball players owned more than $5,000 worth of property. Thus Newark's cricketing community was composed mainly of mechanics with no land or houses, though a sizable minority held some property and were probably self-employed. The data on personal estates reinforces the conclusion that Newark's baseball fraternity was more prosperous than its cricketing community,[66] as do the residential patterns of that city's sportsmen. A lower percentage of Newark's cricketers lived in the more affluent central business district or the "Old Core," while a higher proportion resided in the more socially mixed "inner" and "outer rings."[67]

The elite classes of America's eastern cities contributed a number of first-class players and lesser talents who loved cricket. Among these were Charles Cadwallader and Spencer Meade, who were ranked with the Wisters and Newhalls of Philadelphia. A few men from Newark's upper classes joined the action, including John C. Jennings, a wealthy jewelry manufacturer and president of his town's Mechanics club (who was worth over $30,000 in 1860), and James Douglass Orton of the Newark club, a banker who estimated his personal estate at $10,000 in 1860.[68] The professional ranks of the clergy also produced several cricket enthusiasts, including the Reverend Thomas W. Higginson, a Harvard graduate and advocate of "muscular Christianity" who served as president of the Lincoln Cricket Club of Worcester, Massachusetts.[69] The artistic community contributed William Ranney, a founder of the New York Cricket Club, who gained some fame but little fortune during the 1840s and 1850s as a painter.[70]

Most cricketers never achieved the long-term reputations of Higginson or Ranney, but some achieved modest success as artisans or petty proprietors. One of these was James Higham, a member of the New York club who was a tailor until about 1865, when he opened "The Office," a popular English restaurant that attracted a sporting and theatrical crowd.[71] During the 1850s the Newark Cricket Club enlisted dozens of English and American mechanics who reported little or no property in the 1860 census. Like their equally obscure counterparts in baseball, these men were of humble circumstances.

A few females braved ridicule by joining the boys and men who created the first modern team sports in America during the Civil War era. Women had graced ball fields as spectators since the earliest days of American baseball and cricket, but after 1865 some girls and young ladies preferred to be participants. In 1867 the baseball fever in Bordentown, New Jersey, "reached the female persuasion," and a heated rivalry began between the Belle Vue and Galaxy clubs.[72] At Peterboro, New York, the granddaughter of women's rights advocate Gerrit Smith was the captain of a girls' baseball club that enrolled about fifty members. She and her friends practiced out of town, "away from the gaze of the curious who would naturally crowd around such a beautiful display." Dispensing with "all the riotous petticoats and flummery," they adopted a costume "which must have carried insubordination into the ranks of the male assemblage" and played a public game before a large crowd. They wore "short blue and white tunics, reaching to the knees, straw caps, jauntily trimmed, white stockings and stout gaiter shoes."[73] In Rockford, Illinois, a "picked nine of maidens" defeated a married ladies' club, while at Northwestern Female College at Evanston, two nines from the Diana club attracted many curious spectators. Girls' teams also appeared in Cincinnati and Lancaster, Ohio.[74]

This framentary evidence suggests that white middle-class American-born schoolgirls and young ladies were the pioneers of early women's baseball. They broke down male resistance to female ball playing and at the same time blazed the trail for their sisters of all ages, nationalities, races, and classes to compete on the diamonds of America.

During the mid-nineteenth century, thousands of boys and men—and a few women—from all types of ethnic, racial, and social backgrounds in dozens of American cities and towns exercised their bodies and refreshed their minds through cricket and baseball. They played street and sandlot pickup games and organized more formal contests. Skilled craftsmen, clerks, proprietors, merchants, and professionals sought relief from their toil in the new outdoor sports. Most followed a code of sportsmanship that stressed gentlemanly conduct. The occasional breeches of sporting etiquette demonstrated that the desire to win could sometimes disrupt wholesome amusements and friendly strife. Many of these players joined sports clubs, which provided good fellowship and more opportunity to engage in favorite pastimes. It is these early athletic associations, which created and nurtured modern team sports during the Civil War era, to which we now turn.

NOTES

1. *Porter's Spirit* 1 (January 10, 1857): 309; 3 (January 9, 1858): 292.
2. Steven M. Gelber, "Working at Playing: The Culture of the Workplace and the Rise of Baseball," *Journal of Social History* 16 (Summer 1983): 3–22; " 'Their Hands Are All Out Playing': Business and Amateur Baseball, 1845–1917," *Journal of Sport History* 11 (Spring 1984): 5–27; Warren Jay Goldstein, "Playing for Keeps: A History of American Baseball, 1857–1876" (unpublished Ph.D. dissertation, Yale University, 1983). Both Gelber and Goldstein correctly emphasize the influence of the culture of work on nineteenth-century sport, but both underestimate the persistence of the play element in informal games, club practice sessions, and interclub matches. On the issue of pure play versus serious work in baseball, see Goldstein, "Playing for Keeps," pp. 32–33, 36–37, 42, 94–102.
3. *Newark Daily Advertiser,* August 2, 1865.
4. *Newark Daily Advertiser,* September 5, 1866.
5. *Wilkes' Spirit* 18 (April 4, 1868): 99.
6. *New York Times,* April 30, 1871.
7. Henry Chadwick's scrapbooks, vol. 1 (1871), Albert G. Spalding Collection, New York Public Library.
8. *Jersey City Daily Sentinel and Advertiser,* June 4, 11, 1855. See also *Jersey City Daily Sentinel,* August 11, 1856; *Newark Evening Journal,* November 15, 1858.
9. *Newark Daily Advertiser,* July 31, October 29, 1866; May 13, 1867; July 7, 1869. See also *Jersey City Daily Times,* September 4, 1865.
10. *Newark Daily Advertiser,* May 14, 1860.
11. *Clipper* 14 (September 15, 1866): 179.

12. *Clipper* 5 (April 17, 1858): 411. See also *Newark Daily Advertiser,* November 30, 1857; May 14, 1860; May 2, 6, 1864; *Clipper* 10 (November 1, 1862): 227; 12 (May 28, 1864): 51; *Brooklyn Daily Eagle,* August 27, September 20, 1858; *Porter's Spirit* 5 (August 14, 1858): 380; 7 (September 3, 1859): 4; *Newark Evening Journal,* November 28, 1858; *Wilkes' Spirit* 3 (October 27, 1860): 116; 5 (November 9, 1861): 147; (November 30, 1861): 196; (January 11, 1862): 293; 6 (July 5, 1862): 276; 7 (September 13, 1862): 20; (October 4, 1862): 68; (October 18, 1862): 116; (November 1, 1862): 131; (November 8, 1862): 147–48; (November 15, 1862): 172; 8 (June 20, 1863): 243; (August 29, 1863): 403; 9 (September 26, 1863): 52; (October 3, 1863): 67; (October 24, 1863): 118; (November 28, 1863): 196; (December 12, 1863): 231; 10 (May 21, 1864): 180; (August 13, 1864): 371; 11 (November 5, 1864): 147; 13 (September 2, 1865): 13; (September 9, 1865): 19; (September 16, 1865): 44, 45; (September 23, 1865): 54; (September 30, 1865): 75; (October 21, 1865): 119; (October 28, 1865): 140; (November 4, 1865): 147; (November 11, 1865): 166; (November 18, 1865): 188. Susan E. Hirsch, *Roots of the American Working Class: The Industrialization of Crafts in Newark, 1800–1860* (Philadelphia, 1978), states that some of the Newark jewelry firms had company baseball teams (p. 100). Jewelers did join baseball clubs and probably played informal contests, but I found no evidence of company-sponsored sports teams in New Jersey before the Civil War.

13. *Wilkes' Spirit* 12 (April 8, 1865): 85.

14. *Newark Daily Advertiser,* July 24, 26, September 14, 1867; *Wilkes' Spirit* 13 (December 2, 1865): 208. See also *Clipper* 14 (August 18, 1866): 146; *Spirit* 24 (October 10, 1868): 114; (October 24, 1868): 148.

15. *Clipper* 14 (November 3, 1866): 236.

16. *Newark Daily Advertiser,* July 6, August 11, September 7, 1870.

17. Gelber, "Their Hands Are All Out Playing," 17–18.

18. *Clipper* 7 (October 8, 1859): 196; (November 26, 1859): 252; 8 (September 1, 1860): 155; *Wilkes' Spirit* 3 (September 15, 1860): 26. See also *Wilkes' Spirit* 1 (November 19, 1859): 172; *Newark Evening Journal,* October 25, 1858.

19. *Porter's Spirit* 1 (January 10, 1857): 309.

20. Quoted in Thomas L. Altherr, " 'The Most Summery, Bold, Free, & Spacious Game': Charles King Newcomb and Philadelphia Baseball, 1866–1871," *Pennsylvania History* 52 (April 1985): 73–75.

21. *Spirit* 25 (September 29, 1859): 389.

22. *Clipper* 7 (July 2, 1859): 84; *Porter's Spirit* 6 (April 9, 1859):84. At mid-century a cricket fanatic nicknamed "Old Gruel" played at Hoboken, New Jersey, and became the subject of a satirical

piece in the *Spirit of the Times.* See *Spirit* 19 (December 8, 1849): 498. For prose and poetry extolling the virtues of cricket, see *Spirit* 19 (June 16, 1849): 204; (June 23, 1849): 211; (July 17, 1849): 235; (September 15, 1849): 353; (October 13, 1849): 403; 20 (August 3, 1850): 282; 25 (October 6, 1855): 397; (December 1, 1855): 498; *Clipper* 6 (September 4, 1858): 157; 8 (April 26, 1860): 13. For a humorous story lampooning cricket as dull and too serious, see *Wilkes' Spirit* 1 (December 3, 1859): 204.

23. *Spirit* 16 (August 15, 1846): 300; *Newark Daily Journal,* June 4, 1866; letter to the editor of the *Chicago Tribune,* reprinted in *Ball Players' Chronicle,* September 26, 1867.

24. *Clipper* 9 (November 9, 1861): 236.

25. *Porter's Spirit* 5 (October 9, 1858): 84; 6 (July 9, 1859): 293.

26. *Clipper* 10 (May 24, 1862): 42; (May 31, 1862): 51. See also *Clipper* 11 (September 26, 1863): 190; *Philadelphia Sunday Mercury,* August 9, 1868.

27. For example, see *New York Times,* July 9, 1860.

28. For examples of bad feeling among clubs over gambling, see the discussion in Chapter 7.

29. *Clipper* 9 (November 9, 1861): 234.

30. *Clipper* 9 (November 30, 1861): 258. See also *Wilkes' Spirit* 5 (December 21, 1861): 245.

31. Reported in *Philadelphia Sunday Mercury,* March 4, 1866.

32. *Wilkes' Spirit* 16 (May 22, 1867): 209.

33. *Clipper* 8 (January 19, 1861): 315; (February 16, 1861): 347; 9 (March 1, 1862): 362; 11 (February 20, 1864): 354; 12 (January 21, 1865): 322; (February 4, 1865): 338; (February 18, 1865): 344; *Wilkes' Spirit* 9 (February 27, 1864): 407. A few cricket matches were also played on ice.

34. *Wilkes' Spirit* 15 (January 19, 1867): 324.

35. *Clipper* 12 (June 18, 1864): 242.

36. *Clipper* 15 (May 18, 1867): 45; (May 25, 1867): 52.

37. *Porter's Spirit* 3 (October 17, 1857): 101; 6 (July 30, 1859): 345; 7 (September 3, 1859): 9; *Wilkes' Spirit* 3 (September 29, 1860): 53; (October 13, 1860): 87; *Spirit* 15 (April 26, 1845): 62; 17 (September 25, 1847): 366; (October 30, 1847): 419; 20 (October 19, 1850): 415; 27 (December 19, 1857): 529; *Clipper* 5 (September 26, 1857): 183; (October 24, 1857): 215; 6 (October 2, 1858): 189–90; (January 1, 1859): 293; 7 (May 21, 1859): 4; 8 (November 3, 1860): 225.

38. For a discussion of the methodology used to gather the data and compute the statistics for this study, see the note at the end of this volume.

39. For example, the Jersey City Enterprise and Independence junior clubs; see *Jersey City Daily Courier and Advertiser,* August 16, 1859.

40. *Porter's Spirit* 1 (October 25, 1856): 133; *Brooklyn Daily Eagle,* June 15, 1857; August 10, 26, 1858; July 12, 1859.

41. *Spirit* 24 (August 12, 1854): 306; (August 26, 1854): 336.

42. *Newark Daily Advertiser,* May 5, 1858.

43. *Clipper* 6 (July 3, 1858): 84; (November 27, 1858): 253.

44. *New York Times,* July 6, 9, 1860.

45. John A. Lester, ed., *A Century of Philadelphia Cricket* (Philadelphia, 1951), 9, 11, 16.

46. *Brooklyn Daily Eagle* quoted in Melvin L. Adelman, *A Sporting Time: New York City and the Rise of Modern Athletics, 1820–70* (Urbana, Ill., 1986), 176; *Newark Daily Advertiser,* September 30, 1862.

47. William Still to the Pythian Base Ball Club, January 30, 1869, and Jacob C. White, Jr., to William Still, March 1, 1869, in the records of the Pythian Base Ball Club, American Negro Historical Society Papers, Leon Gardner Collection, Box 8G, Historical Society of Pennsylvania.

48. For a study of Philadelphia's black population in the nineteenth century, see Theodore Hershberg and Henry Williams, "Mulattoes and Blacks: Intragroup Color Differences and Social Stratification in Nineteenth-Century Philadelphia," in Theodore Hershberg, ed., *Philadelphia: Work, Space, Family, and Group Experience in the Nineteenth Century* (New York, 1981), 392–434.

49. Harry C. Silcox, "Philadelphia Negro Educator: Jacob C. White, Jr., 1837–1902," *Pennsylvania Magazine of History and Biography* 97 (January 1973): 75–98.

50. Harry C. Silcox, "Nineteenth-Century Philadelphia Black Militant: Octavius V. Catto," *Pennsylvania History* 44 (January 1977): 53–76.

51. *Newark Daily Advertiser,* October 7, 1865.

52. *Newark Daily Journal,* May 30, 1866; *Newark Daily Advertiser,* September 16, 1868.

53. A player's age is here given as that of his final year of competition.

54. *Clipper* 7 (October 22, 1859): 212; *New York Times,* July 9, 1860.

55. Lester, *Philadelphia Cricket,* 21, 26–27; *Spirit* 28 (July 17, 1858): 271.

56. Adelman, *A Sporting Time,* 125–26, 138. He also presents statistics on officers, delegates to the NABBP conventions, and active participants (pp. 139–42). For a study of post–Civil War Chicago baseball and statistics on white- and blue-collar players similar to Adelman's, see Stephen Freedman, "The Baseball Fad in Chicago, 1865–1870: An Ex-

ploration of the Role of Sport in the Nineteenth-Century City," *Journal of Sport History* 5 (Summer 1978): 55–58.

57. The Jersey City Yacht Club, whose members were among the town's wealthiest citizens, organized informal baseball games at several of its celebrations and outings. Some members of that city's Hamilton Base Ball Club also belonged to the yacht club. See *Jersey City Daily Courier and Advertiser,* November 26, 1859; July 5, November 30, 1860.

58. For property holdings of Newarkers in general, see Hirsch, *Roots of the American Working Class,* 69.

59. For the structure of Newark's eleven wards in 1860, see Hirsch, *Roots of the American Working Class,* 95–97.

60. For statistics on American-born whites, compiled by the Philadelphia Social History Project, see Scott C. Brown, "Migrants and Workers in Philadelphia, 1850 to 1880" (unpublished Ph.D. dissertation, University of Pennsylvania, 1981).

61. *New York Times,* December 3, 1907; December 25, 1902.

62. *New York Times,* May 31, 1919. For examples of other prominent Knickerbockers, see *New York Times,* April 19, 1915; June 11, 1904.

63. *New York Times,* August 7, 1874; *Newark Daily Advertiser,* September 23, 1848.

64. For example, Michael McQuade and Michael Morrissey were Irish laborers who played baseball in Hoboken, New Jersey. See 1860 federal census for Hoboken.

65. Note that because of a small number of extremely wealthy persons, the mean is much higher than the median for New Jersey and especially Philadelphia sportsmen.

66. Baseball players in New Jersey who reported personal estates of at least $100 had a mean worth of about $4,950 (median = $675); cricketers who reported personal estates of at least $100 had a mean worth of $2,340 (median = $425). See 1860 federal censuses for Newark, Jersey City, Hoboken, and Orange.

67. For a more detailed discussion of the characteristics of New Jersey sportsmen, see George B. Kirsch, "The Rise of Modern Sports: New Jersey Cricketers, Baseball Players, and Clubs, 1845–60," *New Jersey History* 101 (Spring/Summer 1983): 53–84.

68. 1860 federal census for Newark, Ward 5, 349; Ward 4, 21.

69. John A. Lucas, "A Prelude to the Rise of Sport: Antebellum America, 1850–1860," *Quest* 11 (December 1968): 54–56; *Porter's Spirit* 4 (April 24, 1858): 117; *Clipper* 6 (June 26, 1858): 75.

70. *Clipper* 5 (December 12, 1857): 271; *New York Times,* November 24, 1857; *Dictionary of American Biography* (New York, 1935), 377–78.

71. *New York Times,* July 10, 1872.

72. *Newark Daily Advertiser*, September 16, 1867.

73. *Spirit* 20 (August 15, 1869): 471; 21 (August 29, 1869): 26. See also *Clipper* 16 (August 15, 1868): 149; (August 29, 1868): 163.

74. *Clipper* 18 (September 3, 1870): 173; (November 26, 1870): 266; *Chicago Tribune,* August 17, 1870; *Chicago Times,* October 11, 24, 1870.

CHAPTER

7

Clubs

ON an autumn evening in 1856, after the Putnam Base Ball Club had defeated the Excelsiors of South Brooklyn, the victorious hosts entertained their rivals and other invited guests at Trenor's Dancing Academy in Williamsburg. There the sportsmen consumed a large meal, then settled back to enjoy several hours of speeches, toasts, songs, jokes, and stories. The Putnams' president praised the "good effects they all experienced, both socially and physically, by the practice of baseball." Cheers greeted his remarks and those of the Excelsiors' captain. A glass was raised to honor the Knickerbockers, as the pioneers of baseball. The gathering joined in a baseball tune, sung "to the air of the old Scotch song of 'Here's a health to fair Scotland, the land of the brave,'" then toasted the press. After the party adjourned the Putnams escorted the Excelsiors to their horsecars, concluding an afternoon and evening of good sport and fellowship.[1]

Such harmony among sportsmen did not always prevail. In the late summer of 1860 the Resolutes of Brooklyn journeyed to Bergen, New Jersey, to play the deciding game of a series with the Mechanics of Jersey City. Foul language and open gambling among the spectators apparently upset the Resolutes' president; after the Mechanics won the hard-fought contest, he reluctantly gave up the game ball and then ignored the victorious captain. A few days later he wrote a scathing letter to a Jersey City newspaper, denouncing the crowd and accusing the opposition of unfairness and interference with his players. Supporters of the Mechanics responded with rebuttals and countercharges, until the newspaper's editor decided that the controversy had taken up enough space. The entire episode served to demonstrate that a "friendly game of ball" could lead to a good deal of discord among the participants.[2]

These two episodes provide a contrast between the ideal beneficial effects of early amateur sport and the all-too-frequent reality of contention and bad feeling. Given the tumultuousness of mid-nineteenth-century America, it is not surprising that in amateur sport the real and the ideal often came into conflict. The populace was faced with trying to maintain order and social stability while divisive forces threatened to tear society apart. Racial, ethnic, religious, and class distinctions increased in importance, while capitalist competition and unrestrained individualism pitted people against each other. Although sports clubs reflected these divisions and tendencies in society, they were also supposed to foster good relations through friendly competition and social interaction. Like other institutions of the era, amateur sports achieved mixed results in promoting social peace.

America's first cricket and baseball clubs were private, voluntary associations. Political, religious, charitable, educational, and cultural societies were popular in colonial and Revolutionary America, and they multiplied during the rapid urbanization of the 1800s. As the pressures of life in the cities intensified, and as social diversity and tensions mounted, city people sought reaffirmation of their identities as well as recreation and relaxation in sports clubs. These small subcommunities were larger than the family unit but intimate enough to preserve a sense of fellowship and group loyalty. Athletic clubs provided social interaction, exercise for health, and various levels of competition for all grades of athletes. They permitted people who shared common values to play together, and their proliferation during the Civil War era marked a critical stage in the development of modern American sports. These clubs embodied and fostered the increasing organization and the beginnings of bureaucracy that would characterize the postwar era of athletics in the United States.[3]

For a social historian, perhaps the most intriguing problem posed by America's first team sports associations is how the members grouped themselves into clubs. A cricket or baseball club was established each time a few enthusiasts succeeded in recruiting enough players who were willing to attend meetings, appear on practice days, and support all club activities. Members generally had more in common than their love of sport, but it is a difficult task to identify precisely which characteristics they shared. However, when one analyzes the players' demographic data by clubs, it is possible to determine whether age, birthplace, race, occupation, wealth, education, religion, or any combination of these factors decided club membership. (The following discussion is based in part on statistics tabulated here and in Chapter 6.)[4]

Whenever ball players formed clubs, age was a decisive factor in choosing members. Skill level, physical maturity, and cultural norms all dictated that men and boys should not play or socialize together. Both sports had three age categories: boys (sixteen and under), juniors (young men under twenty-one), and seniors. There were many exceptions to these limits, of course, as talented boys sometimes played with older adolescents while skilled juniors competed with adults; and in some cases it is difficult to classify an entire team. The *Clipper* reported in 1861 that the two Brooklyn clubs competing for the junior championship were "not composed of boys, but of young men, many of whom [were] older than the younger members of the senior organizations."[5]

Cricket flourished among boys and young men in the Philadelphia region. The Young America club of Germantown originated as a junior club in 1855, when the older boys in town excluded anyone under sixteen from their ranks. The youngsters responded with an "apple barrage" against their elders and banded together to found an organization that grew into one of the premier outfits in American cricket.[6] By the Civil War these Germantown adolescents had become clerks, merchants, and managers; after the conflict they joined Philadelphia's elite. That city had several dozen junior cricket clubs in 1860, while Camden, Newark, Trenton, Lawrence (Mass.), Baltimore, and Milwaukee also fielded a few squads. In New York City there were very few junior clubs, but the leading organizations did sponsor youthful elevens within their own associations.[7]

While only a modest number of junior cricket clubs appeared in the United States before the Civil War, the baseball mania of the 1850s generated several hundred nines of boys and young men. The greatest concentration occurred in Brooklyn, which fielded more than fifty junior clubs before 1861, and Newark and Jersey City each added at least twenty-five more. In the latter two cities it seems that nearly every ward, neighborhood, or even street organized at least one club, most of them composed of a blend of students, apprentices, and clerks from middle- or upper middle-class families. Two of the more prominent of the New Jersey junior associations were Jersey City's Lone Star and Morphy teams (see Table 8). Their members were primarily American-born students and white-collar workers who had been reared in moderately prosperous households. In general, it seems that ward residence was a more important factor for boys and juniors than for adults in determining club membership, probably because most of these teams were formed by boys and young men who became friends and playmates on neighborhood streets.[8]

As public opinion during the 1850s shifted in the direction of a more favorable attitude toward physical education and sport for America's youth, many schools, academies, and colleges sanctioned student-sponsored cricket and baseball clubs. The earliest of these began in 1834 at Haverford College, in Pennsylvania, which became a center for American cricketers for the next several decades. Other colleges with cricket clubs before the Civil War were Assumption, Girard, the United States Naval Academy at Annapolis, New York City's Free Academy (later City College), Oberlin, Holy Cross, the University of Pennsylvania, and Princeton.[9] As the more popular game, however, baseball overwhelmed cricket in America's schools before 1861. Amherst and Williams colleges played the first intercollegiate baseball game in 1859, and there were student-sponsored clubs at New York University, the Free Academy, Yale, Union, Kenyon, Hobart, and Utica colleges. During the Civil War years, nines were fielded at Princeton, Fordham, Seton Hall, Norwich, Harvard, Brown, Bowdoin, Hamilton, Williams, Free Academy, Columbia, New York, and Tufts.[10]

Nationality was a more important factor in the formation of early American cricket clubs than it was for baseball associations. English immigrants, who introduced cricket into America, constituted the core of that sport's leading clubs. While the New York and St. George clubs served their respective subcommunities by

TABLE 8. Birthplace, Age, Occupation, Wealth, and Residence of Members of Jersey City Baseball Clubs, 1855–60

	Hamiltons	Lone Star Jrs.	Morphy Jrs.
BIRTHPLACE (%)			
United States	100.0	81.3	80.0
Great Britain	0.0	18.7	20.0
AGE (years)			
Mean	24.8	21.2	19.3
Median	25.0	21.0	19.0
OCCUPATION (%)			
Student	12.5	22.2	16.7
Unskilled	6.3	11.1	0.0
Semiskilled	6.3	5.6	0.0
Skilled	6.3	16.7	25.0
Low white-collar	50.0	33.3	58.3
High white-collar	18.8	11.1	0.0
REAL ESTATE (%)			
None	66.7	69.2	50.0
$5,000 and under	0.0	23.1	30.0
Over $5,000	33.3	7.7	20.0
Mean ($)	7,133	1,077	2,250
Median ($)	0	0	500
PERSONAL ESTATE (%)			
None	38.5	30.8	20.0
$500 and under	15.4	30.8	50.0
Over $500	46.2	38.5	30.0
Mean ($)	11,915	1,025	1,120
Median ($)	500	500	300
RESIDENCE (%)			
Ward 1	26.7	5.9	0.0
Ward 2	13.3	5.9	8.3
Ward 3	40.0	17.6	8.3
Ward 4	20.0	70.6	83.4
N	16	19	12

preserving and strengthening allegiance to old-world customs, they also admitted an increasing number of Americans during the 1850s and 1860s.[11] In part because of the tendency of immigrants to monopolize play, several associations of American-born cricketers appeared in the Philadelphia area, including the Germantown, Young America, and Union clubs. All three apparently placed restrictions on membership, as did New York's short-lived American Cricket Club, founded in 1860.[12] Clubs organized at Rouse's Point (N.Y.), Lowell (Mass.), and Franklin (N.J.) were virtually all American.[13]

Several prominent cricket teams of this era were nearly evenly divided between Americans and Englishmen. Newark's three leading cricket clubs ranged from 31 percent to 46 percent American-born (this seems to have been the case throughout New Jersey before 1861). In the City of Brotherly Love, the Philadelphia Cricket Club was 90 percent American in 1860, while the less-prominent organizations were 60 percent native (see Tables 8 and 9). Clearly, the rivalry between John Bull and Brother Jonathan created a complicated pattern of ethnic allegiance among early American cricket clubs.

Since modern baseball was home-grown and was promoted by Americans, its club members were overwhelmingly native. Although some English, Irish, and German ball players were active before the Civil War, there were probably very few clubs with a majority drawn from any one of these groups.[14] Nationality certainly had some role in the founding of baseball clubs before 1861, but it was clearly less important than age, occupation, or wealth (see Tables 8, 9, and 10). Ethnic considerations were obviously more vital to cricketers than to baseball players.

Race was a far more decisive factor than nationality in determining club membership, for color restrictions were strictly observed during this period. Baseball fever swept through the black communities of many American cities and towns during the 1860s, and all-black nines appeared in Newark, Camden, New Brunswick, Boston, Chicago, Rockford (Ill.), Ripley (Ohio), Washington, D.C., Harrisburg, Pittsburgh, Philadelphia, Carlisle (Pa.), Brooklyn, New York, Utica, Buffalo, Niagara Falls, Albany, Rochester, Johnstown and Lockport (N.Y), Baltimore, and New Orleans, among other places. Some of these clubs, such as the Philadelphia Pythians,

TABLE 9. Birthplace, Age, Occupation, Wealth, and Residence of Members of Newark Cricket and Baseball Clubs, 1855–60

	Cricket			Baseball				
	Newarks	Mechanics	Essexes	Adriatics	Knicker-bockers	Lafayettes	Newarks	Empires
BIRTHPLACE (%)								
United States	46.5	33.3	31.2	85.7	86.7	80.0	88.0	88.9
Great Britain	46.5	50.0	62.5	9.5	13.3	10.0	3.8	0.0
Ireland	7.0	16.7	0.0	4.8	0.0	10.0	3.8	0.0
Other European	0.0	0.0	6.2	0.0	0.0	0.0	3.8	11.1
AGE (years)								
Mean	33.1	38.8	33.5	31.6	34.1	33.6	31.9	33.7
Median	32.0	40.0	29.5	26.5	35.0	33.0	28.0	28.0
OCCUPATION (%)								
Unskilled	2.0	14.3	0.0	5.0	0.0	0.0	0.0	0.0
Semiskilled	2.0	0.0	6.2	0.0	5.9	0.0	6.9	16.7
Skilled	81.6	78.4	81.3	40.0	23.5	50.0	37.9	55.5
Low white-collar	4.1	7.1	12.5	15.0	52.9	21.4	37.9	16.7
High white-collar	10.2	0.0	0.0	40.0	17.7	28.6	17.3	11.1
REAL ESTATE (%)								
None	59.5	63.6	62.5	38.9	50.0	[1]	60.0	[1]
$5,000 and under	24.3	27.3	25.0	33.3	14.3	[1]	12.0	[1]
Over $5,000	16.2	9.1	12.6	27.8	35.7	[1]	28.0	[1]
Mean ($)	2,678	1,336	1,719	11,278	5,486	[1]	4,340	[1]
Median ($)	200	100	50	300	550	[1]	200	[1]
PERSONAL ESTATE (%)								
None	41.0	50.0	50.0	21.1	35.7	[1]	25.0	[1]
$500 and under	35.9	25.0	37.5	47.4	14.3	[1]	45.8	[1]
Over $500	23.1	25.0	12.5	31.6	50.0	[1]	29.1	[1]
Mean ($)	908	2,725	463	4,811	1,271	[1]	1,558	[1]
Median ($)	200	100	50	300	550	[1]	200	[1]
RESIDENCE (%)								
Central Business District	20.0	14.3	6.2	13.1	0.0	7.1	0.0	12.5
"Old Core"	42.0	28.4	18.6	73.9	76.4	57.1	75.8	49.9
"Inner Ring"	24.0	35.7	62.4	4.3	23.6	21.4	10.3	37.4
"Outer Ring"	14.0	21.4	12.4	8.6	0.0	14.2	13.7	0.0
N	50	15	16	24	17	14	30	18

[1]Insufficient number of cases.

TABLE 10. Birthplace and Age of Members of Philadelphia Sports Clubs, 1855–70

	Pythian Base Ball Club	Philadelphia Cricket Club	Germantown Cricket Club	Young America Cricket Club
BIRTHPLACE (%)				
England and Scotland	0.0	7.3	0.0	0.0
Ireland	0.0	1.2	0.0	0.0
Other European	0.0	1.3	0.0	0.0
United States				
Pennsylvania	66.7	82.9	100.0	100.0
Other U.S.	33.3	7.3	0.0	0.0
Total	100.0	90.2	100.0	100.0
N	39	82	13	17
AGE (%)				
21 and under	25.6	15.9	69.2	88.2
22–29	35.9	30.4	30.8	11.8
30–39	33.4	25.7	0.0	0.0
40–49	5.1	20.7	0.0	0.0
50 and over	0.0	7.3	0.0	0.0
Mean (years)	27.4	32.0	20.9	18.1
Median (years)	26.0	30.0	21.0	18.0
N	39	82	13	17

recruited from the upper ranks of black society, while others enlisted men of lower status—for example, the Chicago Blue Stockings were hotel and restaurant waiters.[15]

The Pythians were one of America's most prominent black clubs during the late 1860s. While its players ranked far below their white counterparts in social status, they were among the black elite of their city (see Tables 10, 11, 12, and 13). Two-thirds were natives of Pennsylvania (compared to 40 percent of the total black population), and one-fifth were born in Virginia or South Carolina. The mean age of these players was twenty-seven, and 69 percent of them were mulattoes (versus only one-quarter of the total black population) at a time when lighter skin meant higher social status. In 1870 three-quarters of Philadelphia's blacks toiled as laborers, porters, waiters, or in other unskilled or semiskilled occupations;

by comparison, only one-quarter of the Pythians worked at those jobs, while nearly 27 percent were artisans and about 44 percent were petty proprietors, clerks, teachers, and other low white-collar workers. In their real and personal estates the Pythians also ranked at the top of black Philadelphia society, with a mean combined wealth of over $3,000. They lived among their poorer black brethren near the waterfront or in the city's seventh ward, but they were clearly a class apart from most of their neighbors. The *Sunday Mercury* described them as "a well-behaved, gentlemanly set of young fellows."[16]

As an elite black sports association, the Pythian club provided its members with recreation and a means of displaying their privileged social status. Many of the Pythians were active in black social and civic organizations, and about two-fifths of them belonged to the Banneker Institute, a literary and debating society that shared a room with the baseball players. One-fifth of these

TABLE 11. Occupation of Members of Philadelphia Sports Clubs, 1855–70

	Baseball					Cricket	
	Pythians	Athletics	Uniteds	Winonas	Olympics	Philadelphia	Washington
UNSKILLED (%)	9.8	0.0	0.0	0.0	0.0	0.0	0.0
SEMISKILLED (%)	14.6	8.3	0.0	9.1	0.0	0.0	0.0
SKILLED (%)	26.8	0.0	10.0	18.2	16.7	3.0	83.3
LOW WHITE-COLLAR (%)							
Petty proprietors	9.8	8.4	10.0	27.2	0.0	3.1	16.7
Clerical	34.1	33.3	50.0	36.4	8.3	23.5	0.0
Total	43.9	41.7	60.0	63.6	8.3	26.6	16.7
HIGH WHITE-COLLAR (%)							
Merchants and managers	4.9	33.3	30.0	9.1	58.3	22.4	0.0
Professionals	0.0	16.7	0.0	0.0	16.7	48.0	0.0
Total	4.9	50.0	30.0	9.1	75.0	70.4	0.0
N	41	12	10	11	12	98	12

TABLE 12. Property Holdings of Members of Philadelphia Sports Clubs, 1855–70

	Pythian Base Ball Club	Philadelphia Cricket Club
REAL ESTATE (%)		
None	78.0	54.1
$5,000 and under	14.6	7.1
$5,000–10,000	0.0	7.1
$10,000–50,000	7.4	23.5
Over $50,000	0.0	8.2
Mean ($)	2,027	19,122
Median ($)	0	0
PERSONAL ESTATE (%)		
None	56.1	36.7
$500 and under	22.0	3.1
$500–1,000	14.7	14.3
$1,000–5,000	2.4	10.2
$5,000–10,000	2.4	10.2
Over $10,000	2.4	18.4
Mean ($)	1,022	12,353
Median ($)	0	1,000
N[1]	41	98

[1]See note to Table 3.

athletes also joined civil rights organizations, such as the Pennsylvania State Equal Rights League and the Social, Civil, and Statistical Association of the Colored People of Pennsylvania. A small minority of activists, including Jacob C. White, Jr., and Octavius V. Catto, were active members of a committee to recruit blacks for the Union army in 1863.[17] Clearly, the Pythians had the leisure time and money to play baseball while most of their brethren suffered from poverty and racism, but a significant number of them also worked to improve the status of blacks in Philadelphia.

Among senior white cricket and baseball players, occupation appears to have been the major factor in club formation, although wealth and ward residence were influential. Cricket clubs were composed of either predominantly white-collar or working-class men, and very few clubs had evenly mixed memberships. Baltimore's Franklin Club, founded in 1859, included compositors, re-

TABLE 13. Residence of Members of Philadelphia Sports Clubs, 1855–70

	Baseball					Cricket			
	Pythians	Athletics	Uniteds	Winonas	Olympics	Philadelphia	Germantown	Young America	Washington
WARDS (%)									
1	3.0								
2		10.0							
3	9.1					0.9			
4	9.1		10.0						
5	6.1		10.0		9.1	2.7			
6					9.1	2.7			
7	36.3					18.2			
8	12.2					28.2	13.3	5.5	
9				18.2		7.3	13.3		
10	3.0		10.0		36.3	8.2	6.7		
12	6.0								
13	3.1	20.0	30.0	18.2	9.1	1.9			
14		20.0	20.0	36.3	9.1	2.7	5.6		
15	3.0	10.0				2.7			
16		20.0		9.1		0.9			
20	3.0	10.0	20.0	9.1	2.7				
21						1.9			8.3
22					9.1	12.7	60.0	83.3	83.4
23		10.0							8.3
24	3.1				18.2	0.9			
26	3.0								
N	33	10	10	11	11	110	15	18	12

porters, editors, clerks, bookkeepers of the printing profession, and also telegraph operators. The leading New York, Philadelphia, and Boston clubs were dominated by merchants, managers, professionals, and other solid citizens of the middle and upper echelons, including a few prosperous skilled craftsmen. In 1859, men of commerce comprised more than half of the St. George club, while skilled craftsmen accounted for only about 15 percent. Although

Porter's Spirit ranked that club "at the head of all the Cricket Clubs in the United States," its membership was not as affluent as that of New York's most exclusive social, literary, jockey, or yacht clubs. Yet the Dragon Slayers were "gentlemen of unexceptionable standing," with "several of wealth and very high position." The New York Cricket Club, which drew more of its members from the city's literary, artistic, and theatrical circles than from its mercantile community, was also probably less affluent than the St. George club.[18]

In Philadelphia, upper-class enthusiasm for cricket made that city the U.S. capital of the English national sport for the second half of the nineteenth century (see Tables 11, 12, and 13). The members of the Philadelphia Cricket Club were mainly men in their thirties and forties. Ninety-seven percent were white collar workers (almost half were doctors, lawyers, or other professionals), and the average combined real and personal estate was over $31,000. Nearly half of these sportsmen resided in Wards Seven and Eight, mostly on fashionable Walnut Street or on or near Rittenhouse Square, while one-eighth lived in suburban Germantown. About 80 percent of these elite cricketers had offices in the central business district. Those who were not neighbors were probably business associates or acquaintances within "Proper" Philadelphian society.

Although white-collar clubs ruled cricket in America, there were numerous working-class organizations in the United States before the Civil War. Artisans had helped to introduce cricket before 1840, and during the 1850s several clubs of skilled craftsmen competed in New York, Massachusetts, Pennsylvania, Maryland, and New Jersey. Many of Philadelphia's less-prominent elevens recruited heavily from the ranks of artisans. In that city thirty printers, most of whom were employed by daily newspapers, formed the Typographical Cricket Club.[19] Weavers from local mills dominated Germantown's Washington club, which was five-sixths craftsmen.

The center of blue-collar cricket was New Jersey, particularly Newark (see Table 9). That city and other factory towns in the state attracted many British craftsmen, who brought with them their love of sport. Skilled artisans, especially jewelers, silver platers, and tailors, controlled all three of the city's top organizations—the Newark, Mechanics, and Essex clubs—although the Newarks were slightly more affluent. The three clubs drew players from most of the city's eleven wards, but 62 percent of the Newark club lived in the central business district or "Old Core," compared to 43 percent of the Essexes. The Essex club was apparently more of a neighborhood team than either of its rivals, for it had a high concentration (44 percent) of its members in the seventh ward. All of this suggests that there were important residential (and also probably economic) differences among working-class cricket clubs in Newark and elsewhere.

In some of these artisan-based organizations, factory owners were either officers, patrons, or influential members. We can assume that journeymen joined with at least a few of their bosses to play cricket. It should be remembered that before the Civil War the industrial revolution had not yet completely separated workers from the manufacturing classes. Many shop owners still toiled as master craftsmen and thus had close relationships with their employees. At least in the case of Newark, the various cricket clubs probably did not enhance a feeling of shared working-class consciousness. Rather, these organizations probably strengthened the ties between the bosses and their hired men. In that sense, these particular clubs retained some premodern characteristics.[20]

America's first baseball clubs present a more complex problem when one tries to categorize them by occupations. Although some were either predominantly white- or blue-collar, many were fairly evenly mixed. All of the baseball cities had their prominent white-collar clubs of merchants, managers, lawyers, doctors, clerks, actors, and petty professionals. These included the New York Knickerbockers and Metropolitans, the Brooklyn Excelsiors, Esculapians, and Enterprise, Jr.'s, the Boston Olympics, Bay Staters, and Tri-Mountains, the Newark Knickerbocker Antiquarians, the Jersey City Hamiltons, and the Philadelphia Olympics, Athletics, and Mercantiles.[21]

While large numbers of middle- and upper middle-class men joined these white-collar clubs, perhaps an equal or greater number of blue-collar players formed working-class clubs (see Tables 8, 9, 10, 11, and 13). Unlike the numerous factory and trade nines discussed in the previous chapter, these were formally organized associations that existed apart from any company or business connection. Brooklyn boasted two of the most powerful teams of skilled workers—the Atlantics and the Eckfords. Francis Pidgeon, a member of the latter, described his teammates as shipwrights and mechanics who could only practice once a week.[22] The Newark Empires were nearly three-fourths skilled artisans, including jewelers, masons, cloth workers, and other tradesmen. Half of the players lived in the city's "Old Core," but the club recruited its members from eight of the town's wards.[23] In Philadelphia, the Pennsylvania club was made up of printers, "whose in-door sedentary occupation [rendered] some out-door exercise highly necessary to preserve their health."[24]

Since these blue-collar clubs were not under the direct influence of factory, shop, or company owners, they were free to demonstrate independence and class consciousness, though we do not know the extent to which these teams asserted the solidarity and feelings of working men. The clubs did combine premodern and modern characteristics in their mixture of drinking and horseplay with serious, hard practice and intense competitiveness, and there were occasional instances of class identification by their supporters during match play—as, for example, when the Atlantics or the Eckfords played (see Chapter 8).

American baseball fielded several clubs with an evenly divided blue- and white-collar membership during its amateur era. The Newark Base Ball Club, as well as that city's Adriatic and Lafayette nines, represented this type. The Newark club, founded in 1855, included a variety of skilled craftsmen, petty proprietors, clerks, and bookkeepers of moderate wealth. Three-quarters of them lived in the city's "Old Core." The Adriatics were primarily jewelers, merchants, and professionals—clearly the most affluent of Newark's baseball fraternity, as their real and personal estates attest. That club also drew about three-quarters of its members from the "Old Core." The Lafayettes brought together men from the building and leather trades, along with some clerks and merchants. All of these examples suggest that when blue- and white-collar workers formed a baseball club, their common economic status or residence outweighed their vocational differences. In fact, even those clubs that were predominantly working-class had some white-collar members, and vice versa.

Education, religion, family background, or affiliation in any number of institutions may have been as important as occupation, economic status, or residence in shaping the membership of these early athletic associations. For example, volunteer fire companies often sponsored baseball clubs; and some of these clubs had close ties with political parties. The most notorious example of a baseball team with a fire company connection was New York's Mutual club, which eventually became an instrument of Boss Tweed after the Civil War.[25] There is some evidence that a few churches sponsored teams, despite religion's traditional coolness toward sport. The players on New York's Alpine club belonged to the Jane Street Methodist Episcopal Church, for which "religion and healthful out-of-door exercise [were] not incompatible."[26] In 1865 a group of prominent Philadelphia clergymen formed a baseball club and appeared in public "as athletes, in true club style—belts, caps, and all."[27] New York's St. Nicholas club was composed principally of gymnasts who met regularly to train at a local gymnasium.

Whenever a group of boys, young men, or adults joined to form a cricket or baseball club, they sacrificed some of the freedom of informal play for the social and athletic benefits of organized sport. In so doing they submitted to many rules and regulations governing their personal conduct. Members were expected to fulfill all of their group obligations and do all that was necessary for the club's welfare. Although they were required to yield to club restrictions, they expected to gain good fellowship, recreation and amusement, healthful exercise, and opportunities to improve their athletic skills and participate at various levels of competition. The rationalization and bureaucratization of cricket and baseball replaced the spontaneity of "folk-ball" with the structure of modern sport. For thousands of antebellum American sportsmen, what was gained in joining a club far outweighed what was lost in personal liberty.

Before a group of players could consider themselves a cricket or baseball club in good standing, they had to choose a name, ratify a constitution and bylaws, and find a playing ground. The selection of a name was the simplest of these procedures: cricketers generally titled their associations after home cities, towns, or counties,[28] while baseball players showed more imagination by choosing patriotic, sporting, Indian, or other names in addition to local place names. In the New York metropolitan area the most common names reflecting nationalism were Union, Independent, Liberty, Washington, Lafayette, Hamilton, Pioneer, Columbia, Empire, Continental, Eagle, Americus, Young America, and National.[29]

Within the sporting category, Olympic, Athletic, and Exercise were popular; and among the other types, Excelsior, Active, Alert, and Enterprise were favorites.

When these sportsmen banded together as an athletic club they invariably followed the traditional American democratic procedures that governed voluntary associations. They wrote and ratified a constitution, which spelled out the rules for the selection of members and officers as well as their respective duties.[30] The president and vice president presided over meetings and ceremonies, while the secretary kept track of the membership rolls and challenge matches. The treasurer collected initiation fees, dues, and any special assessments to cover the expenses of renting and maintaining a ground and clubhouse, purchasing equipment, and paying any entertainment costs. A committee of directors usually issued and reviewed challenges for matches with rival clubs.[31] A club's bylaws listed the financial and personal obligations of each member, which generally included an initiation fee of from two to five dollars and annual dues, with five dollars being the standard.[32] Voluntary assessments for elaborate meals on match days were often paid by the most affluent players. The principal expense for new members was the purchase of a uniform, for each player was expected to appear ready for action in proper shoes, pantaloons, shirt, cap, and belt. The *Clipper* reported in 1860 that "the expense of joining a Ball Club is comparatively a mere nominal sum,"[33] and it does appear that membership was within the means of most working-class and all white-collar workers.

In addition to the financial obligations, each club member was expected to attend practices and behave in a gentlemanly fashion. Officers levied fines ranging from ten cents to one dollar for disorderly conduct, arguing with umpires, disobeying captains, and using profane language. The Knickerbockers even fined members fifty cents for opening another player's locker or wearing someone else's apparrel without permission.[34]

While most clubs preferred to sign up only active players, many organizations were willing to accept applications from men who did not intend to participate on a regular basis, or at all. Depending upon the number of active and "contributing" players, clubs enrolled anywhere from a few dozen to several hundred members. Nominations of new recruits were essential to the welfare of even the most successful outfits. Most welcome were men who were both skilled athletes and socially desirable. The famed Excelsiors of Brooklyn developed into a "crack club" in part because they recruited star performers from their city's junior squads, yet they retained their standing as a gentlemen's club. The New York Knickerbockers placed more weight on social status but also respected athletic ability. When Anson Palmer nominated A. Dewitt Baldwin for admission, he wrote: "Mr. B. is a member of the legal fraternity (i.e. is a *respectable lawyer*) has had considerable experience in ball playing—and I cheerfully recommend him, being convinced the Knickerbockers will find him an acquisition to their Club."[35]

Philadelphia's oldest and most prestigious ball club, the Olympic, claimed city championships in both townball and baseball while remaining exclusive in its admission policy. In 1862 an admirer explained that while the club stressed skillful playing and victories, "respectability has always been the ruling desire . . . ; hence, no gratuitous additions have been sought for or admitted to build up and strengthen a first nine. One of the commendable objects of the club, always kept in view, has been to make it socially agreeable. Therefore, in weighing the claims of an applicant for membership, due attention is given to his merits in this respect."[36]

Club members remained in good standing as long as they paid their dues and fines and appeared reasonably often on practice days. Some inactive players realized that they might be taking a place someone else could better fill and usually resigned. For example, Daniel L. Adams quit the Knickerbockers with great reluctance after fifteen years with the club, "but in accordance with a determination, long since formed, never to remain an inactive, non-playing member." However, many clubs tolerated inactive members as long as they paid their dues and assessments. The annual reports of the grounds committee of the Philadelphia Cricket Club lamented the lack of interest in practice sessions. In 1856, for example, only thirty-five of eighty-four members appeared either for matches or play days. Early in 1861 the club listed seventy-six men on its roll, yet an official complained that there were no more than twenty active members and that it was not unusual for only ten members or so to show up on a practice day. "Unless our members show more energy and interest in the game," he noted, "we will lose our reputation as the foremost club in the city."[37]

Many sports clubs of this era lasted only a few seasons because of mismanagement or failing interest. One club officer complained: "As a general rule, cricket clubs do not pay. A club is raised, the players practice enthusiastically for a year, pay their fees once, and then the club goes down. The secretary and president . . . run the club almost at their own expense, and then get tired and adieu, cricket club." Severe reform saved this particular outfit, with strict policies on fees and ungentlemanly conduct, and no liquor "for those who punish the beer more than the bowling." The club survived with fewer enrolled but also "a larger revenue, no bad debts, no nominal members, no useless expenditures, and . . . the esteem of its neighbors."[38] Of course, the paying of dues, required attendance, and laws prohibiting swearing, arguing, or misbehaving were all a far cry from the old style of "folk-ball" played behind country barns or on village greens. A few old-timers remembered the informality of earlier ball games and lamented its passing.[39]

Before a sports club could practice or play intrasquad or interclub matches, it had to secure a suitable ground. This posed few problems in the premodern era, when farms and villages provided plenty of open space for such pastimes, but it was not so simple in America's rapidly expanding towns and cities of the 1850s, where vacant lots and fields of sufficient size were becoming increasingly scarce. The sportsmen's need to reserve and improve grounds for their weekly sessions was a major factor in stimulating formal club organization. The clearing and leveling of land, the rental or purchase price, and perhaps the construction of a clubhouse or the raising of a tent all required a commitment of time and money by the players. As the new urban environment of mid-nineteenth-century cities encroached upon traditional playing space, it hastened the creation of modern forms of sports organization.

City expansion often forced teams to move and sometimes contributed to their demise. In the mid-1840s the Knickerbockers abandoned the Murray Hill section of Manhattan for the greener pastures of the Elysian Fields, in Hoboken, New Jersey, apparently because their play area had become more valuable as residential and commercial property. Jersey City's first clubs, the Pioneers and the Excelsiors, did not survive their second season in part because "they lost their first grounds in the 4th Ward, in consequence of the march of improvement, such as filling in streets, etc., which flooded them out. Their second ground was destroyed, because the Erie Rail Road had the impudence to put a Rail Road immediately through it."[40] On a few occasions landlords raised the rent on ball grounds, thereby forcing clubs to find other locations. Such a dispute drove New York City's second oldest baseball club, the Gothams, across the Hudson River to Hoboken in 1857. The owner of the field had demanded $200 a year and informed the club members that if they did not choose to take it at that rent, "they could leave it—that, rather than hire it for a less sum, he would turn it into cow sheds—that he had little regard for ball clubs; their patronage was not desirable." He then "indulged in abusive epithets, reflecting upon the character and respectability of ball players." Insulted by this treatment, the Gothams left Harlem for a field next to the Eagles' ground in Hoboken, a relocation that cost them a few of their players.[41]

By the late 1850s most of New York's leading baseball and cricket clubs were playing at the Elysian Fields.[42] There were still ample vacant lots in Brooklyn to accommodate the baseball mania that swept the city,[43] but the problem of finding a place to play in Manhattan inhibited the formation of more clubs. In 1858 *Porter's Spirit* pointed out that within a few years New York's baseball players would have to go several miles out of town to find a large enough field. The National Association of Base Ball Players appointed a committee to negotiate with the city to secure fields in the newly constructed Central Park, but park officials were rather cool to the idea. They were willing to agree to ball playing "under certain restrictions, one of which is that no club shall be permitted to use the grounds unless two-thirds of the members be residents of this city."[44] Before the Civil War, baseball enthusiasts were unsuccessful in their attempts to reserve space in Central Park for ball grounds, and most New Yorkers ferried across the river for their pastimes. By the late 1860s the park commissioners had allowed schoolboys to use the lawns for ball play, but adults and the prominent ball clubs were still barred.[45]

Cricket organizations had more trouble with their home fields than did baseball teams, for their sport required a well-manicured grass surface. (Baseball did not need so fine a "pitch," although in an era before fielders wore gloves, a smooth surface protected fingers and teeth.) New York cricketers crossed the Hudson River to play in Hoboken, in part because the Central Park commissioners ruled that the game was too dangerous and barred both boys' and men's clubs. The Newark Cricket Club played its inaugural matches during the late 1840s on a lot near a chemical factory, then moved several times before it settled on a new field on Railroad Avenue in 1855. The surface of the latter did not meet the standards of the cricket reporters of New York City's sporting periodicals, all of whom severely criticized the Newark grounds. The Mechanics of Newark played on property adjacent to the home of one of the club's most prominent members, a city alderman named James A. Pennington. The Essex club had to travel to East Newark for its sport.[46]

Once these amateur sports clubs secured a suitable playing space, they scheduled play days and arranged contests with rivals to provide their members with various types of competition. Most practiced two afternoons a week but not on Sundays. Saturdays brought hundreds of players to Boston Common, since many of that city's mercantile firms closed after lunch to permit their clerks to pursue their pastimes.[47] Boston and Brooklyn also had several clubs that practiced in the early morning on weekdays, between five and seven o'clock.[48] On exercise days captains would make up sides from members who appeared on time, and if places remained open they would invite visitors on their grounds to join in the game. These scrimmages were used to select the club's first and second teams, with the worst players constituting a "muffin" squad. St. Louis's Old Hickory club used a novel method of choosing its first eleven: its bylaws restricted eligibility to those cricketers who weighed at least 200 pounds![49]

Clubs also held special intrasquad matches, and their methods of choosing sides reveal traditional cultural distinctions that antebellum Americans drew among themselves. For both cricket and baseball clubs, by far the most common method was to match the married members ("Benedicts") against the single men ("Bachelors"). *Wilkes' Spirit* contrasted these playful encounters with the more serious interclub challenges: "These contests . . . are among the most enjoyable of the season, as the members meet on the ground more for recreation than for earnest work, time not being of so much importance in these matters as it is on occasions when the credit of the club is to be maintained against skillful opponents;

more leisure being had, in the former case, for social intercourse, and of course for more genuine enjoyment."[50] Another favorite pitted the heavyweights against the lightweights, as in 1866 when Philadelphia's Keystone Fat Nine edged the Thins, 31–28. The city's *Sunday Dispatch* noted that the losers did not have a "ghost of a chance, and were driven from the field by the Falstaffs." The *Clipper* described the contest as "Fat and Greasy versus Lank and Leany"; it was a "very laughable game . . . which almost convulsed the lookers-on with merriment."[51]

Other intrasquad games matched seniors against juniors, with the division usually at thirty-two years of age. Cricket clubs sometimes played members from the north counties of England against the south or American members versus "old countrymen." "Muffin" contests were exercises in ineptitude and provided amusement for participants and spectators alike. There were also a few political contests staged by the Chicago Excelsiors, including an 1860 encounter between the club's Douglas and Lincoln partisans and an 1868 game between the supporters of Grant and Seymour. Cricketers participated in alphabet contests ("A" to "M" versus "N" to "Z"), and the Newark Cricket Club played right-handers against left-handers and even tall players versus short ones. The New York Cricket Club once placed its powerful first eleven against the rest of the club, with the top players required to use baseball bats as a handicap. All of these contests show the spirit of playfulness in early amateur sports yet reveal significant personal, political, social, and athletic distinctions within organizations.[52]

Since amateur sports clubs were social organizations, too, they scheduled periodic entertainments to supplement their regular business meetings and play days. After the successful season of 1856, New York area teams maintained their spirits over the winter with "a series of *soiree* amusements, convivial, dansante, and musical, both vocal and instrumental." During the next few years the wealthiest club members hosted extravagant parties and fancy winter balls or "hops," while the middle-class white-collar and artisan associations held more modest affairs. Many clubs scheduled annual dinners at the beginning and end of each season, the 1858 celebration of the New York Cricket Club being typical of these all-male affairs. Members and guests ate, drank, sang, told stories, and reminisced until the "gentlemen received an inward admonition that the solemn hour of midnight was fast approaching, and that their fond wives and little ones were anxiously awaiting their return home."[53] Newark's Mechanics club concluded its winning season of 1856 with an intrasquad game, after which the men and their guests retired to Mr. T. Smith's "Punch Bowl" to consume a fine supper and partake of rounds of toasts and cricket songs until the wee hours.[54] These social events were as popular among working-class clubs like the Brooklyn Eckfords[55] as they were with the more affluent St. George Cricket Club or the Knickerbockers. Some organizations even promoted intellectual pursuits, meeting in winter for debate, discussion, and fellowship.[56]

While "muffins" and orators enjoyed their play days, parties, and meetings, the better athletes competed in interclub matches that generated excitement and promoted their sport. Before the Civil War many clubs fielded both first and second nines, but after 1865 there were fewer contests between reserves. In 1867 one second-stringer complained: "The first nines of our clubs monopolize the games too much. . . . the second class players of a club should be entitled to as much of the sport of the season as the first nine, but they do not get a third of the chances for playing." He added that the "regular amateurs" got only about two or three games a season at most.[57]

Secretaries and match committees had the delicate task of issuing and responding to challenges for a "friendly game of ball." Normally, clubs preferred to play against those organizations with a similar age and social class membership. They also preferred playing local rivals, although intercity and even interstate contests were common, especially among clubs in the New York City vicinity. A few of the elite clubs, such as the Knickerbockers, restricted their play to other white-collar teams or those that shared their home grounds.[58] Antebellum baseball also saw numerous interclass matches among both junior and senior players. In cricket, there were many contests that pitted mechanics against white-collar players. For example, the Newark Cricket Club regularly played both first- and second-eleven matches with the New York and St. George clubs. In a few factory towns, leading citizens matched their skills against machine operators, as in Waltham, Massachusetts, when the Rumford club, composed mostly of the town's elite, defeated the Uniteds, who were mainly factory workers. One observer viewed this as an example of cricket's democratic tendencies, "where employers and employees meet in friendly strife and intercourse, where all distinction is for the time being, entirely removed."[59]

At most matches sportsmen observed traditional rituals and customs. In cricket, the hosts treated their guests to an elaborate lunch between innings, despite the bad effects "on the digestive organs, of a hot dinner eaten with hearty appetites on a hot day, and immediately followed by active and violent exercise."[60] After cricket and baseball matches the president or captain of the defeated side invariably presented the game ball as a trophy to an official of the victorious team. Often the ball would be wrapped in gold foil, with the score and date of the game inscribed. Brief speeches accompanied this ceremony, as each side praised the sportsmanship and skill of the opposition. Sometimes special prizes or bouquets of flowers were awarded to the highest scoring batsmen.[61] While the newspapers refer to a few challenges for prize money, most clubs condemned the idea of competing for cash. Albany's Knickerbockers believed that playing for money "would have a tendency to destroy [baseball's] present enviable reputation as a field sport, and to cause unfriendly rivalries between those clubs that now maintain the most harmonious relations."[62]

The postgame dinner after most major baseball challenges could be quite elaborate.[63] During the late 1850s this lavish socializing created sufficient tension, with clubs competing at the dinner table as well as on the field, that the NABBP recommended the abolition of refreshments after matches. Many people felt that the custom had degenerated into a practice that was "seriously detrimental to the interests of the game, owing to the spirit of emulation that arose among the clubs, each aspiring to excel each other in the expense and splendor of these entertainments."[64] The tradition persisted into the early 1860s in several cities,[65] but after the Civil War these lavish dinners were no longer common. In New York City the leading clubs resolved in 1865 not to entertain each other at matches, although they felt obliged to give special attention to rivals from other cities. While on tour, the Philadelphia Athletics tried to discourage the home team from hosting expensive dinners or suppers, preferring simple refreshments after the game.[66] When Brooklyn's Excelsior club wined and dined the Nationals of Washington, D.C., adding a sightseeing tour of the city, the *Clipper* noted the extravagant "palatial feasts" and criticized the team for violating "an express rule of the Association prohibiting this style of thing."[67]

Black clubs emulated the white associations in their organizations, social life, match play, intercity tours, and competition for state and national black championships. The Pythians, a black Philadelphia club, issued and received formal challenges to compete against rivals from Camden, West Chester, Washington, D.C., Brooklyn, and Harrisburg; and they, too, entertained their guests at lavish dinners. Their great success on the ball field was due in part to recruiting outsiders to bolster their first nines for special matches, just as many white clubs did, even though this was in violation of NABBP rules.

The leading black baseball clubs of Brooklyn, Newark, Philadelphia, and Washington, D.C., were on good terms with the white organizations and frequently obtained permission to use their grounds for feature contests. White umpires sometimes even officiated at blacks' games. The Pythians enjoyed harmonious ties with the Athletics, who were generous with their facilities and support. In 1868 the Pythians' secretary, Jacob C. White, Jr., congratulated the Athletics after a "brilliant victory" that upheld "the pride of Philadelphia on the base-ball field." The secretary of the Athletics thanked White for "these manifestations of confidence from our brethren in the city, that have met with us on all sides."[68]

Although white and black baseball players generally got along well, there was still much resistance among the white fraternity to the recognition of equality inherent in interracial competition. This opposition was overcome to some degree in Philadelphia in September 1869, thanks to the efforts of Col. Thomas Fitzgerald, a former president of the Athletics and editor of a local newspaper, the *City Item*. Although the Athletics had refused his overtures, Fitzgerald succeeded in arranging a match between the Olympics and the Pythians (who prepared for the historic encounter by recruiting outsiders from New Jersey). The Olympics defeated the Pythians, 44–23, in front of a large crowd attracted by the novelty of the match. The *Spirit* praised the experiment, declaring that "old-time prejudices are melting away in this country." It noted that interracial sporting contests were common in England and other countries and added, "It is not considered outside our own territory a lessening of dignity nor in the least disparaging to white men that they contend with blacks." It was hoped that "now the prejudice has been broken through here, it will be entirely swept away."[69] A few weeks later the Olympics of Washington, D.C., manhandled a black club, the Alerts, 56–4, in front of a large assembly of men and women, both black and white, as well as many government officials.[70]

In the majority of interclub contests, good will and sportsmanship ruled the day. Yet there is evidence that controversy and hard feelings marred many early matches. America's players were raised in an intensely competitive culture, where individual/group achievement and success were stressed as much as good manners. Club officials and sportswriters encouraged an atmosphere of amicable competition, but winning and losing mattered a great deal. As early as July 1858, the *Brooklyn Daily Eagle* noted a disturbing trend in cricket contests, praising the harmony that was apparent in a game between the East New York and New Durham teams while reminding readers that the sport "was originally intended for amusement, recreation, and interchange of good feeling; not for a test of exclusive strength and supremacy." The paper added: "We have often witnessed cricket matches, and often have been disgusted with the manifest want of respect, good fellowship, and hospitable bearing between the opposing clubs. There has been no feeling in common—there has been too much hostility developed—too much of the *vulgar brag* unbecoming to cricketers and men."[71] The *Clipper* commended the Queens County and East New York clubs for their "very friendly and kindly feelings" during a contest but also noted: "That acrimonious spirit, resulting from the too general desire to win at all hazards, provided the mere letter of the law is adhered to, has been generally creeping into cricket matches, alike to the detriment of the best interests of the game, and the entire prevention of all pleasure in the contests that are marked by it. Cricket is a game designed for the *recreation* of all classes and conditions of men, and is eminently a *social* game, and one in which the amenities of social life are of vital importance to its existence."[72]

Baseball generated more friction among clubs than did cricket, in part because of the greater number of matches but also because so many classes and groups fielded nines. The stresses and strains of American society were more likely to be played out on the baseball diamond than the cricket pitch. New York's junior teams, especially those in Brooklyn, were notorious for being quarrelsome. The secretary of the Niagaras explained that his club would not play the North Stars because "they would come down on the ball-grounds in South Brooklyn, and swagger up to some of our members, and say, with oaths: 'If we cannot whip you with bats and ball, we can with FISTS.'"[73] Senior clubs in several cities also exhibited hard feelings, both before and during the Civil War. When the *Clipper* complimented "a spirit of manly courtesy and gentlemanly conduct" between the Hamilton and Exercise teams in 1860, it also pointedly noted that "the contrary course of conduct . . . has frequently marked leading contests this season."[74] An observer of the Philadelphia baseball boom argued that "petty jealousies, unmanly criticism, and childish bickerings, not only between rival clubs, but members of the same club . . . retard the popularity of the game, and injure the success of the clubs."[75] Another Philadelphia sportsman asked: "When will the Philadelphia clubs learn that it is much more creditable to give up a ball with equanimity, than to fall into the manners and customs of blackguards? The club that cannot stand a defeat is unworthy of victory."[76]

Among the many specific causes for such controversies and ill will, the most frequent were differences over access to grounds, the eligibility of players, rules and umpires' decisions, gambling and other forms of interference by spectators, and championship competition. In some cases one or more of these escalated existing class tensions among rivals. Organizations that shared the same playing field normally got along well; but there were exceptions in both cricket and baseball.[77] In Philadelphia, for example, bad blood between the Olympic and Athletic clubs was evident in 1862 when the latter team was deprived of its two play days at Camac's Wood. One player charged that the Olympics had circulated reports that the Athletics had disbanded so as to bid for and obtain the field.[78]

The eligibility of players to participate in interclub matches sometimes led to heated exchanges. Following the English custom, cricketers often played on more than one team without objection, but on a few occasions clubs did challenge this practice. The Long Island and Satellite (Brooklyn/Williamsburg) clubs refused all matches against players who competed for more than one club, arguing that the use of outsiders discouraged the regular members and thus hurt the cause of American cricket. According to this logic, weaker players would have a greater incentive to practice if they had a better chance of making the first eleven. Others rejected this thinking, claiming that multiple memberships gave everyone more chances on more play days and reminding players and fans alike that the system had worked well in England to popularize cricket. There is some evidence that American cricketers felt that multiple memberships tended to give preferential treatment to Englishmen.[79]

Baseball clubs would sometimes permit outsiders to play in match games if both captains consented, but this was clearly the exception to the rule. In 1856 some teams complained that their rivals were recruiting good players from other clubs for special matches. Members of the Knickerbockers were upset when a superior player from the Union club of Morrisania (in the Bronx) joined the Gothams just prior to a game against their nine, without first resigning from the Unions. The latter club immediately passed a resolution that disapproved of the fellow's action and stated that it would not play matches against clubs with players from other nines, nor would it admit anyone who was a recognized member of another organization.[80] In 1857 the first baseball convention prohibited men from playing for more than one club, although this did not stop the practice or the complaints that ensued.[81]

Even in second-string contests, winning was important. The strong feelings generated by the rivalry among Newark's three leading senior cricket clubs surfaced in the summer of 1857 during a controversy that marred an easy victory by the Mechanics' second eleven over the first team of a new outfit, the Essexes. A few of the spectators accused the Mechanics of taking unfair advantage of the Essex eleven by fielding too many strong players.[82] Disputes over umpires' decisions and interpretaions of rules also indicated the intensity of interclub rivalries. In 1862 the *Clipper* editorialized that "the sooner the custom of attributing the loss of matches to erroneous decisions of an umpire ceases the better for the interests of the game. It is very annoying, we know, to lose a game under such circumstances, but when it is considered that a match lost in this way not only detracts nothing from the skill of the defeated party, but materially lessens the *eclat* of the victory, we should think that unnecessary censure of the umpire would only tend to make matters worse."[83]

The most intense interclub cricket feud of the antebellum era resulted from an 1857 contest between the New York and St. George clubs. On that occasion the former eleven was forty-four runs behind with only one wicket remaining when its captain refused to permit his last player to bat because of a six o'clock curfew and the approaching darkness. After the umpire decided that the match should continue, the New York side withdrew its players and refused to concede defeat. Both clubs appealed to the foremost sporting journal of England, *Bell's Life in London*. The acrimony intensified over the next winter, as the two captains argued their positions on the pages of *Porter's Spirit* and the *Clipper*. In February 1858 a prominent observer of the New York cricket scene, William M. Bradshaw, tried to mediate, pointing out that the clubs' animosity was "doing more harm than good to the game, . . . promulgating an opinion in the public mind that this noble exercise is a BITTER CONTENTION instead of FRIENDLY STRIFE."[84] In the summer of 1859 the two clubs agreed to binding arbitration by a third party from Albany, New York, who ruled in favor of the St. George club. The New Yorkers finally gave up the ball, and in 1860 they refused to play at the Dragon Slayers new enclosed ground because of the ten-cent admission charge. During the Civil War the old rivals did play a few practice and second-string contests, but it was not until 1865 that the clubs resumed their series of first-eleven matches.[85]

Baseball, too, was not immune to controversy over umpires' verdicts. *Porter's Spirit,* in discussing the settlement of disputes between players, umpires, and referees, advised sportsmen "to assume the referee to be *ever in the right,* and to bow to his decree whether it be *right or wrong.*" An 1860 match between Philadelphia's Equity and Athletic clubs was marred by an argument over an umpire's decision, and two years later that city's Athletics blamed their losses to the Olympics on the official, R. F. Stevens.[86] Most of the senior clubs of New York and Brooklyn avoided confrontation with umpires, but the junior nines were notorious for arguing with the officials. A Jersey City reporter blamed an 1858 defeat of his city's Lone Stars by Brooklyn's Enterprise club on its home ground on poor decisions by the umpire.[87]

Local, state, and national championship matches in baseball also generated ill will among rival teams and spectators, especially when they were accompanied by gambling and fan interference.[88] After the Eurekas of Newark defeated the Kearneys of Rahway in 1866 for the "championship of New Jersey" by a score of 45–6, the losers skipped the usual postgame ritual; and the Eurekas were forced to climb through the clubhouse windows to retrieve their street clothes.[89] The troubled relations among Brooklyn's three top teams—the Excelsiors, the Atlantics, and the Eckfords—best exemplifies the negative consequences for sportsmanship of these intense rivalries. The Excelsiors and the Eckfords never played each other after a dispute over the 1858 New York versus Brooklyn all-star series. The Atlantics and the Excelsiors were on better terms, but the disorders that ended their 1860 series created much ill will. Clubs like the Knickerbockers withdrew from the challenges for the unofficial championship and played only for exercise and fun. In 1860 the *Clipper* called for more cordiality and friendship among Brooklyn's three leading teams, stating that "when the rivalry between clubs is carried to an extent that leads to mutual jealousy and ill feeling, it is about time that matches should cease to be played."[90]

Black clubs sometimes also displayed the animosity and contentiousness exhibited by white organizations. When the Philadelphia Excelsiors challenged the Uniques of Brooklyn/Williamsburg for the black championship of the United States in the fall of 1867, their chaotic contest went from bad to worse. According to *Wilkes' Spirit,* "wrangling, disputing, bullying, charging, denying, cursing, and countering from first to last were the order of the meeting." At 5:30 P.M., with the Brooklyn club at bat and likely to win, the Excelsiors "profited by the examples set them by their white brothers, declared that it was too 'dark' to continue the game, and the umpire called it and awarded the ball to the Philadelphians." Only police intervention prevented the ensuing tumult from turning into a full-scale riot.[91]

America's earliest amateur ball clubs aimed to provide healthful recreation and promote good will among players, and to a considerable extent they succeeded. But they could not escape the athletic and social tensions inherent in competition. While the goal was "friendly strife," the aim of each contest was victory; winning was joyous, while defeat was bitter. In cities that were diverse in religion, nationality, and economic class, interclub rivalries inevitably involved personal and social as well as athletic conflicts. While sport helped to provide a sense of fraternity and cohesion that was lacking in mid-nineteenth-century America, at times it also contributed to further contention and fragmentation. Yet Americans continue to enjoy the combination of athletics and social life so evident during the formative years of team sports in this country.

NOTES

1. *Porter's Spirit* 1 (November 8, 1856): 165.
2. *Jersey City Daily Courier and Advertiser,* September 8, 10, 11, 1860.
3. Benjamin Rader, "The Quest for Subcommunities and the Rise of American Sport," *American Quarterly* 29 (Fall 1977): 355–69.
4. These statistics were computed only for those teams and categories with data for at least ten players.
5. *Clipper* 9 (December 7, 1861): 271.
6. John A. Lester, ed., *A Century of Philadelphia Cricket* (Philadelphia, 1951), 23–25; *Clipper* 7 (March 10, 1860): 372.
7. *Spirit* 22 (August 7, 1852): 294; *Porter's Spirit* 4 (May 15, 1858): 164; *Clipper* 6 (May 15, 1858): 28; 8 (June 2, 1860): 53; (June 9, 1860): 60; Constitution of the Philadelphia Cricket Club, February 10, 1854, in its Minute Book, Historical Society of Pennsylvania.
8. A few junior clubs named their teams after city streets, but most of them copied the names of well-known senior clubs.
9. *Spirit* 15 (September 27, 1845): 363; *Wilkes' Spirit* 1 (November 26, 1859): 181; (December 3, 1859): 205; (December 10, 1859): 215; *Clipper* 5 (May 2, 1857): 10; (September 5, 1857): 155; (October 3, 1857): 188; 7 (August 13, 1859): 132; (August 27, 1859): 148; 8 (April 7, 1860): 407; *Porter's Spirit* 1 (September 20, 1856): 37; (October 25, 1856): 133; Lester, *Philadelphia Cricket,* 11.
10. *Porter's Spirit* 3 (November 21, 1857): 180; *Wilkes' Spirit* 1 (November 19, 1859): 165; 2 (June 23, 1860): 250; (July 7, 1860): 283; 3 (October 13, 1860): 86; 9 (September 19, 1863): 36; (October 31, 1863): 141;

(November 7, 1863): 147; 10 (July 9, 1864): 292; (July 16, 1864): 308; (August 13, 1864): 371; 11 (September 17, 1864): 36; (October 22, 1864): 116; (November 5, 1864): 147; (December 3, 1864): 212; 13 (October 21, 1865): 119; *Clipper* 11 (September 19, 1863): 178; (October 10, 1863): 202; 12 (July 2, 1864): 92; (July 16, 1864): 107; (August 13, 1864): 141.

11. For the St. George club, see Melvin L. Adelman, *A Sporting Time: New York City and the Rise of Modern Athletics, 1820–70* (Urbana, Ill., 1986), 111–12.

12. *Clipper* 7 (March 10, 1860): 372.

13. *Clipper* 5 (April 30, 1857): 19; (July 4, 1857): 85; *Newark Daily Advertiser,* May 3, 1855.

14. Partial evidence from box scores and the 1860 census indicates that the Washington club of Hoboken, New Jersey, consisted of mostly Irish laborers, while the Columbia team of Orange, New Jersey, included many Irish hatters. In both cases occupation was probably as important as ethnicity in club formation.

15. *Newark Daily Advertiser,* October 23, 1866; October 2, 4, 1867; *Clipper* 14 (October 13, 1866): 210; 15 (July 6, 1867): 99; (July 13, 1867): 107; (July 27, 1867): 123; (October 19, 1867): 220; 17 (October 2, 1869): 203, 205; 18 (April 23, 1870): 18; (July 23, 1870): 123; (July 30, 1870): 131; (September 3, 1870): 171, 173; (September 10, 1870): 179, 180; (September 24, 1870): 197; (October 8, 1870): 213; (October 15, 1870): 220; (November 19, 1870): 258; (November 26, 1870): 266; *Wilkes' Spirit* 17 (October 5, 1867): 133; *Spirit* 20 (August 14, 1869): 407; 21 (September 4, 1869): 39; (September 11, 1869): 55; (September 18, 1869): 68; *Philadelphia Sunday Dispatch,* October 7, 1866; *Chicago Tribune,* August 24, 1870.

16. *Philadelphia Sunday Mercury,* July 21, 1867. These statistics on Philadelphia's black population were compiled from data gathered by the Philadelphia Social History Project at the Center for Philadelphia Studies, University of Pennsylvania.

17. Catto and White were both recording secretaries of the 1866 session of the Pennsylvania State Equal Rights League. For their comments on civil rights issues, see *A Synopsis of the Proceedings of the Pennsylvania Equal Rights League* (Philadelphia, 1866).

18. Adelman, *A Sporting Time,* 103, 116–18, 122–23, 125–26, 138–41; *Porter's Spirit* 6 (April 2, 1859): 73; (June 11, 1859): 228.

19. Other artisan cricket clubs composed principally of American-born mechanics played at Rouse's Point and New Brighton (on Staten Island), New York, and at Waltham and Berlin, Massachusetts. See *Clipper* 5 (July 4, 1857): 85; (September 5, 1857): 156; 6 (July 10, 1858): 91; (August 14, 1858): 133; 7 (August 20, 1859): 143.

20. Labor historians in general have paid very little attention to sports clubs in their studies of nineteenth-century American working-class culture. For recent examples of works that are very illuminating on several aspects of blue-collar life except sport, see Bruce Laurie, " 'Nothing on Compulsion': Life Styles of Philadelphia Artisans, 1820–1850," *Labor History* 15 (Summer 1974): 337–66; Paul Faler, "Cultural Aspects of the Industrial Revolution: Lynn, Massachusetts, Shoemakers and Industrial Morality, 1826–1860," *Labor History* 15 (Summer 1974): 367–94. See also Paul Faler, *Mechanics and Manufacturers in the Early Industrial Revolution: Lynn, Massachusetts, 1780–1860* (Albany, N.Y., 1981), esp. chaps. 9, 10; Alan Dawley, *Class and Community* (Cambridge, Mass., 1976).

21. Adelman, *A Sporting Time,* 125–26; *Clipper* 5 (November 7, 1857): 232; 9 (October 5, 1861): 197; *Porter's Spirit* 1 (December 20, 1856): 260; 4 (August 28, 1858): 405; *Jersey City Daily Courier and Advertiser,* September 1, 1858.

22. *Porter's Spirit* 3 (January 10, 1857): 309.

23. In 1857 this club played a few intrasquad games that matched a side of jewelers against nine other tradesmen. *Newark Daily Advertiser,* May 7, June 30, 1857.

24. Scrapbook of newspaper clippings on baseball, Historical Society of Pennsylvania; for other examples of blue-collar nines see *Clipper* 6 (July 10, 1858): 91; 7 (November 26, 1859): 252; *Jersey City Daily Courier and Advertiser,* August 3, 20, September 8, 1860; *Wilkes' Spirit* 3 (December 1, 1860): 196.

25. Ted Vincent, *Mudville's Revenge: The Rise and Fall of American Sport* (New York, 1981), 101–4.

26. *Newark Daily Advertiser,* August 25, 1860.

27. *Clipper* 13 (October 7, 1865): 203.

28. There were exceptions, of course, especially in Philadelphia. Among that city's minor clubs were the Chippewas, Olympians, Eagles, Stars, and Aramingos. New Jersey had the Uniteds of Beverly, Mechanics of Newark, Mohawks of Camden, and two clubs named Independent, of Bordentown and Boonton.

29. For a more complete discussion of the relationship between baseball clubs and American nationalism, see Chapter 5.

30. See, for example, *Constitution and By-Laws of the Beaman Base Ball Club, of West Boylston* (Worcester, Mass., 1858). A model constitution was published in *Clipper* 8 (February 18, 1860): 349. For examples of cricket club constitutions, see also *Clipper* 5 (August 29, 1857): 148; 6 (May 8, 1858): 20; *Constitution and By-Laws of the Philadelphia Cricket Club, 1858* (Philadelphia, 1858).

31. See, for example, the records and correspondence of the Knickerbocker Base Ball Club, Correspondence, vol. 1, New York Public Library; Minute Book, Philadelphia Cricket Club, vol. 1 (1854–79).

32. *Porter's Spirit* 4 (March 20, 1858): 37; *Clipper* 5 (May 23, 1857): 34.

33. *Clipper* 8 (March 10, 1860): 372. See also *Porter's Spirit* 3 (December 5, 1857): 212; (December 19, 1857): 244; *Wilkes' Spirit* 10 (May 28, 1864): 196.

34. Knickerbocker Correspondence, vol. 1; *Eagle Base Ball Club Constitution, Bye-Laws, and Rules* (New York, 1858), at the New-York Historical Society. The latter also has published constitutions and bylaws of the Brooklyn Base Ball Club (New York, 1860) and the Hudson River Base Ball Club of Newburgh (New York, 1859).

35. Knickerbocker Correspondence, vol. 1.

36. *Clipper* 10 (May 3, 1862): 19.

37. Knickerbocker Correspondence, vol. 1; Minute Book, Philadelphia Cricket Club, vol. 1 (1854–79).

38. *Wilkes' Spirit* 11 (September 24, 1864): 61.

39. *Jersey City Daily Courier and Advertiser,* October 16, 1858; see also two letters responding to these comments, on October 19, 1858.

40. *Jersey City Daily Sentinel,* September 9, 1856.

41. *Porter's Spirit* 2 (May 16, 1857): 173; (May 23, 1857): 180; *Clipper* 5 (May 16, 1857): 26.

42. Among the clubs that did not relocate were the Baltic (86th Street and Second Avenue); Harlem (123rd Street and Fifth Avenue); Manhattan, Metropolitan, Monumental, and Stuyvesant (Hamilton Square—65th Street and Third Avenue); and Young America, Jr. (115th Street and First Avenue).

43. Among the clubs that played at Brooklyn locations were the Atlantic (Bedford); Charter Oak (Sackett, Degraw, and Smith streets, in South Brooklyn); Excelsior (Smith, Hoyt, Carrol, and President streets); and Independent (Sackett, Hoyt, Union, and Smith streets).

44. *Clipper* 6 (January 22, 1859): 314.

45. *Clipper* 16 (May 23, 1868): 51; (October 24, 1868): 226; *Spirit* 20 (February 20, 1869): 9; *Ball Players' Chronicle,* July 25, August 1, 1867.

46. Newspaper clipping, letter to the *New York Times,* undated, Satterthwaite scrapbooks, New Jersey Historical Society; *Spirit* 22 (June 5, 1852): 192; 24 (August 26, 1854): 336; 26 (May 31, 1856): 87; *Clipper* 6 (July 17, 1858): 101; (July 24, 1858): 110; 7 (June 11, 1859): 60; *Wilkes' Spirit* 10 (August 27, 1864): 403.

47. *Porter's Spirit* 4 (May 29, 1858): 196.

48. *Clipper* 5 (May 7, 1857): 19; *Brooklyn Daily Eagle,* September 2, 18, 1858.

49. *Porter's Spirit* 6 (May 7, 1859): 149.

50. *Wilkes' Spirit* 6 (May 31, 1862): 195.

51. *Philadelphia Sunday Dispatch*, June 24, 1866; *Clipper* 14 (June 30, 1866): 91.

52. *Spirit* 12 (October 15, 1842): 385; 13 (July 1, 1843): 210; 15 (May 31, 1845): 158; (June 14, 1845): 177–78, 188; 23 (November 5, 1853): 451; *Porter's Spirit* 2 (June 20, 1857): 245; (July 11, 1857): 292; 3 (September 5, 1857): 4; (November 21, 1857): 180; *Wilkes' Spirit* 2 (August 11, 1860): 363; *Clipper* 5 (May 30, 1857): 45; (July 11, 1857): 95; (August 29, 1857): 151; (September 5, 1857): 159; 6 (May 22, 1858): 36; 7 (May 7, 1859): 19; *Brooklyn Daily Eagle,* September 24, 1855; October 26, 1856; October 14, 1858; July 12, 1859; *Newark Daily Advertiser,* May 12, 1857; July 17, 1858; May 3, June 16, 1859; *Newark Evening Journal,* August 25, September 3, 1858; May 4, June 15, 1859; May 15, November 14, 1860; *Chicago Times,* October 27, 1868.

53. *Porter's Spirit* 5 (November 15, 1858): 176; *Spirit* 28 (December 11, 1858): 522.

54. *Spirit* 26 (November 22, 1856): 487.

55. *Clipper* 8 (February 4, 1860): 332; *Newark Daily Advertiser,* December 12, 1859; *Newark Evening Journal,* December 7, 15, 1859.

56. *Clipper* 5 (November 7, 1857): 231; (November 28, 1857): 252; 6 (December 11, 1858): 270; 7 (May 7, 1859): 19; 8 (April 28, 1860): 13; *Wilkes' Spirit* 1 (December 10, 1859): 214; (January 14, 1860): 294; 3 (December 15, 1860): 228; *Brooklyn Daily Eagle,* October 6, 1858; *Porter's Spirit* 4 (August 7, 1858): 356.

57. *Ball Players' Chronicle,* September 5, 1867.

58. For example, see *Porter's Spirit* 3 (September 5, 1857): 4; 4 (August 28, 1858): 404.

59. *Clipper* 5 (September 5, 1857): 156.

60. *Clipper* 12 (July 2, 1864): 91.

61. *Newark Evening Journal,* October 16, 1858.

62. *Clipper* 9 (November 23, 1861): 251; 8 (October 20, 1860): 213; *Newark Daily Advertiser,* September 29, 1859; *Porter's Spirit* 3 (December 5, 1857): 212.

63. For examples, see *Wilkes' Spirit* 3 (October 20, 1860): 100; *Spirit* 29 (September 17, 1859): 376.

64. *Beadle's Dime Base Ball Player,* 1864, 9–10.

65. See F. Cresson Schell, quoted in *Philadelphia Bulletin,* April 13, 1936, in scrapbook of newspaper clippings on baseball, Historical Society of Pennsylvania.

66. *Clipper* 13 (June 17, 1865): 75; (June 24, 1865): 82.

67. *Clipper* 14 (July 14, 1866): 107–8.

68. J. C. White to Philidore S. Bell, Esq., September 7, 1868, and Bell to White, September 14, 1868, in the records of the Pythian Base Ball Club, American Negro Historical Society Papers, Leon Gardiner Collection, Historical Society of Pennsylvania. See also "Rules for Government of the Room—Shared with the Banneker Institute," March 13, 1867; report of Jacob C. White, Jr., November 4, 1868; O. V. Catto to Mr. McCullough, August 12, 1869; Charles R. Douglass to J. C. White, September 10, 1869; O. V. Catto to Alert Base Ball Club, June 30, 1867; Catto to E. Hicks Hayhurst, July 12, 1867; Catto to the president of the Athletic Base Ball Club, July 12, 1867.

69. *Spirit* 21 (September 11, 1869): 55. See also *Philadelphia Sunday Dispatch,* September 5, 1869.

70. *Clipper* 17 (October 2, 1869): 205

71. *Brooklyn Daily Eagle,* July 1, 1858. See also *Clipper* 12 (May 28, 1864): 51.

72. *Clipper* 8 (May 12, 1860): 31.

73. *Porter's Spirit* 4 (July 17, 1858): 309.

74. *Clipper* 8 (July 21, 1860): 108.

75. "Looker-on," *Clipper* 10 (May 15, 1862): 42.

76. *Clipper* 12 (August 20, 1864): 151.

77. For example, see *Clipper* 6 (July 10, 1858): 91; (July 17, 1858): 102.

78. *Clipper* 10 (May 31, 1862): 50–51.

79. *Wilkes' Spirit* 2 (August 25, 1860): 396. See also *Clipper* 6 (October 3, 1858): 214; (November 6, 1858): 229.

80. *Porter's Spirit* 1 (September 13, 1856): 28; (September 20, 1856): 37; *Clipper* 4 (September 13, 1856): 167; *New York Sunday Mercury,* August 24, 1856.

81. *Porter's Spirit* 3 (November 28, 1857): 197; (December 5, 1857): 212; *Clipper* 7 (November 26, 1859): 255; (December 3, 1859): 259.

82. *Spirit* 27 (July 18, 1857): 267. See also *Newark Daily Advertiser,* June 22, 25, 1857.

83. *Clipper* 10 (October 25, 1862): 219.

84. *Clipper* 6 (February 27, 1858): 354. See also *Clipper* 5 (August 15, 1857): 152; (January 16, 1858): 306; (February 20, 1858): 348; 7 (May 7, 1859): 19; *Porter's Spirit* 3 (January 30, 1858): 341; (February 27, 1858): 405; *Spirit* 27 (September 19, 1857): 373.

85. *Clipper* 10 (July 12, 1862): 103; 11 (August 8, 1863): 135; 12 (September 10, 1864): 170; *Spirit* 22 (September 25, 1852): 379; (October 9, 1852): 402. See also *Clipper* 6 (May 8, 1858): 20; (May 15, 1858): 27; (June 5, 1858): 52; (July 24, 1858): 109; (August 21, 1858):

141; (September 18, 1858): 173; 7 (July 9, 1859): 92; (July 23, 1859): 108; 8 (August 4, 1860): 124; 11 (September 19, 1863): 180; 12 (July 9, 1864): 79; *Porter's Spirit* 4 (August 7, 1858): 356; 5 (October 16, 1858): 101; (November 13, 1858): 171; (November 27, 1858): 196; 6 (July 30, 1859): 341.

86. *Porter's Spirit* 4 (April 3, 1858): 69; *Philadelphia Morning Pennsylvanian,* November 13, 1860; *Clipper* 8 (October 20, 1860): 210; (November 24, 1860): 250; (December 8, 1860): 271; 10 (May 31, 1862): 50.

87. *Jersey City Daily Courier and Advertiser,* October 29, 1858.

88. Gambling and spectator influence are discussed in Chapter 8.

89. *Newark Daily Advertiser,* July 11, 1866.

90. *Clipper* 8 (November 3, 1860): 228.

91. *Wilkes' Spirit* 17 (October 5, 1867): 133; *Clipper* 15 (October 19, 1867): 220. See also *Newark Daily Advertiser,* October 19, 1867.

CHAPTER

8

Spectators

On the morning of October 4, 1859, at the freshly sodded and rolled St. George ground at Hoboken's Elysian Fields, several thousand spectators watched the All-England Eleven warm up for their grand encounter with a select squad of twenty-two United States cricketers. The host club provided tents for the contestants, seats for many ladies, and refreshments and other accommodations for the public and the press. By afternoon the crowd had swelled to nearly 8,000—a throng so numerous "that it was a great difficulty to find room for the hits of the Eleven, which were brilliant in the extreme." Probably many in the multitude were disappointed with the results of the first day's play, which ended with the English side forty-four runs ahead with only two wickets lost.

Another huge crowd of about 10,000 turned out on the second day to watch the British athletes continue their thrashing of the Americans. The contest aside, everyone seemed to enjoy "the beautiful view, the lofty strains of music from Dodsworth's band, the gay regalia of Britain and America fluttering in the breeze, and the presence of so many beautiful women." Those who saw the English eleven complete their rout on the third day did not attend because they anticipated an exciting conclusion; rather, they were intrigued by the English celebrities. The grand international contest evidently attracted mostly those prosperous people who could afford to pay fifty cents or one dollar for daily tickets, or five dollars for a weekly subscriber's pass. Each of the crowds formed a "respectable and orderly assemblage," and "the decorum of the vast circle . . . gave it the look almost of a family party."[1]

The pleasant atmosphere at the Elysian Fields in the fall of 1859 contrasts sharply with the riotous scene at the Putnam Base Ball Club's ground on August 23, 1860. About 15,000 people packed around that Brooklyn field to witness the deciding game of the championship series between the Atlantics and the Excelsiors. These two crack teams had split the opening contests—the Excelsiors won the first game easily but lost the second by a single run. The excitement among the baseball fraternity was intense, as rumors circulated that the Excelsiors would not be allowed to win a close contest. During the early play one of the Atlantics agitated part of the crowd by refusing to yield immediately to an umpire's call. Then, in the top of the sixth inning, with the Excelsiors ahead 8–6, a group of rowdies renewed their "insulting epithets and loud comments on the decision of the umpire." Joseph Leggett, the Excelsiors' captain, warned the spectators that his team would withdraw if the hooting continued. Members of the Atlantics appealed to their supporters to let the game go on, as one hundred policemen tried to restrain the unruly crowd. But the troublemakers only increased their yelling and abuse of the umpire and the Excelsiors, prompting Leggett to order his players off the field. A large crowd pursued them and pelted their omnibus with stones as they drove off. Most newspapers blamed the disorders and interference on gambling and condemned the behavior of those spectators who had disrupted the contest. It was unfortunate that "sports which are healthful and respectable in themselves should be rendered disreputable by their surroundings," commented the *Brooklyn Daily Eagle,* which then added that "a little further decadence will reduce the attendance at ball matches to the level of the prize ring and the race course."[2]

These two episodes in antebellum American sport provide dramatic proof of the importance of spectators during the formative years of baseball and cricket. Interclub and special all-star matches were more than just competitions among the players. They were also public entertainments and major events in the recreational life of thousands of city dwellers. To fully understand the cultural aspects of modern sport in the United States during the formative years, it is thus important to know who attended these contests, why they came, how they experienced them, and how they influenced the games and the sports themselves. Unfortunately, there is very little reliable documentation about spectators of mid-nineteenth-century sports. The following analysis therefore depends mostly on newspaper accounts and includes some speculation where direct evidence is lacking. A comparison of cricket and baseball spectators also helps to explain in part the relative popularity of the two sports in the United States during the nineteenth century.[3]

The power of baseball to attract large audiences during its formative years merits special consideration because of the sport's lasting appeal and because contemporary commentators continue to search for the magic that has enthralled so many generations of fans. Scholars and journalists have argued that the fascination with baseball derives from its pastoral qualities, its scientific and statistical aspects, its capacity to evoke strong feelings of nostalgia for childhood and youth, its hero worship, its peculiar combination of individualism and teamwork, its analogy to war, and so on. Most of these theories come from people who have pondered the meaning of their favorite sport without really consulting those who pack the stadiums and follow the games on television. While it is hard to extract the essence of baseball's appeal from today's crowds and viewers, it is much more difficult to explain its popularity during its first few decades, as early spectators left scant records of their feelings toward baseball. Yet, enough material exists to provide some answers and to warrant the conclusion that many of the forces that drew people to games before the 1870s are still important influences behind the attraction of modern baseball.[4]

During the early years of team sports in America, amateur clubs generally did not restrict attendance at their matches. An early cricket manual defined the policy that baseball officials also observed: "Respectable and quiet strangers" could witness either play or practice as long as they understood that their presence on the ground was "a privilege, not a right."[5] Before the 1860s promoters charged admission fees only for the all-star baseball games and for international cricket contests. Since spectators also had to pay for their transportation, these special matches tended to attract those from the middle- and upper-income groups. When leading teams played interclub games on neighborhood ball grounds, however, especially in Brooklyn, Newark, and Jersey City, the crowds included many people who were not financially comfortable. For example, when the Knickerbockers played the Excelsiors before about 6,000 people in August 1859, it was noted that "a means of rational enjoyment was offered freely to all who chose to avail themselves of it, the only passport requisite being, orderly conduct while on the ground, thus giving to those of the community whose circumstances prohibit their participation in any sport attended with expense, an opportunity to relieve themselves temporarily at least of the cares and anxieties of daily life."[6] On Boston Common, at Camac's Wood in Philadelphia, at Hoboken's Elysian Fields, and at virtually all of the early ball fields, both blue- and white-collar workers and their families watched amateur antebellum team sports.[7]

After the Civil War promoters and clubs charged an admission fee for many of the top matches, in part because they wished to exclude spectators from the poorer classes. Yet there is considerable evidence that baseball games continued to draw fans from a wide variety of social groups during the 1860s. In describing the huge throng that attended an 1865 contest between the New York Mutuals and the Brooklyn Atlantics, the *Clipper* commented on the variety of people in attendance, with minority representation of "roughs," the "blackleg fraternity," and pickpockets. An 1867 upstate New York championship game brought out an assortment of "judges, lawyers, bankers, doctors, clergymen, merchants, clerks, mechanics, students, railroad men, laborers, farmers, officials, editors, printers' devils, boot-blacks, and so on, all anxious to see a good game." When the champion Unions of Morrisania (in the Bronx) invaded Paterson, New Jersey, in 1867 to play the hometown Olympics, the audience of about 5,000 included a "large number of young ladies and a few old ones; men of all grades, ages, and standing—the young and strong, the aged and feeble, crippled, blind, and maimed; garrulous, patient, enthusiastic, passive, combatible and non-combatible, in truth a motley group, comprising everything."[8] The sporting press also recorded the presence of blacks at a few contests between white clubs in the South and noted occasional interracial fights.[9]

The events that generated the most excitement and attracted the largest crowds before the Civil War were the biennial United States versus Canada cricket contests, the annual eleven Englishmen versus eighteen Americans cricket matches, the 1858 New York City versus Brooklyn all-star baseball series at the Fashion Race Course, the 1859 encounters between the All-England Eleven and the twenty-two United States cricketers at Hoboken and Philadelphia, and the 1860 Atlantic versus Excelsior baseball games in Brooklyn. Most of these drew crowds of at least 5,000, with a few going well over 10,000.[10] Many who came to the first of the ball games at the Fashion Race Course were prosperous, arriving in fancy wagons and coaches. But apparently not all who watched the third and deciding game were as well heeled, for "a large deputation of overgrown boys from Brooklyn occupied a prominent position in the Grand Stand, and they materially interfered with the pleasure of the game by their noisy and very partial comments on the decisions of the Umpire, when unfavorable to the Brooklyn Nine."[11] The visit of the All-England Eleven brought out a high proportion of well-to-do spectators, while a broader spectrum of society attended the contests between the Atlantics and the Excelsiors.

The popularity of early American baseball and cricket cannot, however, be judged solely by how many people witnessed these special matches, because they were exceptional public amusements that received a great deal of newspaper publicity. A better indicator of the relative appeal of each sport is the attendance at the regular contests among the leading and lesser clubs. In New York, Brooklyn, Philadelphia, Boston, and a few other large cities the premier baseball games regularly attracted a few thousand people, despite inconvenient travel and hot weather. The *Clipper* estimated the throng at the 1865 Mutuals-Atlantics match at 18,000–20,000, "closely packed together, some five to eight deep, standing beneath the burning rays of an August sun." This was "proof positive that there is an innate attraction in the sport not possessed by any other out-door recreation in vogue." According to the *Ball Players' Chronicle,* in 1867 about 6,000 spectators braved the torture of an hour's ride in hot, dusty cars and then stood for more than three hours under the burning rays of a July sun to see a match between Morrisannia's Union club and the New Jersey Irvingtons.[12] In Newark and Jersey City, and in smaller towns in several states, crowds of a few hundred were more typical.[13]

Early American baseball's capacity to excite the masses was not matched by the English pastime. Interclub cricket contests drew far fewer people than did baseball games. While the all-star and international matches continued to attract thousands during the late 1850s, the leading cricket clubs of New York, Brooklyn, and Newark played before small groups of one hundred or fewer spectators. When the Dragon Slayers of the St. George club defeated the Newark Cricket Club in June 1860, for example, "at no time were there fifty spectators present, although the weather was very pleasant on both days."[14] More people watched cricket in Philadelphia, but the audiences there did not equal those for baseball in other cities.

People attended these early sporting events for widely different reasons and experienced the games in many different ways. Players frequently appeared at important matches to observe the skills of their fellow athletes and future opponents. Sportswriters such as Henry Chadwick stressed the aesthetic appeal of baseball and cricket—they commonly referred to "the beautiful game of baseball"—and often presented a detailed critique of the quality of play, complimenting clever bowling or pitching, fine fielding, and strong batting.[15] Charles King Newcomb, a Philadelphia man of letters, thought that baseball provided object lessons in art and science. He appreciated a pitcher's "statuesque posture" and wrote that the sport was also a "proof of physics": the "rush & lines of the balls in their passage through the air" reminded him of "the action of planetary orbs."[16]

Many spectators enjoyed hard hitting, while others appreciated the fine points of scientific batting and acrobatic fielding. In 1860 the *Newark Daily Advertiser* observed that strong-armed batters who drove the ball a long distance "cannot fail to elicit applause."[17] But the *Clipper* complained that "the majority of spectators of a ball match are ignorant of what constitutes scientific batting, and consequently they applaud only the long, heavy hits for home runs." It criticized both the lively balls then in use and the tendency of batters to try to satisfy the fans' desire to see the long ball. While the *Clipper* heralded a dead ball and carefully placed singles, clearly the masses did not follow suit.[18] Other writers considered fielding to be the "essence of the game" and lobbied for the elimination of the rule permitting an out when a ball was caught on the first bound, arguing that taking it "on the fly" was more difficult and more exciting for spectators.[19]

A major attraction of both sports was the excitement of the competition, especially for local, state, and national championships, coupled with the uncertainty of the outcome. A surprise upset intensified interest, as when the upstart Newark Cricket Club stunned the heavily favored New York club in the autumn of 1851. The *Spirit of the Times* called that match "the most exciting and amusing of any we have seen for years, and proved the 'glorious uncertainty' with a vengeance."[20] Baseball also had its share of triumphs by the underdog. When the Brooklyn Atlantics crushed the favored Gothams of New York by a score of 44–11 in 1857, the *Clipper* commented on the startling result: "If one man or party of players were sure of winning each time, it would be useless playing . . . and . . . the beautiful game of Base Ball would be numbered among the things that were."[21]

The advent of unofficial championships and open professionalism after the Civil War drew thousands of spectators to ball parks but also raised suspicion about the legitimacy of some of the contests, which sometimes dampened enthusiasm among the fans. The rivalries among the Athletics, Atlantics, Mutuals, Red Stockings, and other great teams certainly stimulated interest.[22] But as admission fees became more common during the late 1860s, journalists began to demand that the patrons of baseball get their money's worth. Several newspapers complained about clubs that charged a price for practice or exhibition games. In 1866 Philadelphia's *Sunday Dispatch* scolded the Athletics for displaying a "miserly spirit" in collecting ten cents for an intrasquad session "wherein the players are only anxious to 'keep their hands in,' and not to show their skill." The *Clipper* took the Atlantics and the Athletics to task for not informing the public in advance about whether several contests were exhibitions or regular matches.[23]

According to several of the sporting weeklies, rumors of fixed games did reduce the size of the crowds during this era. The *Clipper* asserted that games that called out 10,000–15,000 spectators in 1867 and 1868 did not attract 5,000 fans in 1869. The *Spirit* estimated that in 1870 only 1,000 people witnessed a Chicago White Stockings victory over the Atlantics. It explained that the Brooklyn club was "getting into such bad repute, from the constantly flying rumors of 'sells' and 'thrown' games, that few people care to expend their time and money in going to witness what may turn out to be merely a 'hippodroming' exhibition."[24]

The vicarious involvement of the spectators in the game was as obvious in the 1850s and 1860s as it is today. Every team had its "club followers," those who identified with their heroes and came to root them to victory—although sometimes they revealed their loyalties all too plainly. The annual match between eleven Englishmen and eighteen Americans generated much national feeling, and when the native side (including seventeen Philadelphians) earned their first victory in the series in 1860, "the anxiety of the large number of the English spectators, and the enthusiasm of the immense throngs of Americans" was obvious to all. At the moment of triumph, "never were heard such cheers on a cricket ground."[25] In the fall of 1861, when the Olympics and Athletics played a baseball game for bragging rights in Philadelphia, "the manifest feeling among the spectators in favor of the Athletic nine was too marked for the good of future play."[26]

Partisanship intensified after the Civil War, especially among the fans of the leading nines. In commenting on a thrilling victory by the New York Mutuals over the Atlantics, the *Spirit* declared: "No other games throughout the year arouse the same amount of excitement that the Atlantic-Mutual games do. Irrespective of the fine play . . . there is a certain amount of party feeling imported to the game which appears to make the spectators feel as if they themselves were engaged in the strife and not merely lookers-on." The many instances of spectators jeering the opposition or hissing the umpire also demonstrated intense party feeling.[27]

Although undoubtedly there were many who flocked to these matches for the fine plays and excitement of the competition, some certainly had a more pecuniary interest. Sports gambling already had a long history in America when the first cricket and baseball games were played. Not only did the public wager on these events, but so did some of the contestants. During the 1850s clergymen and other leaders of public opinion continued to condemn gambling, yet the many references to wagering in the daily press seem to indicate that the public had come to tolerate it. More than a few people were still quite sensitive about the moral respectability of the new pastimes, however. A contributor to *Porter's Spirit* was upset when that journal mentioned "very large bets" made on a contest between Brooklyn's Enterprise and Star junior teams. "Was it necessary to drag this in the newspapers," he asked, "in order to let the public know that ball-playing begins to assume some of the worst features of sport? I think not."[28]

The first American cricketers of the 1830s and 1840s followed the English custom of playing the sport for prize money and side bets. When the Albany and Schenectady clubs competed in a return match in the fall of 1837, the odds shifted back and forth during the contest and "bets were freely offered." One year later two teams of men from Nottingham and Sheffield played in Brooklyn for $100. When a select eleven of Canadians defeated New York's St. George club in 1845, "a good deal of money . . . exchanged hands" and "one gentleman in New York backed Canada for $7,000." After the 1850s there was less competition for prize money, although gambling remained commonplace.[29]

Wagering on baseball was a nearly universal practice during the sport's formative years, even though the National Association of Base Ball Players prohibited participants from betting. The NABBP had no means of enforcing such bans, however, especially since many of the New York area clubs and the large majority of clubs from other states were not even members. It is true that whenever gambling produced ugly incidents at contests, some of the prominent clubs passed resolutions against the practice.[30] But this did not prevent New York's spectators from placing their bets, and many players probably continued to wager in private as well. In Massachusetts, "large stakes were staked in different quarters" on the result of a championship match in 1859 between the Unions of Medway and the Winthrops of Holliston. The New England version of baseball also produced a few challenges to play for prize money.[31]

When the new Hamilton club of Jersey City challenged the Newark Adriatics in 1858, "any amount of 'lucre' could be had on the defeat of the Hamiltons." After the Mechanics of Jersey City defeated the Resolutes of Brooklyn in September 1860, one of the losers complained about "the free flourish of money, shaken in the faces of bystanders and the loud and frequent offers to bet upon the game, together with the low and profane language used." A spokesman for the Mechanics charged that a supporter of the Resolutes had opened the wagering, and he asked if that club "would like to undertake to stop outsiders from betting on the game?" "If they do," he wrote, "I think they will get more kicks and cuffs than pence."[32] As long as ball games had winners and losers, little could be done to stop gambling.

After the Civil War the baseball boom fed a gambling fever, especially at championship matches. In 1867 a reporter for the *Newark Daily Advertiser* described the scene at an Athletic-Atlantic game: "A few men, with their hands full of greenbacks, were walking around the skirts of the crowd calling for takers of bets at a hundred dollars to twenty that the Athletics will beat two to one." He estimated that "over one hundred thousand dollars changed hands." The next year, pools of bets were sold at a game between the Atlantics and the Haymakers of Troy, New York. According to the *Troy Budget,* it was "lamentable to see what an extent the betting mania reaches." That paper declared that betting "pervades all classes. At the game played with the Mutuals on Tuesday women brought their money and bet on their favorite Haymakers to the last cent in their possession. We hear of Lansingburg sewing girls who sent down their five, ten, and twenty dollars each by male friends to bet on the Haymakers."[33]

While the artistry of players, the excitement of competition, and the chance to profit were all major attractions of early American team sports, many people also enjoyed the spectacles the leading events provided. As Warren Goldstein has pointed out, there were important similarities between the cultures of baseball and the theater during this era. The sportsmen played out the drama of a match on their special stage, dressed in costumes that symbolized their club affiliation. Like the world of the theater, baseball had associations with both respectable society and the less-reputable life of Victorian popular amusements. People flocked to games for many of the same reasons they attended plays produced for the masses; their tastes were both high-brow and low-brow. Some simply wanted to watch an exciting contest on a beautiful day, while others anticipated a good time spiced with some liquor and wagering.[34]

A match between two prominent clubs or an all-star or international contest played on a sunny day before an enthusiastic audience produced quite a show. A reporter for the *Clipper* waxed poetic as he described the melodious birds and fragrant trees in bloom at Hoboken, the setting for an 1857 cricket encounter between an eleven from the New York club and sixteen men from Newark.[35] A cricket enthusiast from Philadelphia believed that his favorite sport offered spectators much to admire, including "the fresh and level green, the tents gleaming in the sunlight, the little flags floating jauntily in the breeze, and the telegraph announcing the stages of the play."[36] Early baseball staged its spectacles as well. When the best players of New York and Brooklyn met for their first game at the Fashion Race Course in 1858, *Porter's Spirit* reported that "no race day the Fashion Course has ever seen, presented such a brilliant numerical array. . . . The *coup d'oeil* . . . was brilliant in the extreme."[37] Artists and photographers, including Matthew Brady, and illustrators employed by Currier and Ives often attended the feature matches to capture these novel scenes for those unable to witness them in person.[38]

The special events that drew thousands of spectators produced a carnival atmosphere, as the great crowds attracted con artists, traders, vendors, and thieves. At the Fashion Race Course series, spectators arriving at the entrance encountered "thimble-riggers and card sweaters" who were trying to swindle a few dollars out of the "greenies." At the second game between the Atlantics and the Excelsiors in August 1860, on the outskirts of a huge throng of onlookers were "various itinerant tradesmen and vendors of eatables and drinkables." Fans crowded into fancy colored tents to quench their thirst with beer or stronger spirits, such as "Jersey lightning," which increased the business of the police force.[39] Pickpockets plagued these and other contests, prompting newspapers to report their activites and warn people to be on the alert.[40] After the war, pickpockets flocked to feature events, "such a favorable opportunity seldom occurring for picking up stray pocket-books, watches, etc." At an 1867 game between the Mutuals and the Irvingtons, several "Newark rowdies" staged a fight in order to give some thieves an opportunity to work the crowd.[41]

Most sports clubs made a special effort to encourage ladies to attend their matches by providing them with tents, seats, refreshments, and other accommodations. Sportsmen believed that female spectators would enhance the respectability of their pastimes while also restraining the behavior of males in the crowds. The sporting weeklies and daily press cooperated by urging women to patronize both cricket and baseball. The *Brooklyn Daily Eagle,* for example, recommended baseball as "a rational and manly pastime, which our wives, sisters, and sweethearts can witness, and enliven us with their presence, without the fear of a word or deed that would call the blush to the cheek of the most fastidious."[42] Frank Queen, editor of the *Clipper,* suspected that women attended sporting events primarily for social reasons, and he wanted them to exert their positive influence on troublemakers: "Let our American ladies visit the cricket grounds, the regattas, the baseball matches, and the most rough or rude among the spectators would acknowledge their magic sway. . . . When ladies are present . . . no class of our population can be found so debased as not to change their external behavior immediately, and that change is always for the better."[43] Before the war *Porter's Spirit* remarked that contestants exerted extra energy to perform well in front of the ladies and speculated that "more than one of them attends the ground with the view of sharply measuring among the players the qualities of what might make a serviceable future husband."[44] During the Civil War the sporting press continued to applaud sportsmen who welcomed women at their contests.[45]

Females did appear in sizable numbers at ball grounds, especially for the premier interclub, all-star, and international contests. On several occasions they showed their approbation of the new team sports as moral, wholesome recreations by presenting the participants with American flags or bouquets of flowers. In 1859, in the small town of Danvers Centre, Massachusetts, a bevy of ladies presented the Stars and Stripes to the local Essex Base Ball Club. One of them praised the men for their healthy exercise, which she believed was far preferable to the frequenting of the "gilded saloon, or the table of chance." When Amherst College defeated Williams College in the first intercollegiate baseball match in 1859, some spectators on the nearby roof of the Young Ladies Institute waved a "Star Spangled Banner" at the players.[46] In New Jersey, delegations of women frequently participated in postgame awards rituals.[47] Newspaper descriptions of their attire suggest that most of the women who attended these matches, albeit primarily for social reasons, were from the "respectable" classes. Others came out of curiosity or because of the beauty and excitement of the play. More than a few were well acquainted with the fine points of the sport and were vociferous fans. When Harvard defeated the Lowell club for the championship of New England in 1867, the crowd included "the fair friends of the Lowells donning blue and white badges, and those of the Harvards purple and white."[48] Some women apparently joined in the gambling as well—for example, at the second game of the 1858 Fashion Race Course series.[49]

The presence of female spectators at baseball and cricket matches proved that the two sports had achieved respectability, but it is doubtful that the women really inspired the players or restrained the hecklers, gamblers, and rowdies. At the Harvard-Lowell contest in 1867, late-arriving male spectators stood in front of the assembled women, obscuring their view. The umpire refused to start play until the "well dressed but excedingly rude and ungallant crowd" sat down or relocated. In 1868 Philadelphia's *Sunday Mercury* complained that "a number of boors" sat in seats reserved for ladies and annoyed the women by spitting tobacco juice.[50] The presence of women also had little impact on those spectators who liked to be active and vocal during the games. Heated rivalries generated much emotion, which led to physical and verbal interference and fighting by club followers and assorted troublemakers. Baseball players and club managers were sensitive to the problem of crowd control and attempted to cope with it by appeals to the spectators, which usually worked.[51] Some of the Brooklyn baseball clubs owned their own grounds and hired police to maintain order and remove objectionable persons. The Excelsiors enjoyed a reputation for preserving peace at their field in South Brooklyn, while the Atlantics of Bedford did not control their grounds and therefore had trouble with unruly spectators.[52] On a few occasions, such as the deciding game of the Atlantic-Excelsior series in 1860, even the police were unable to restrain the crowd.

During the amateur era, most of the baseball matches were played on open grounds. When thousands appeared to witness a contest, clearing the field of spectators was no easy task, and keeping them away from the players during the game could also be difficult. Generally the crowd cooperated by staying behind lines marked as bounds, but sometimes club followers got too close to the action—for example, outfielders might have to retrieve balls from among a forest of legs. Fans of the home team could make life miserable for visitors, as in 1858 when Brooklyn's Excelsior club defeated the New York Gothams with the help of an immense crowd that surrounded the contestants and interfered with the progress of the game. The Atlantics were also adept at driving the ball to left field, "an ugly corner they seem especially fond of sending the balls to," where, an observer remarked, "the crowd 'backed [them] up' . . . [and] so annoyed the Gothams that they resigned in disgust." During Philadelphia's first summer of baseball in 1860, police were hired to keep spectators away from the base lines, but at one game a local paper reported "quite a crowd backing up the third base" and complained that "players on the second base are frequently at a loss to know whether the third base is occupied or not."[53]

More common and annoying than physical interference was heckling. Prominent sportswriters blamed gamblers for engineering many instances of verbal abuse by spectators, which irritated the umpire, the players, and others in the crowds. A *Clipper* reporter (probably Henry Chadwick) believed that "these outside parties, these excresences of ball matches . . . are generally the very persons that create all the trouble and ill feeling that ever occurs on these occasions." He continued:

> Many of the spectators at ball matches assume to themselves the power belonging solely to the captains and umpires, directing players how to act, and loudly deciding upon points of the game as umpires, not according to the merits of the question, but solely in reference to their peculiar wishes as to the result. From this source has arisen the complaints made by clubs of different localities, that they cannot visit this or that ground without having to encounter the opposition of a large delegation of "club followers" as well as the nine of the club they play with, the former invariably being the parties most to be feared.[54]

When the Excelsiors defeated the Niagaras in a Brooklyn junior contest in 1857, "some of the Niagara's friends did not behave as gentlemen should." Whenever the Excelsiors were about to strike the ball, some people in the crowd yelled "such remarks as 'shanks,' 'Shanghai,' and other words not quite as decent as the above." They also cried out "foul" for fair hits in order to trick the Excelsiors into putouts.[55] The *Clipper* reported and condemned many such incidents of bad manners by uncouth onlookers.[56]

Fights and other disturbances among boys and men also created problems for baseball clubs. In July 1860 a Jersey City resident reported that "spectators are seriously annoyed on the Hamilton's grounds by the misconduct and noise of rude and rowdyish boys." He urged officials "to see that good order is preserved, and that the nuisance caused by groups of yelling, hooting and wrestling boys mixing themselves with the quiet spectators, and sometimes insulting the visiting club, should be prevented." The *Daily Courier and Advertiser* suggested that "a policeman be engaged to keep order among the noisy and ill-bred urchins who intrude themselves among the spectators and annoy and disturb every one in the vicinity with bad language and rough conduct." This advice was apparently not followed, for one month later the same newspaper noted that a contest was "marred as usual by the misconduct of a set of rowdies whom there was no policeman present to keep in check."[57] In Philadelphia, a game between the Equity and Winona nines was disturbed by "the very reprehensible conduct of a number of small boys, who, by shouting and running between the bases distracted the attention of the players." An old-timer remembered that in the 1860s the conduct of the players was excellent, but he recalled "many nasty melees among spectators after the games." He was among those who followed "an adherent of the Atlantics . . . several blocks to a drugstore where his wounds from gunshot were treated. Near-riots were frequently the results of clashes between hucksters and drivers who on top of their vehicles in Columbia av. hurled remarks at each other until these ended in fistic encounters. But this was all off the field of honor."[58] There were also a few fights reported between white and black spectators, including one at Charleston, South Carolina, in 1869.[59]

The intense partisanship that frequently marked baseball matches reflected a contentiousness that plagued most antebellum American cities. Urban violence and mob activity were commonplace in the divided and tumultuous world of these fast-growing centers. The riot that ended the Atlantic-Excelsior series was symptomatic of the nationalism and social class antagonism that troubled many communities—the Irish, working-class Atlantics versus the Excelsior gentlemen, for example. A *Clipper* editorial identified the true cause of disorder as "the *spirit of faction* . . . in which the foreign element of our immense metropolitan population, and their native offspring, especially, delights to indulge." While noting that gambling contributed to the trouble, the paper stated that the real evil lay in "the bitterness of party spirit and sectional strife," in fire department fights, in lower-class gangs, and in sectarian religious jealousies. "In short," it continued, "whether it is 'our country,' 'our party,' 'our company,' 'our club,' or 'our church,' the same evil spirit rules the actions and paralyzes the virtuous tendencies of all who succumb to its baneful influence, replacing kindly feelings with bitter hatred, and manly emulation and generous rivalry with revengeful retaliation." According to the *Clipper,* the remedy lay "in the self control of contending clubs and parties, and in a strict adherence to the rules that guide the actions of a man of honor and a gentleman."[60] Of course, proper conduct among the contestants did not guarantee peace and quiet among the spectators. When issues of social class or nationality appeared, as they apparently did in the Atlantic-Excelsior matches of 1860, there was always the potential for problems in the crowd.

The commercialization of baseball after the Civil War did not bring any drastic changes in the behavior of spectators. Some promoters and enthusiasts thought that the trend toward enclosed grounds and admission fees ranging from ten to fifty cents for most games would lead to a more select and well-mannered crowd. But this was not usually the case, in part because many people from the lower classes were willing to pay to see feature events. Also, thousands of fans congregated outside the fences and often found ways to view the sport over or through the barriers. One reporter marveled at the number of persons waiting at the entrance to deposit their quarters to see a Mutuals-Athletics contest in 1867: "One would imagine that in these times of high rents and low wages that the patronage of the base ball arena would be somewhat limited at such a high tariff as a quarter of a dollar; but the fact is a quarter is nothing for such an hour or two's exciting sport as a well contested ball match yields."[61]

Those who were unable or unwilling to pay could still find ways to see the action and often create a disturbance. When the Athletics routed the Atlantics in 1868 at the Union Grounds in the Williamsburg section of Brooklyn, "several thousands managed to witness the game without disbursing the required admittance fee."

The *Clipper* reported that "owners of trucks and other vehicles drove a brisk trade by stationing their establishments close to the high fence surrounding the ground, and letting out 'standing room only' to those who preferred this method of looking on. Others secured the prominent 'peek-holes' in the fence, while others still, after the game was under way and the attention of officers was centered in the exciting contest, boldly took up their position on the fence and held them to the close."[62]

Charging admission to enclosed fields did lead to better accommodations for ladies, the press, and the general paying public, but it did not eliminate fan interference, fights, or crowd disorders. An 1866 contest between the Athletics and the Atlantics ended in the bottom of the first inning after a fight between police and spectators and a rush of people onto the field that disrupted play.[63] Fisticuffs in the stands also were commonplace. Henry Chadwick chastised the daily press for reporting prizefights in detail, arguing that this encouraged "those, who, in a crowd of spectators at a ball match, at the cry of 'fight, fight,' rush from the manly excitements of such a contest to seek gratification for their brutal tastes in witnessing and encouraging bloody encounters between two or three blackguards."[64] People who paid twenty-five or fifty cents for admission also fought over good seats and were enraged when others blocked their view or that of their lady friends.[65]

While early amateur baseball attracted and excited thousands of orderly as well as riotous spectators, cricketers generally played before smaller and less involved crowds. An exception was in Philadelphia, where major interclub challenges attracted sizable, fashionable, and enthusiastic audiences. Apparently in that city the rowdiest fans were not exclusively working-class or English but also included upscale Americans. A *Clipper* reporter complained that cricket crowds in the City of Brotherly Love "lack considerably in courtesy to strangers, as they frequently express their exhultation at the success of their own players, and their chagrin at any discomfiture of their friends in a manner anything but proper or pleasant to their guests." He noted that "members of the clubs . . . try to suppress the yelling and unruly comments as much as possible, but they cannot always succeed."[66]

In the New York City region there is some evidence that cricket officials believed that both the foreign- and American-born laboring classes misbehaved at sporting events and thus should be discouraged from attending matches. In 1852 the *Spirit* urged the Newark Cricket Club to purchase its own field so that it could be better manicured for play but also to allow them to "keep off intruders, and make the lookers on more select."[67] In the spring of 1860, New York's St. George club began charging admission to its new ground at Hoboken, and although the Dragon Slayers maintained that this policy was necessary to defray expenses, the *Clipper* dismissed that argument by noting that the club was financially very secure. The paper hinted that the real motive was to restrict the spectators to members of the higher social classes, a policy "calculated to be detrimental to the future progress of the game." "Free access to cricket-grounds, for all persons who conduct themselves in an orderly manner, and ample accommodation for the fair sex . . . should be the policy of all clubs who desire to promote the popularity of the game," the *Clipper* editoralized. "As it is now, when scarcely a hundred spectators can be induced to visit a cricket-ground, for the purpose of witnessing an ordinary contest, it is a very questionable procedure to diminish the number by interposing the obstacle—however trifling the fee charged, in amount—of a charge for admission to grounds."[68]

St. George's first match on its fenced field drew only about 200 persons, including less than one dozen ladies, despite a strong rival in the Philadelphia Cricket Club and delightful weather on the second day. To the *Clipper,* a sporting journal dedicated to the promotion of all outdoor sports, this proved that the new ten-cent admission charge was "bad as a general rule, and especially so in this vicinity, with such an attractive game as baseball to rival cricket."[69] While the native Philadelphians apparently welcomed all classes of spectators and were more successful in promoting cricket, the Englishmen who controlled New York cricket pursued a more exclusive policy. Thus while baseball expanded its appeal and had to contend with disturbances among its enthusiasts, cricket tended to withdraw from the masses and therefore had few if any serious troubles with crowd control, at least in the New York area.

By 1872 the new team sports had demonstrated that they could attract at least as many spectators as horse racing or pedestrianism and often more. They were popular because they provided artistry, excitement, and opportunities for gambling; they also proved to be colorful and respectable public amusements. Thousands of people attended the special contests that excited the sporting fraternity, while smaller but equally enthusiastic crowds witnessed lesser matches. Early amateur cricket and baseball gave the players a chance to exercise and have fun, while creating a new form of public recreation that all could enjoy. As fans flocked to these ball games for their own particular reasons, they also experienced them in their own special ways. Baseball proved its great popularity and showed its potential for commercialism, which promoters would exploit after 1865. Although American cricket was less promising from the standpoint of profit, it still appealed to a small but devoted following, especially in the Philadelphia region. The remaining years of the nineteenth century would reveal the differences in each sport with respect to their audiences and their capacities for generating income.

NOTES

Portions of this chapter first appeared in a slightly different form in George B. Kirsch, "Baseball Spectators, 1855–1870," *Baseball History* 2 (Fall 1987): 4–20.

1. *New York Times,* October 3–6, 1859; *Clipper* 7 (October 15, 1859): 202; *Wilkes' Spirit* 1 (October 15, 1859): 83, 89; (January 28, 1860): 327; *New York Herald,* October 4–5, 1859.

2. *Brooklyn Daily Eagle,* August 24, 1860. See also *Wilkes' Spirit* 2 (September 1, 1860): 404–5; *New York Sunday Mercury,* August 26, 1860; *New York Times,* August 24, 1860.

3. For a survey of sports audiences from antiquity to modern times, as well as an analysis of sociological and psychological theories about contemporary fans, see Allen Guttmann, *Sports Spectators* (New York, 1986).

4. For some recent attempts to explain baseball's contemporary appeal, see Allen Guttmann, *From Ritual to Record: The Nature of Modern Sports* (New York, 1978), 91–116; David Lamoreaux, "Baseball in the Late Nineteenth Century: The Source of Its Appeal," *Journal of Popular Culture* 11 (1977): 597–613.

5. Quoted in *Porter's Spirit* 3 (December 12, 1857): 228.

6. *Brooklyn Daily Eagle,* August 3, 1859.

7. An exception was New Orleans, where some spectators came by invitation only. See Dale Somers, *The Rise of Sports in New Orleans, 1850–1900* (Baton Rouge, La., 1972), 51.

8. *Clipper* 13 (August 12, 1865): 138; *Wilkes' Spirit* 17 (November 2, 1867): 213. See also *Wilkes' Spirit* 18 (June 6, 1868): 273; *Chicago Tribune,* July 22, 1868. Guttmann maintains that antebellum baseball crowds were middle-class but that after the war the lower classes predominated. See *Sports Spectators,* 111–15.

9. *Clipper* 17 (August 14, 1869):147; *Spirit* 20 (August 7, 1869): 391.

10. For various crowd estimates for these events, see *Porter's Spirit* 2 (June 6, 1857): 212; 4 (August 21, 1858): 388; *Clipper* 6 (July 24, 1858): 106; *Brooklyn Daily Eagle,* August 18, 1858.

11. *Porter's Spirit* 4 (July 24, 1858): 332; 5 (September 11, 1858): 36; *Brooklyn Daily Eagle,* August 18, 1858.

12. *Clipper* 13 (August 12, 1865): 138; *Ball Players' Chronicle,* July 11, 1867.

13. *Spirit* 29 (June 5, 1859): 193; (September 17, 1859): 376; *Clipper* 6 (July 3, 1858): 183; 7 (August 13, 1859): 132; *Brooklyn Daily Eagle,* June 11, July 9, 1858.

14. *Clipper* 8 (June 30, 1860): 85. See also *Clipper* 8 (July 7, 1860): 91.

15. *Clipper* 5 (November 7, 1857): 231. See also *Clipper* 6 (July 17, 1858): 102.

16. Quoted in Thomas L. Altherr, " 'The Most Summery, Bold, Free, & Spacious Game': Charles King Newcomb and Philadelphia Baseball," *Pennsylvania History* 52 (April 1985): 77.

17. *Newark Daily Advertiser,* May 14, 1860.

18. *Clipper* 18 (July 9, 1870): 109.

19. *Clipper* 5 (September 19, 1857): 175; *Porter's Spirit* 4 (July 9, 1858): 292.

20. *Spirit* 21 (November 1, 1851): 438.

21. *Clipper* 5 (September 12, 1857): 163.

22. *Clipper* 18 (June 25, 1870): 92–93. See also *Clipper* 15 (September 7, 1867): 171; *Philadelphia Sunday Mercury,* September 1, 1867.

23. *Philadelphia Sunday Dispatch,* June 3, 1866; *Clipper* 18 (July 2, 1870): 98.

24. *Clipper* 17 (November 13, 1869): 253; *Spirit* 23 (October 1, 1870): 100.

25. *New York Times,* July 9, 1860.

26. *Clipper* 9 (November 23, 1861): 251.

27. *Spirit* 22 (August 13, 1870): 407; *Newark Daily Advertiser,* September 5, 1867; *Ball Players' Chronicle,* June 13, 1867.

28. *Porter's Spirit* 3 (December 12, 1857): 228.

29. *Spirit* 7 (October 7, 1837): 272; 8 (September 15, 1838): 246; (October 13, 1838): 278–79; *Porter's Spirit* 3 (June 13, 1857): 229;

Clipper 5 (August 8, 1857): 122; John Lester, ed., *A Century of Philadelphia Cricket* (Philadelphia, 1951), 15, 16, 21.

30. *Clipper* 8 (July 21, 1860): 107.

31. *Wilkes' Spirit* 1 (October 15, 1859): 84; 2 (May 5, 1860): 143; (August 26, 1860): 389; *Clipper* 8 (July 21, 1860): 107.

32. *Jersey City Daily Courier and Advertiser,* October 7, 1858; September 8, 10, 1860.

33. *Newark Daily Advertiser,* August 23, 1867; *Troy* (N.Y.) *Budget* quoted in the *Philadelphia Sunday Mercury,* August 16, 1868.

34. Warren Jay Goldstein, "Playing for Keeps: A History of American Baseball, 1857–1876" (unpublished Ph.D. dissertation, Yale University, 1983), 214–34. Goldstein presents an interesting analysis of how proper uniforms gave baseball players the appearance of respectability that was so important to Chadwick and other promoters of the sport.

35. *Clipper* 5 (June 6, 1857): 53.

36. *Clipper* 7 (July 2, 1859): 84.

37. *Porter's Spirit* 4 (July 24, 1858): 332.

38. *New York Sunday Mercury,* August 12, 1860; *Porter's Spirit* 1 (September 20, 1856): 37; 6 (August 13, 1859): 372; *Newark Daily Advertiser,* May 27, 1857; *Spirit* 26 (September 20, 1856): 379.

39. *New York Times,* July 21, 1858; *Brooklyn Daily Eagle,* August 10, 1860.

40. *Jersey City Daily Courier and Advertiser,* August 25, 1858; *New York Times,* July 21, 1858.

41. *Clipper* 13 (August 12, 1865): 138; *Wilkes' Spirit* 16 (July 6, 1867): 347; *Newark Daily Advertiser,* May 17, 1867.

42. *Brooklyn Daily Eagle,* August 3, 1859.

43. *Clipper* 7 (May 14, 1859): 29.

44. *Porter's Spirit* 1 (September 6, 1856): 13.

45. *Clipper* 12 (September 3, 1864): 163; *Wilkes' Spirit* 5 (October 26, 1861): 116; 6 (April 5, 1862): 76.

46. *Clipper* 7 (August 20, 1859): 141; (July 16, 1859): 99. Such flag waving reveals the early connection between baseball, traditional moralism, and nationalism. See also *Clipper* 14 (June 23, 1866): 84; *Ball Players' Chronicle,* June 13, 1867; *American Chronicle* 1 (May 28, 1868): 172.

47. *Newark Daily Advertiser,* September 29, 1859.

48. *Wilkes' Spirit* 16 (June 8, 1867): 268. See also *Clipper* 15 (June 8, 1867): 66; 18 (July 9, 1870): 109; *Philadelphia Sunday Mercury,* June 16, 1867.

49. *Porter's Spirit* 4 (August 21, 1858): 388.

50. *Wilkes' Spirit* 16 (June 8, 1867): 268; *Philadelphia Sunday Mercury,* August 16, 1868.

51. *Clipper* 8 (July 14, 1860): 101; (September 22, 1860): 180.

52. *Clipper* 8 (July 21, 1860): 107.

53. *Porter's Spirit* 5 (October 30, 1858): 135; *Philadelphia Morning Pennsylvanian,* August 27, 1860.

54. *Clipper* 8 (June 2, 1860): 51.

55. *Porter's Spirit* 3 (September 5, 1857): 4.

56. *Clipper* 7 (November 5, 1859): 229; 8 (June 23, 1860): 76. See also *Porter's Spirit* 3 (December 5, 1857): 212; *Jersey City Daily Courier and Advertiser,* October 29, 1858. For the antics of the Eckford fans, see *Clipper* 10 (September 6, 1862): 163; *Wilkes' Spirit* 7 (October 18, 1862): 100.

57. *Jersey City Daily Courier and Advertiser,* July 12, 24, August 28, 1860.

58. *Philadelphia Morning Pennsylvanian,* July 24, 1860; *Philadelphia Bulletin,* April 13, 1936, in a scrapbook of newspaper clippings on baseball, Historical Society of Pennsylvania.

59. *Clipper* 17 (August 14, 1869): 147; *Wilkes' Spirit* 20 (August 7, 1869): 391.

60. *Clipper* 8 (September 8, 1860): 164.

61. Newspaper clipping from the *Morning Programme,* city unknown, Henry Chadwick's scrapbooks, vol. 8, Albert G. Spalding Collection, New York Public Library.

62. *Clipper* 16 (September 12, 1868): 178. See also *Ball Players' Chronicle,* August 22, 1867; *Philadelphia Public Ledger,* September 1, 1868; *New York Daily Tribune,* September 17, 1868.

63. *Wilkes' Spirit* 15 (October 13, 1866): 109; *Philadelphia Sunday Mercury,* October 7, 1866.

64. *Ball Players' Chronicle,* August 22, 1867.

65. *Philadelphia Sunday Dispatch,* July 8, 1866. For an account of crowd behavior when the Brooklyn Atlantics stopped the Cincinnati Red Stockings' long winning streak in 1870, see *Harper's Weekly* 14 (July 2, 1870): 427.

66. *Clipper* 8 (July 14, 1860): 99.

67. *Spirit* 22 (June 5, 1852): 192.

68. *Clipper* 8 (April 21, 1860): 7; (June 16, 1860): 68.

69. *Clipper* 8 (June 16, 1860): 68.

CHAPTER

9

Baseball's Boom and Cricket's Survival

In October 1865 the *Newark Daily Advertiser* announced that a "carnival of Base Ball" had run riot in the city. The return of peace had ignited a new boom for the national pastime, prompting the paper to conclude that "when, indeed, we see the general interest manifested among all classes in this manly and healthful sport, not only in our own city but throughout the country, we must acknowledge that it is rightfully called the National Game of America."[1] The fever infected players of both sexes and all ages, races, and levels of skill. While the famed Atlantics, Athletics, Mutuals, and other first-class nines battled to be recognized as the baseball champions of the United States, the lesser known of all shapes and sizes emulated their heroes on the ball fields of urban and rural America. In 1866 Philadelphia's *Sunday Mercury* proclaimed that "baseball is truly a national game, and not confined exclusively to Young America. . . . we have had our 'Fat and Thin' matches; the 'Ponies and Muffins' have given us a touch of their quality, and the 'Broken-winded Nine' of a prominent club have come in for a share of base ball honors, but they all dwindle into insignificance when compared with the efforts of the 'Invalids.'"[2]

Proof of the masses' passion for baseball during the late 1860s appeared in the urban bazaars and rural fairs that awarded rosewood bats and silver balls to the club that received the highest number of votes in popularity contests. At indoor social gatherings, ladies and gentlemen amused themselves with a new board game—

"Sebring's Parlor Base Ball Field."[3] From the rocky coast of Maine to the Golden Gate of California, from upstart Chicago to the reconstructed states of Dixie, a baseball mania swept the land. Yet in April 1865 few if any promoters of the national game could predict the fantastic success or the host of difficulties it would experience over the next half decade. With the populace rejoicing that four years of terrible war had come to an end, baseball players greeted the return of spring by flocking to playing fields instead of battlefields. Several clubs in northern cities postponed their opening days out of respect for the memory of the slain president, but after a brief period of mourning they returned to their diamonds. Others, including the Philadelphia Mercantiles, passed resolutions expressing sorrow over Lincoln's death.[4]

The baseball season of 1865 began a new chapter in the sport's history. The same forces that had fueled its prewar development fed its expansion during the late 1860s. As before, personal contacts (now enriched through military service), the press, interclub competition, urban rivalries, regional tours, and state and national organizations all contributed in varying degrees to new rounds of baseball excitement.

Baseball historians in general have stressed the importance of the army experience in popularizing the sport after the war. The *Clipper* declared in 1865 that "when soldiers were off duty, base ball was naturalized in nearly every state in the Union, and thus extended in popularity," and it is true that the pastime remained popular among soldiers stationed in the West and South after 1865.[5] However, many players who enjoyed baseball before the war but never served in the military helped to promote the sport in the cities to which they relocated after the conflict. Former residents of Philadelphia and Washington, D.C., for example, organized the first game of baseball ever played in Fayetteville, Tennessee, in October 1868, as the KKK club defeated "nine Carpetbaggers." Contestants in an 1868 match between Macon and Savannah, Georgia, clubs included former members of New York City, Newark, Irvington, and Philadelphia nines. A group of Washingtonians wandered "to the land of gold and silver, found it impossible to forget their old pastime," and formed the Star City Club of Eastern City, Nevada, in 1870. Philadelphians in San

Francisco founded four clubs before the Cincinnati Red Stockings arrived there on tour in 1869.[6]

National, regional, and local newspapers and magazines also gave an enormous boost to baseball, as publishers, editors, and reporters appreciated the intimate connection between the fortunes of the new sport and the prospects of their respective publications. Before the war, detailed coverage of the game appeared only in the New York City sporting weeklies, such as the *Clipper* and the various versions of the *Spirit of the Times*. But beginning in 1865, family publications such as *Harper's Weekly* and *Frank Leslie's Illustrated* devoted more space to feature matches and leading players. Henry Chadwick's *American Chronicle of Sports and Pastimes,* the first publication to specialize in ball games, survived only thirteen months, from June 1867 to July 1868.[7]

City dailies and Sunday papers began to expand their baseball reporting, as a few editors who were prominent officers of ball clubs used their positions to popularize both their teams and their papers. In Philadelphia, for example, Col. Thomas Fitzgerald, a founder and former president of the Athletics, published the *City Item*. The *Clipper* credited him with turning interest in that town from cricket to baseball and recalled a time when it was difficult to get Philadelphia's newspapers to print a box score.[8] Fitzgerald's arch-rival was William Meeser, editor of the *Philadelphia Sunday Mercury*. A vice president and an intensely partisan champion of the Athletics, he carried on running controversies with both Fitzgerald and Chadwick in his columns. When sporting weeklies and the daily papers became overwhelmed with baseball material during the peak months, they presented only summaries of minor matches, and by the late 1860s many had begun to charge a fee for announcements of club meetings and elections of officers. Some, like the *Philadelphia Press,* refused to cover ball games unless the clubs advertised in their columns.[9]

The reciprocal relationship between baseball and the media included the use of the telegraph as well as newsprint. With public excitement at fever pitch for major intercity contests, crowds besieged newspaper and telegraph offices for the latest results. When the Philadelphia Athletics opened a three-game road trip in New York City in August 1867, "citizens, some of them venerable in years," sought out the offices of the *Sunday Mercury* and "hovered around the doors, mistaking every running boy as a messenger bearing us the intelligence." The telegraph offices also were jammed, and people packed the sidewalks until news came of the Athletics' victory over the Unions of Morrisania. Many fans lingered to speculate on the chances of their heroes on the next day, and "at a late hour two of the *Mercury*'s staff were serenaded by the American Glee Club, in honor of the Athletics' success."[10] That same month the Newark telegraph office and the adjoining sidewalk were filled with people anxiously awaiting the score of the game between the hometown Eurekas and the Unions of Lansingburg, New York. Closing time came and went, yet the "eager crowd . . . defied the power of the operator to put them out." Police kept a passage open for pedestrians, in a scene reminiscent of previous gatherings awaiting news of the Civil War.[11]

While participants and press sang its praises after 1865, intercity competition provided most of the excitement that fanned baseball fever. Traditions of local pride, urban rivalries, and city boosterism spurred hometown clubs and newspapers to seek glory for their nines and communities. Quaint country villages, modest settlements, burgeoning upstart towns, small cities, and giant metropolises all competed for unofficial championships at local, state, regional, and national levels. The New York City area still claimed to be the baseball capital of the United States, and its sporting journals boosted local teams even as they claimed to be impartial in their reporting. In 1866 the *Clipper* urged the Philadelphia Athletics to use only hometown players and hoped that the club would "be encouraged by the people of that city, the same as the Atlantics are by the people of New York and Brooklyn." It added: "If Philadelphians would take a more lively interest in their own affairs instead of toadying to New York . . . its institutions, its clubs, and its general business would be placed on a more sound footing." The paper admitted "that in all of our sports and recreations we prefer that New York shall hold the supremacy, but when we are beaten by outside 'villagers' or 'country clubs,' we desire that due credit be given to the victors"; it promised "to give honor to whom it is due, be it to the Squeedunk Yacht Club, the wild cat race horses, or the Tinicum Town Pump Base Ball Club. It is only by friendly strife that we can hope to build up the sporting interests of America."[12]

Winning nines could propel quiet country towns and sleepy villages into the limelight, especially if they defeated or fought a close battle with celebrated metropolitan teams. The Unions (Haymakers) of Lansingburg rocketed to prominence with victories over the New York City Mutuals and other major clubs. In New Jersey, the Irvingtons shocked the baseball world with an 1867 triumph over the Atlantics, and the *Newark Daily Advertiser* declared that baseball had "brought more people into that quiet village than its most sanguine property holders could have hoped." According to the paper, "a few months ago comparatively few knew anything about the place. Now there is a lively interest to know 'where that Irvington Club comes from.' Yesterday hosts of strangers saw."[13] In Marshalltown, Iowa, "the fever broke out in its most virulent form, and it was not many weeks before the entire town had gone base-ball crazy, the fever seemingly attacking everybody in the place save the baby in arms." The Marshalltown team held the state championship for several years during the late 1860s, prevailing in a heated rivalry with Des Moines. When the famed Forest City club of Rockford, Illinois, barnstormed through Marshalltown, everyone went wild with excitement. The Forest City club was an upstart "country Club" in the eyes of easterners, but to the Iowans they were big-city giants. Although the Forest City nine destroyed their hosts in two lopsided games, their visit boosted the sport in Marshalltown and many other villages throughout the Midwest.[14]

State fairs and groups of sporting entrepreneurs organized many baseball tournaments during the late 1860s to capitalize on the new mania. Popular in the Midwest, they often brought together nines from small and large towns and cities, as well as some rural teams. A few offered prize money or gifts to entice crack clubs from the East to seek more fame and fortune further west. Detroit, for example, hosted a "World's Base Ball Tournament" in 1867, with a first prize of $300 (in greenbacks) and a gold-mounted rosewood bat, valued at $75. The organizers promised $700 to the Atlantics and the Athletics to play the last game, but neither team accepted.[15] Local tournaments were generally open to all entrants, with the exception of black teams. The organizers of an 1870 Chicago amateur competition barred that city's Blue Stockings, an all-black club. The Blue Stockings' secretary speculated that the club was excluded because the white clubs were afraid "of us beating them." However, the *Chicago Tribune* maintained that officials had rejected the team because it was considered too weak to be competitive with the white nines. The *Tribune* did concede that "probably their social standing had somewhat to do with the matter" and pointed out that Chicago's white amateur clubs included young men from some of the best families in the city who "were not disposed to burlesque the tournament by the admission of a colored club of inferior capacity, even though the gate receipts should suffer thereby."[16]

Urban boosterism contributed to the baseball boom, especially in such midwestern cities as Chicago, Cincinnati, and St. Louis, where competition for railroads, commerce, and industry was mirrored by these cities' baseball teams. Chicagoans were obsessed with dominating local and distant rivals in baseball and eveything else, so when a neighboring Forest City nine upset the touring Nationals of Washington, D.C., in 1867, the *Chicago Times* crowed. When the Nationals then routed the hometown Excelsiors, however, Chicago's dailies accused the Nationals of intentionally losing the Forest City game to increase the wagering on the Excelsior match. After recovering from their humiliating defeat, the Excelsiors recruited a few new players from the East and Midwest and triumphed over a number of regional rivals. The *Chicago Times* resumed its boasting about the Excelsiors: "They have obliterated Bloomington. They have annihilated Rockford. They have left little of Detroit save a grease spot. They have done everything . . . save to beat a third-rate club of treasury clerks from Washington." The Excelsiors were urged to meet "foemen worthy of their steel" and "challenge Chicago's only remaining rival—New York."[17]

The next two years brought defeat and embarrassment to the "Garden City" as the Excelsiors suffered a number of losses and disbanded in the fall of 1868. The *Chicago Tribune* announced the club's demise with a call to action, demanding that Chicago form a nine that could beat "any and all clubs in America."[18] When the Cincinnati Red Stockings swept eastern and western honors in 1869, Chicagoans were distraught by the success of the club from "Porkopolis." That summer Chicago's baseball enthusiasts reported that the game was thriving on the junior and amateur levels but was nonetheless a failure in their city because of the lack of a first-class nine. They blamed the situation on inadequate support by the business community and inferior local players, prompting fifty Chicagoans, including several prominent businessmen and a future United States senator named Potter Palmer, to found a nine that "should play ball and nothing else; a nine which should beat the world." The Board of Trade promised support, and by Thanksgiving the new baseball club had issued stock certificates and raised $5,000.[19]

The Chicago White Stockings hired James Wood from the Brooklyn Eckfords to captain the team and added a few of his mates and some crack players from the Haymakers of Troy, New York. In the spring of 1870 they swept through the South, demolishing all opponents, including a 47–1 rout of the Unions of St. Louis and a 157–1 destruction of the Bluff City nine of Memphis. In May the White Stockings returned to a rousing welcome and a newly prepared home ground at Dexter Park Race Course, with grandstand, clubhouse, and room for 30,000 spectators.[20] But a July tour of the East turned into a disaster, as the Chicago team lost to the Atlantics, the Mutuals, and the Athletics, then suffered more setbacks at home in August. The *Spirit* ridiculed Chicago's pretensions: "New York was to be wiped from the map of the United States in the matter of playing base-ball, as it had been commercially and socially long ago by the Garden City. Well, not one of these dire results has yet been brought about."[21]

As the White Stockings' fortunes improved in the fall of 1870, so did the city's spirit. Chicago went wild when the team triumphed 10–6 over their arch-rivals from Cincinnati. Thousands welcomed the returning heroes, who sported scarfs made of small red stockings; perched on the front seat of their carriage was a baby pig adorned with a pair of small red hose and draped with a placard that read "Porkopolis, September 7, 1870." The *Chicago Tribune* gloated: "Our Cincinnati friends . . . were routed, horse, foot, and dragoons, and not a Porkopolian has heart enough left to tell of the defeat. . . . it was necessary in order to teach the Cincinnatians a wholesome lesson. If they will profit by it, and learn that their place is on a back seat, Chicago . . . in time may accord them the place of second best."[22] After a second win over Cincinnati and a series of victories over all their eastern rivals, the White Stockings claimed the championship for 1870, but the fans were frustrated when the Mutuals refused to yield their pennant after a disputed eight-inning loss to Chicago in early November. Nonetheless, the Garden City nine replaced the Cincinnati Red Stockings as the Midwest's premier team, with St. Louis struggling to assemble a nine that could wrest championship honors away from its commercial and industrial rivals.[23]

While these regional rivalries popularized baseball, intersectional matches accelerated the national growth of the sport. Once the eastern clubs began a series of long-distance tours via railroads and steamships, western and southern nines followed suit. In 1867 the Nationals of Washington, D.C., ventured beyond the Alleghenies and electrified western towns with a nine composed mostly of government clerks, lawyers, and students. They covered five states, traveling over 3,000 miles by train and boat at a cost of more than $5,000. Club officials, friends, and baseball reporters joined this pioneer barnstorming excursion, which became the prototype for future sporting tours.[24] The following year the Atlantics, the Athletics, and the Unions of Morrisania swept through the Midwest, creating a sensation in Pittsburgh, Cincinnati, Louisville, Indianapolis, St. Louis, Chicago, Buffalo, Cleveland, Detroit, Milwaukee, Forest City, and Bloomington, Illinois, and elsewhere. Midwestern clubs also took to the road, journeying east for return matches with the great teams of New York, Brooklyn, Newark, and Philadelphia. New Orleans's Southern club was greeted upon its return from a western swing in 1869 by a grand torchlight procession of local clubs, a band, and a crowd of enthusiastic citizens. A local reporter wrote that the trip gave "a new impulse to base ball in our city."[25] The Cincinnati Red Stockings' 1869 tour to California via the newly completed transcontinental railroad was the most ambitious and successful of all, as they capped an undefeated season with lopsided victories in the San Francisco region.[26]

Intersectional baseball competition also had an impact on North-South relations immediately after the Civil War. Some observers viewed the revival of baseball in the border and southern states as a positive force in reuniting the nation. In 1865 the *Clipper* noted that "Maryland [was] fast being reconstructed on this base-is" and hoped to see that state as the " 'Centre field' of our National game," adding that "there would have been fewer 'hands lost' and 'foul balls' had this been the case four years ago." While declaring that "base ball fever is rapidly assuming the form of an epidemic among the constructed and reconstructed denizens of the former stronghold of the extinct Davisocracy [Richmond, Va.]," the journal scolded the southerners of the Richmond club for refusing the challenge of that city's Union nine, which was composed of businessmen and federal officals: "We regret to learn of such petty feeling and sectional animosity being evinced by any party of Southern gentlemen calling themselves ball players. Our national game is intended to be national in every sense of the word, and, until this example was set by the 'Richmond Club,' nothing of a sectional character has emanated from a single club in the country."[27]

Northern and southern journalists believed that the tours of the great eastern ball clubs would help to heal the bitter wounds of war. When the Nationals of Washington, D.C., visited Brooklyn in July 1866, the Excelsiors treated them to a lavish dinner, in violation of a National Association of Base Ball Players rule prohibiting expensive entertainments. The *Clipper* argued that the Brooklynites' extravagance showed southerners that "the ball players' 'policy of reconstruction' is one marked by true fraternal regard, irrespective of all political opinions or sectional feelings, the National Association knowing . . . 'No North, no South, no East, no West,' but simply the interest and welfare of the game itself, and the cultivation of kindly feelings between the different clubs."[28] When the Nationals stopped at Louisville in 1867, however, *Wilkes' Spirit* reported that "a crowd of the most unruly partisan boors and rowdy boys" gave the so-called invading Yankees a greeting that "was not at all in accordance with the reputation for chivalric sentiments which the Southern cities have hitherto claimed." The newspaper singled out the female spectators for special criticism and urged that all sectional feeling be kept out of the game. "The Nationals . . . though from the shores of the Potomac, had too much of the North about them apparently to merit the favor of Southern women."[29]

During the summer of 1868 the Athletics received a warmer reception in Louisville, and Philadelphia's *Sunday Mercury* defended the Louisville players and their grey uniforms, which "had been held up to scorn, and those who wear it denounced as rebels."

A reporter from the City of Brotherly Love "did not inquire the political status of the Louisville Club," not caring "whether they were former rebels or Union men" because that "has got nothing to do with our National Game." He concluded: "if Jefferson Davis . . . was to meet me on the ball field, and salute me as a gentleman, I would endeavor to prove to him that I was one."[30] A New Orleans newspaper announced the upcoming trip of its Southern club to Memphis and St. Louis with players who "organized during the war while prisoners of war at Johnson's Island." Its editor wondered, along with his northern counterparts, "Would it not be pleasant to see the hatchet buried in the great national game, 'spite of the efforts of politicians to keep up ill feeling between the sections?"[31] The *Spirit,* reporting on the Mutuals' December 1869 excursion to New Orleans, observed: "This National Game seems destined to close the National Wounds opened by the late war. It is no idle pastime which draws young men, separated by two thousand miles, together to contest in friendship, upon fields but lately crimsoned with their brothers' blood in mortal combat."[32]

As baseball enthusiasts, journalists, and touring nines spread the gospel of the new pastime across America, national, state, and local sports organizations attempted to guide the game's growth. The New York City–based NABBP acted in a number of ways to recognize and encourage regional and national expansion. It voted to rotate the annual meeting site among several cities, including Philadelphia (1867), Washington, D.C. (1868), and Boston (1869), making its conventions accessible to more players and clubs. It also elected officials from a variety of cities in a conscious attempt to broaden representation. In 1866 the *Clipper* urged the selection of Senator Arthur P. Gorman of the Washington Nationals as the new NABBP president. It argued that in view of the ongoing reconstruction debate, "the [baseball] fraternity should prove to the world that sectionalism is unknown in our national game." Since "for the first time the South will enter the convention," the paper maintained, "the election of the president of the 'Champion Club of the South' would go far to prove the absence of any narrow sectional ideas in the National Association."[33] The convention did choose Gorman as president and later greeted southern delegates with loud applause.[34] The following year the Philadelphia gathering selected a president from Cincinnati and the remaining officers from Madison (Wisc.), Jersey City, Rockford (Ill.), Brooklyn, and Lowell (Mass.).[35]

In another move toward regional and national expansion, the NABBP shifted its system of representation from individual clubs to state associations, allowing one delegate for each ten clubs in the state bodies. The *Clipper* declared that the welfare of baseball depended upon bringing in state and regional organizations as branches of the parent association and thus advocated support of this new system, which would "bring under the influence and control of the playing rules of the National Association . . . hundreds of clubs in distant towns and cities who would other wise be 'out in the cold' . . . and deprived of the advantages of being enrolled as Association Clubs."[36] In 1868 the NABBP formally adopted this scheme of state representation, although it did permit a few individual clubs to send delegates if their states lacked a formal association.[37]

At the regional and state levels, clubs joined together to standardize rules, regulate competition, sanction championships, debate issues, and instruct delegates to the national meetings. Advocates of the formation of state associations believed that they would serve many needs of ball players and clubs, especially in arranging games and resolving disputes.[38] These associations struggled to establish themselves as thriving bodies, but most of them only enrolled a small fraction of all baseball clubs in their jurisdiction. Apathy plagued their efforts to organize, while their annual gatherings were increasingly marred by interclub disputes and dissatisfaction over professionalism, commercialism, and corruption. For example, only twenty clubs sent delegates to the 1867 Pennsylvania state association meeting at Harrisburg, including a few men who represented nonexistent nines. The 1870 conventions of the New York and New Jersey groups drew only nine and twelve clubs respectively, even though each state (like Pennsylvania) had more than one hundred teams.[39]

The national and state associations tried to enlist large numbers of white clubs while excluding black nines that were eager to join. Although the latter often shared playing fields and enjoyed good relations with white teams, they were denied equal representation in baseball gatherings, as they were excluded from Reconstruction-era politics in the North. The 1867 NABBP convention flatly refused to admit clubs with black delegates,[40] and state meetings followed the same segregationist policy. The Philadelphia Pythians sent an emissary to Harrisburg in 1867 to present the club's credentials to the Pennsylvania gathering, but he found that only a few friends from the Athletics and other clubs favored admitting the all-black Pythians. Supporters advised a discrete withdrawal to avoid humiliation, and the Pythian delegate concurred. "Whilst all expressed sympathy for our club," he reported "a few only . . . expressed a willingness to vote for our admission, while numbers of the others openly said that they would in justice to the opinion of the clubs they represented be compeled, tho against their personal feelings, to vote against our admission." He was treated with courtesy and respect, receiving an invitation to attend an afternoon game and a free railroad pass home, but his club was not welcome in the state association.[41] Similarly, the New York state association approved a motion in 1870 that if any of the clubs admitted were found to be composed of gentlemen of color, their association membership would be voided. The *Clipper* objected, stating: "Thus, for the first time in the history of the National Association, was a political question introduced as a bone of contention in the council of the fraternity." The paper later advised black clubs to organize "a National Association of their own."[42]

With baseball earning its reputation as America's national game after 1865, the NABBP rules proved far more popular than any of the prewar, premodern versions. A few diehards still clung to the "Massachusetts game" in New England, including eleven clubs that gathered in 1866 in Boston to organize a new association based on the old regulations.[43] But they were overshadowed by the Harvard, Lowell, and Tri-Mountain nines, which popularized the new pastime. The *Clipper* singled out the latter for special praise, comparing the Tri-Mountains to the "veteran Knickerbockers of New York."[44] Variations of townball remained popular among old-timers in Newark and in parts of Kentucky adjacent to Cincinnati, although some of these clubs switched to baseball in 1866.[45]

As baseball conquered America, its apostles dreamed of preaching the gospel around the world. In 1867 the outgoing president of the NABBP, Arthur P. Gorman, suggested the creation of a sinking fund to defray expenses incurred in sending eighteen players to Europe to demonstrate the progress of the sport.[46] While nothing immediately came of this idea, during the next few decades baseball missionaries barnstormed around the world.[47] More significantly, before 1871 American sailors, expatriates, and tourists introduced the sport in South America and Europe. Officers of the U.S. flagship *Powhatan,* for example, defeated a club composed of residents of Callao, Peru, in what was perhaps the first baseball match ever played in South America. Philadelphia's *Sunday Mercury,* reporting that Valparaiso, Chile, had two clubs, concluded: "Cricket is played in all parts of the world where there are Englishmen—why not base ball where there are Americans?"[48] Americans residing in Germany and Switzerland played baseball and entertained and recruited some travelers and natives,[49] while back in North America a New Yorker founded a club in Montreal in 1869 and the sport continued to grow in the Ontario cities of Woodstock and London.[50] Although baseball did not become an international sensation during the 1860s, its adherents did try to carry it to other countries. Later decades would bring greater success in Asia and the Caribbean than in Europe.

The coming of peace and spring in April 1865 encouraged American cricketers to return to their wickets and resume their favorite sport. Unfortunately, the prospects for cricket in the United States after the Civil War were not nearly as bright as those for baseball. Wartime disruptions had inflicted more damage on the English game, while America's national pastime had already surpassed cricket in popularity in all regions of the country. However, both British and American-born sportsmen kept cricket alive for the next decade and laid the foundation for the revival of the sport during the 1870s. Many of them also contributed to its golden era, which stretched from the 1880s to World War I. White-collar professionals and businessmen and blue-collar artisans and workers competed in cities and in factory towns in New England, the Middle Atlantic region, the South, the Midwest, and along the Pacific coast.

The five major factors that shaped the growth of American cricket prior to 1861 continued to influence the sport's development after the war. However, their cumulative effect did not match that of the prewar period. A proper understanding of postwar American cricket requires an analysis of the impact of personal mobility, the press, intercity competition, conventions, and special all-star and international matches. A review of each of these topics suggests both the difficulties faced by American cricket and its modest standing as of the early 1870s.

The continuing migration of British officials, businessmen, and skilled craftsmen to the United States after the war prevented cricket from dying out in areas where clubs had existed before 1861. Fresh blood from England reinvigorated both white- and blue-collar organizations. In San Francisco the California Cricket Club, founded in 1867, met in the same rooms as the British Benevolent Society, and its president was the British consul, William Lane Booker.[51] In Trenton, New Jersey, potters from Staffordshire, England, were prominent in that city's industrial and recreational life. They formed lodges affiliated with the Sons of St. George and organized cricket clubs to secure and strengthen their ethnic identity, even as they also stimulated interest in cricket among the natives in New Jersey's capital throughout the 1860s and 1870s. Their promotion of the sport in Trenton repeated the earlier contribution of English craftsmen in Newark before the war.[52]

The national sporting weeklies and the daily newspapers continued to editorialize on the virtues of cricket, but they decreased their coverage of contests as the game's popularity waned. In reporting an 1865 feature match between the St. George and Philadelphia elevens, *Wilkes' Spirit* expressed admiration for the "beautiful sight" and noted "how beneficial to health" these matches were. A Philadelphia journal declared that cricket was "an educator. It makes men appreciate the value of muscle and nerve, a clear eye, and great physical endurance, and it also gives both players and spectators precious days in the vital open air."[53] Still, most journalists ignored the game or gave it minimal attention. Before the war *Wilkes' Spirit* provided detailed accounts of contests, but in 1868 it explained that it had discontinued that practice because "a long and professional report of cricket, filled with the technicalities of the game, cannot be of any interest to any save the immediate players."[54]

Henry Chadwick and Frank Queen continued to admire cricket, but they also realized that it no longer merited feature stories in their publications. Both remained extremely critical of the St. George club for what they considered its abuse of the press. When the men of St. George sponsored the 1868 all-England visit to New York City, they tried to woo those they had snubbed before, but the *Clipper,* at least, was not impressed. It noted that the club had "heretofore paid very little attention to the press in its endeavors to give correct reports of matches, but on this occasion was very obsequious when it became a matter of dollars and cents."[55] Club officials in Boston, Philadelphia, and other cities enjoyed better relations with sportswriters, but in general only the major intercity matches and especially the visits of English teams received much notice in the newspapers.

Intercity competition excited cricket followers after 1865, even though there was no official or even informal championship system comparable to that of baseball. While newspapers sometimes referred to Philadelphia's Young America club as the champions of the United States, the *Clipper* noted that no such title was recognized in cricket.[56] Still, cricket fans eagerly awaited the contests between the Dragon Slayers of the St. George club and the leading elevens of Philadelphia. The Boston Cricket Club also toured the Middle Atlantic region and hosted sides from New York City and Philadelphia. In 1867 the *Clipper* commented rather optimistically that, "judging by the number of matches which have of late taken place and the unusually large attendance of spectators, the national game of England is regaining something of the popularity which it enjoyed in this country in former years."[57] The lesser-known clubs of the Midwest and the South also arranged contests with rivals from neighboring towns.[58]

By the late 1860s many cricketers realized that their sport needed state, regional, or national associations that would institute reforms and promote the game across the United States. In 1867 Philadelphia's Olympic club issued a call and a plea for a gathering of delegates who would act to perpetuate a pastime that "now is at such a low ebb, and in danger of being numbered among the 'lost arts.'" The announcement proposed a rule for a forfeit if a side appeared late for a match and also suggested a curb on lavish entertainments. Delegates from at least ten clubs in Washington, D.C., New Jersey, and Pennsylvania met in Philadelphia to found the American Cricketers' Convention. They elected officers and drafted a constitution and bylaws but did not seem to have accomplished anything else. Indeed, there is no further record of the organization's meetings or its activities.[59] Small groups of sportsmen continued to meet periodically to select sides for special all-star and international matches, but all efforts to form a regular cricket association failed before 1878.[60]

The organizers of special events hoped that they would inaugurate a revival of American cricket, but instead they yielded only modest gains. Not surprisingly, the feature attractions were most successful in Philadelphia. In 1865 a select eleven from that city defeated an all-star New York City side in a benefit game that honored the retiring veteran Tom Senior. The *Clipper* described it as a victory for Americans over the British. During the next few years the Young America club (all native amateurs) played a series of contests against select English resident elevens that included a few professionals. These matches at Germantown attracted fashionable and sizable crowds and were highlights of both the social and athletic seasons in Philadelphia.[61]

American cricketers renewed international challenges after the war, hoping that matches between American and Canadian or English elevens would prove as popular as they once were. In 1865 a Bostonian welcomed the impending revival of the United States versus Canada series, which had been suspended since 1860: "Stir up the cricketers, East and West, and make them appreciate the great importance of these matches. They will eventually make the game a national one here, and then the time will come when we shall be able to send our 'eleven' over the water fit to contend with the Old World for supremacy in cricket."[62] The United States team (with only ten men) won that low-scoring encounter by one wicket. Unfortunately, cricketers on both sides of the border were unable to arrange another match until 1879, although it is not clear whether lack of interest or (more probably) differences over selection of sides led to the long interregnum.[63] Notwithstanding this lack of formal North American competition, several groups of American and Canadian cricketers did arrange interclub games. In 1866 the Boston Cricket Club played five matches against teams in the British Maritime Provinces, while two years later a Canadian military eleven visited New York City. Out on the West Coast, in 1869, a

California club split two matches with a select side from Victoria, British Columbia.[64]

Postwar cricket's major events were the visits by all-star squads from England. Canadian and American enthusiasts recalled the success of the 1859 all-England tour and arranged another sporting excursion in 1868. Edgar Willsher of Maidstone, Kent, contracted to bring a professional eleven to North America that autumn to play six matches in Canada and the United States. Each of his players received $250 in gold and $7.50 per day plus all travel expenses. To increase excitement and income, the promoters planned a few baseball games between the Englishmen and the Americans, with the visitors pocketing one-third of the gate money from the novel contests. New York's St. George club assumed half of the liability for the events in the United States, with the other half the responsibility of the Philadelphia, Germantown, and Young America organizations.[65]

The idea of a transatlantic cricket series stirred great excitement in Philadelphia but got a mixed reaction in the New York City vicinity. In the former, promoters tried to court the baseball fraternity when they advertised the international match at an Athletics-Atlantics contest,[66] but in the latter sentiment was divided because of the sport's lack of popularity, dislike for the sponsoring Dragon Slayers, and doubts about the propriety of subsidizing a group of foreign professional athletes. While the daily press and the *Spirit* gave modest support and coverage to the matches, the *Clipper* blasted the arrangements. Frank Queen's editorials attacked the idea of paying English professionals to visit the United States when American sportsmen who toured Britain received no pay and no expense money: "Have English cricketers no pride? Are there no *gentlemen* cricketers in England to make us a visit; Or are they all on the 'play and pay' system?" He urged the "hired cricketers" to stay home and after their arrival continued his criticism: "Base Ball so greatly overshadows the game of Cricket in this country that we are surprised at their coming here for speculative purposes."[67]

The Englishmen opened their North American tour in September with a 175–149 one-innings rout of twenty-two English residents of the New York, Willow, and St. George clubs at Hudson City,

New Jersey. Crowds ranged from about 1,500 on the first and third days to around 3,000 on the second. While the size of the audiences was impressive by the standards of American cricket, the numbers fell far short of the average for feature baseball games. More important, the turnout was significantly below that for the 1859 international match at Hoboken. The English eleven next traveled to Montreal, where their match against twenty-two Canadians was called by rain with the English leading 310–28. The visitors continued their march of conquest in Boston with an easy 180–76 victory. As might be expected, the Philadelphians gave the British their greatest test, as twenty-two amateurs (all natives except one) lost by only two wickets in a very close, exciting contest.[68] In a game held at Germantown, a combined amateur and professional twenty-two (including five men born in England) lost to the Englishmen, 181–109. The professionals ended their journey in North America at Hudson City in mid-October with a 143–138 one-innings triumph over a side of twenty-two players selected by the St. George club. In their five victories and one draw they had outscored their opponents 1,113–623.[69]

Since the sponsors of this international series anticipated that many people would be eager to see the English guests try the American national pastime, they scheduled baseball games to follow the cricket contests. Although the British players had no knowledge of or training at baseball, they agreed to play seven matches against American teams. At most of these games natives skilled at the sport joined the English side, but at least two contests matched nine English cricketers against nine American baseball players. The British defeated a group of cricketers from the St. George club who were even more inept at baseball than they were, but they lost to the Unions of Morrisania, the Athletics, and a composite team from the Lowell, Tri-Mountain, and Harvard clubs of Boston. Their experiences apparently taught the English something about the sport, while their efforts may have aided the cause of baseball among American cricketers. However, it is doubtful whether these games had any positive impact upon the fortunes of cricket in the United States. In a letter to the *Brooklyn Union,* "Old Chalk" criticized the English belief "that their national game is the game of games, while ours is but the 'Americanized England Game of Rounders' . . . a sort of mere child's play by the side of 'ye noble game of ye cricket.'" He noted that if baseball was in fact so simple a sport, the English athletes should have been able to play it better after seven or eight practice games, although he gave them credit "for the example they have set the old fogy cricketers in this country in taking up our game as one of their American specialties." Another columnist remarked that the British visitors "have shown our resident English cricketers an example of the absence of that prejudice against every game but their own, which it would be well for the interests of cricket in this country if they would follow."[70]

Four years later another elite group of cricketers from England journeyed across the Atlantic to challenge Canadian and United States sides of twenty-two. This select amateur team of twelve gentlemen, all highly skilled and captained by R. A. Fitzgerald, included the famed W. G. Grace. Although it was not made up of professionals, the team received $600 in gold for each match. The twelve men began their tour with five victories in Canada, and on September 18, 1872, they arrived in Hoboken, New Jersey, to play a New York City squad selected by the St. George club. Several thousand people found their way to an isolated, remote ground that R. A. Fitzgerald described as " 'out of humanity's reach'; approached by unfinished streets, and surrounded by 'carcases' of houses in an advanced stage of non-completion." The English amateurs repeated the one-innings massacre that the 1868 professionals had inflicted on the New Yorkers, winning 249–110.[71]

In 1872, as in 1868, the invading cricketers met their toughest test in the City of Brotherly Love. The Englishmen downed twenty-two determined natives by three wickets in a match that remained exciting to the conclusion. The *Clipper* was more favorably disposed to this English excursion and called the Philadelphia encounter "the only legitimate international match at cricket yet played in America." Fitzgerald was impressed with the crowds that reached about 7,000, which he compared to the throngs that flocked to Epsom Downs on Derby Day. He also was startled by cricket's popularity in Philadelphia: "We were not prepared for the interest taken in the match by the spectators, nor were we aware of the hold that cricket has taken upon the youth of Philadelphia. It was an agreeable surprise."[72] The Englishmen wound up their trip with a draw played on a miserably wet field in Boston. Their hosts actually held the lead as dusk fell on a match limited to one day's play.[73]

An evaluation of the significance of the 1868 and 1872 British sporting adventures yields mixed results for both the cause of American cricket and the future of international athletics. In Hoboken and Philadelphia the matches attracted sizable crowds and turned respectable profits.[74] The contests greatly encouraged the leading cricketers in the East, both natives and resident Englishmen, strengthening their resolve to keep cricket alive in America. Unfortunately the two series did little if anything to popularize cricket among baseball players or the American masses. Fitzgerald doubted that the English tour "advanced the cause of cricket as against baseball," but he believed "that a great stir was made by our advent, and that many returned to cricket who had abandoned it, and that some will take it up who have never tried it." *Bell's Life in London* remarked: "There exists at Philadelphia and at Boston a strong undercurrent of enterprise that will not let the game expire. At New York a healthy English element alone preserves it." That publication advocated additional cricket expeditions to secure the sport among Americans.[75] In truth, even in Philadelphia the excitement of the British visit did not generate much interest in regular interclub competition. A reporter expressed disappointment that, after the immense crowds at the international contests, only about twenty-five people turned out for a game between the Philadelphia and Germantown elevens in late 1872. He concluded sadly: "The task of making cricket popular in this country seems almost impossible of accomplishment. The warmest and most sanguine friends of the game are fast being forced to reluctantly concede this point. It is a healthy and manly sport, has never been degraded as base ball has been, and we should like to see it flourish."[76]

The English visits did lay the foundation for the more frequent cricket contests between England and America during the late nineteenth and early twentieth centuries. In the long run these matches promoted closer cultural ties and more harmony between at least some of the people of the two nations, which would soon become the chief justifications for international sport. As Philadelphia's *Evening Telegraph* noted in praise of the 1872 events, international sport prompted "more genial fellowship, and . . . mutual pleasure and good will." The cricket matches produced "international sympathy in what may be called the amenities of life."[77]

An overview of the status of American cricket between 1865 and 1872 shows some life in each region of the United States but real vitality only in the Philadelphia vicinity. In New England the Massachusetts Cricket Association listed six clubs from Boston, Salem, Chelsea, Needham, and Waltham. A scattering of elevens remained in the factory towns and smaller cities of Maine, New Hampshire, and Connecticut.[78] In the New York City area, only the Dragon Slayers of St. George were in a sound condition, although even that organization experienced sparse attendance on practice days and was forced to relocate several times. The New York Cricket Club struggled through the 1860s before it finally expired in 1871, and only a few more Manhattan and Brooklyn outfits survived.[79] Across the Hudson, New Jersey cricket did not display the enthusiasm of the prewar period, but there were a few clubs that played in Newark, Paterson, Trenton, Jersey City, Belleville, Lambertville, and Orange.[80]

The English national game prospered in Philadelphia after the war, especially among the city's elite, who patronized the four major associations—the Philadelphia, Young America, Germantown, and Merion clubs. The sport also retained some following among the region's English factory workers as well as students at a few schools and colleges, especially Haverford and the University of Pennsylvania. However, the rise of baseball diminished cricket's appeal among the Philadelphia masses, and the number of minor elevens dropped well below the prewar level.[81] The chief concerns among the elite associations involved increasing membership and maintaining proper grounds. The Philadelphia Cricket Club experienced more difficulty than its rivals in both areas, and in 1872 it finally abandoned its field in Camden and agreed to share time and expenses at the Germantown club ground at Nicetown.[82] The Young America club continued to restrict its rolls to natives and to prohibit outsiders from competing on its first eleven, which was dominated by the Newhall family. Its pitch was at Turnpike Bridge during the war, and later it also shared the facilities at Nicetown.

During these years Charles Cadwalader launched a reorganization of the Germantown club, which moved to the estate of Henry Pratt McKean. In 1867 the club listed 235 junior and senior members. West Philadelphians founded the Merion Cricket Club in the fall of 1865, and the following April a majority of members defeated a move by one faction to switch to baseball. The cricketers opened play near the Wynne Wood station on the Pennsylvania Central Railroad, on a typical pitch where "Proper" Philadelphians could emulate the English. The *Spirit* noted that "in Philadelphia cricket is the favorite pastime with the fashionable world, the ladies of the Quaker City especially taking a great interest in it. . . . the attendance is always of the most distinguished character, the carriages of the wealthier classes surrounding the field, and the leading belles of the city crowding the reception-rooms of the club-houses." It further advised "any English cricketer who wishes to revive some of his youthful recollections" to go to Germantown "to make him imagine he is once more witnessing an Eton and Harrow, or an Oxford and Cambridge match at Lord's ground."[83]

While baseball was invading practically every corner of America during the late 1860s, there were pockets of support for cricket in the South, Midwest, and Far West. Below the Mason-Dixon line the English game survived in Baltimore, Washington, D.C., New Orleans, and St. Louis. Cricketers pitched wickets in Chicago, Detroit, Cincinnati, Cleveland, Indianapolis, Louisville, and as far west as the San Francisco Bay area. British residents and American enthusiasts were not always able to maintain prewar levels of interest, but they did prevent cricket from being wiped out completely by the tidal wave of baseball.[84] As the *Clipper* stated in 1866, "Notwithstanding the general merging of cricket clubs into baseball organizations throughout the country, there are still some to be found who remain true to their first love."[85]

NOTES

1. *Newark Daily Advertiser,* October 7, 1865.

2. *Philadelphia Sunday Mercury,* September 30, 1866.

3. *Philadelphia Sunday Mercury,* March 11, 1866; *Clipper* 14 (December 22, 1866): 291.

4. *Wilkes' Spirit* 12 (April 29, 1865): 132; *Philadelphia Public Ledger and Transcript,* May 12, 1865.

5. *Clipper* 13 (May 27, 1865): 50; (August 12, 1865): 138; 16 September 5, 1868): 173; *Philadelphia Sunday Mercury*, March 22, 1868.

6. *Clipper* 16 (May 16, 1868): 45; 17 (March 19, 1870): 380; *Philadelphia Sunday Mercury*, October 18, 1868; October 3, 1869.

7. See *Philadelphia Sunday Mercury*, March 31, 1867.

8. *Clipper* 14 (August 25, 1866): 156.

9. *Wilkes' Spirit* 14 (July 7, 1866): 296; *Philadelphia Sunday Mercury*, March 18, 1866; *American Chronicle* 1 (June 4, 1868): 180.

10. *Philadelphia Sunday Mercury*, August 25, 1867; *Newark Daily Advertiser*, May 27, 1868.

11. *Newark Daily Advertiser*, August 7, 1867.

12. *Clipper* 14 (November 10, 1866): 242; (March 23, 1867): 394.

13. *Clipper* 14 (August 18, 1866): 146; *Newark Daily Advertiser*, August 6, 1867.

14. Adrian C. Anson, *A Ball Player's Career* (Chicago, 1900), 37–44.

15. *Clipper* 15 (August 3, 1867): 131; (August 24, 1867): 157; *Wilkes' Spirit* 16 (July 7, 1867): 294; (July 14, 1867): 310; 17 (October 12, 1867): 147; (October 19, 1867): 167; (October 26, 1867): 193; (November 16, 1867): 243. See also *Clipper* 13 (October 7, 1865): 204; 14 (September 22, 1866): 189; 16 (May 30, 1868): 59; (June 27, 1868): 91; *Wilkes' Spirit* 13 (September 30, 1865): 75; (October 21, 1865): 118, 119; 18 (March 21, 1868): 73; (June 29, 1868): 327; *Spirit* 29 (August 24, 1868): 7; (August 31, 1868): 27; (September 28, 1868): 108; *Ball Player's Chronicle*, October 31, 1867.

16. *Clipper* 18 (September 24, 1870): 194; *Chicago Tribune*, September 17, 1870.

17. Quoted in *Ball Players' Chronicle*, August 8, October 31, 1867.

18. *Chicago Tribune*, November 7, 1868.

19. *Chicago Tribune*, July 29, September 1, October 2, 8, 13, 24, November 7, 25, 1869. See also *Philadelphia Sunday Mercury*, August 2, 1868; October 17, 1869; *Wilkes' Spirit* 14 (May 26, 1866): 198.

20. *Chicago Tribune*, January 23, February 18, March 13, 22, 27, 30, April 20, 30, May 14, 27, 1870; *Spirit* 21 (October 9, 1869): 119; 22 (April 23, 1870): 154; Stephen Freedman, "The Baseball Fad in Chicago, 1865–1870: An Exploration of the Role of Sport in the Nineteenth-Century City," *Journal of Sport History* 5 (Summer 1978): 42–64; *Clipper* 17 (October 16, 1869): 219; (October 30, 1869): 237.

21. *Spirit* 22 (July 9, 1870): 324. For reports on games played, see *Chicago Tribune*, July 6–7, 12, 24, 26–27, August 2, 6, 11, 1870.

22. *Chicago Tribune*, August 31, September 8, 10, 1870; *Spirit* 23 (September 17, 1870): 69.

23. *Chicago Tribune,* September 24–25, 27–28, October 14, November 2, 16, 1870; Greg Lee Carter, "Baseball in Saint Louis, 1867–1875: An Historical Case Study in Civic Pride," *Missouri Historical Society Bulletin* 21 (July 1875): 253–63; *Clipper* 18 (October 29, 1870): 237.

24. *Wilkes' Spirit* 16 (July 27, 1867): 407; Albert G. Spalding, *America's National Game* (New York, 1911), 103–12.

25. Quoted in *Spirit* 21 (September 4, 1869): 39. For more on club tours, see *Wilkes' Spirit* 12 (June 24, 1865): 259; (August 5, 1865): 365; (August 12, 1865): 380; 13 (September 9, 1865): 19, 20; (September 16, 1865): 45; (September 23, 1865): 54; (September 30, 1865): 75; (October 7, 1865): 86; (October 14, 1865): 102; (October 21, 1865): 119; (October 28, 1865): 140; (November 4, 1865): 147; 14 (June 9, 1866): 230, 231; (July 7, 1866): 294; (July 14, 1866): 310; (August 4, 1866): 364; 15 (September 19, 1866): 68; 16 (June 15, 1867): 285; (June 22, 1867): 307; (July 20, 1867): 388; (July 27, 1867): 407; (August 3, 1867): 427; (August 31, 1867): 433; 18 (June 6, 1868): 273; (June 13, 1868): 299; (June 20, 1868): 316, 317; (July 4, 1868): 355, 356; (July 11, 1868): 376; *Clipper* 13 (July 29, 1865): 123; 14 (September 29, 1866): 195; 15 (June 22, 1867): 84, 85; (June 29, 1867): 93; (July 27, 1867): 123; (August 31, 1867): 162, 164; (September 7, 1867): 171, 173; (September 14, 1867): 179; (September 28, 1867): 194, 196; (October 12, 1867): 213; (November 2, 1867): 236; (February 8, 1868): 347; 16 (June 13, 1868): 75; (June 20, 1868): 83; (June 27, 1868): 91; (July 5, 1868): 99, 101; (July 11, 1868): 111; (July 18, 1868): 114; (August 8, 1868): 139; (September 5, 1868): 173; 17 (August 28, 1869): 163; (January 8, 1870): 315; (January 15, 1870): 325.

26. See Robert Knight Barney, "Of Rails and Red Stockings: Episodes in the Expansion of the 'National Pastime' in the American West," *Journal of the West* 17 (July 1978): 61–70; Brian McGinty, "The Old Ball Game," *Pacific Historian* 25 (Spring 1981): 13–25.

27. *Clipper* 13 (November 11, 1865): 242; 14 (August 11, 1866): 140; (October 6, 1866): 202. For postwar baseball in Virginia, see W. Harrison Daniel, " 'The Rage' in the Hill City: The Beginnings of Baseball in Lynchburg," *Virginia Cavalcade* 28 (Spring 1979): 186–91.

28. *Clipper* 14 (July 14, 1866): 107–8.

29. *Wilkes' Spirit* 16 (July 27, 1867): 407.

30. *Philadelphia Sunday Mercury,* June 14, 1868.

31. Quoted in *Clipper* 17 (July 17, 1869): 115.

32. *Spirit* 21 (December 18, 1869): 281, 283; (January 8, 1870): 331.

33. *Clipper* 14 (December 1, 1866): 266.

34. *Clipper* 14 (December 22, 1866): 290; *Ball Players' Chronicle,* July 11, 1867.

35. *Clipper* 15 (December 21, 1867): 291.

36. *Clipper* 14 (December 1, 1866): 220. See also *Ball Players' Chronicle,* November 28, 1867.

37. The number of clubs represented at the annual conventions had increased to nearly 350 before the new system of state delegates was instituted. See Harold Seymour, *Baseball: The Early Years* (New York, 1960), 45–46.

38. See, for example, Aaron B. Champion's call for an Ohio state association in *Ball Players' Chronicle,* August 29, 1867.

39. *Philadelphia Sunday Mercury,* October 20, 1867; *Clipper* 18 (November 19, 1870): 258, 260. See also *Philadelphia Sunday Mercury,* September 30, 1866; October 25, 1868; November 21, 1869; *Clipper* 13 (November 11, 1865): 242; (December 23, 1865): 290; (April 7, 1866): 412; 14 (June 16, 1866): 75; (January 5, 1867): 308; (March 9, 1867): 378; (March 23, 1867): 395; (March 30, 1867): 405; (April 6, 1867): 413; 15 (May 18, 1867): 45; (August 31, 1867): 162; (September 7, 1867): 173; (October 26, 1867): 227; (November 16, 1867): 251; (November 23, 1867): 261; (March 21, 1868): 395; 16 (April 25, 1868): 18; (May 9, 1868): 35; (September 19, 1868): 187; (November 21, 1868): 258; *Wilkes' Spirit* 14 (March 24, 1866): 55; (April 7, 1866): 85; 15 (December 8, 1866): 236; 16 (May 22, 1867): 209; (July 13, 1867): 367; *Newark Daily Advertiser,* November 7, 1868; November 10, 1870.

40. *Clipper* 15 (December 21, 1867): 291.

41. "Report of a Delegate of the Pythians to the Pennsylvania State Convention," October 18, 1867, American Negro Historical Society Papers, Leon Gardner Collection, Historical Society of Pennsylvania; *Philadelphia Sunday Mercury,* October 20, 1867.

42. *Clipper* 18 (November 19, 1870): 258; (November 26, 1870): 266. See also *Spirit* 23 (November 19, 1870): 212.

43. *Wilkes' Spirit* 15 (September 29, 1866): 68.

44. *Clipper* 15 (June 29, 1867): 91. See also *Clipper* 13 (February 18, 1865): 344; 15 (June 15, 1867): 75; *Wilkes' Spirit* 15 (September 8, 1866): 29; James D'Wolf Lovett, *Old Boston Boys and the Games They Played* (Boston, 1907), 149–50.

45. *Wilkes' Spirit* 14 (August 4, 1866): 364; 15 (September 22, 1866): 60; *Newark Daily Journal,* May 30, 1866; *Newark Daily Advertiser,* October 12, 1865.

46. *Clipper* 15 (December 21, 1867): 291.

47. For more on American baseball missionaries after 1872, see David Voigt, *America through Baseball* (Chicago, 1976), 92–105; Peter Levine, *A. G. Spalding and the Rise of Baseball* (New York, 1985), 97–109.

48. *Philadelphia Sunday Mercury,* March 10, 1867.

49. *Clipper* 17 (August 14, 1869): 149; *Spirit* 22 (July 9, 1870): 323.

50. *Clipper* 14 (January 12, 1867): 315; 17 (June 26, 1869): 93; (August 14, 1869): 149; *Wilkes' Spirit* 17 (October 19, 1867): 167.

51. Roberta J. Park, "British Sports and Pastimes in San Francisco, 1848–1900," *British Journal of Sports History* 1 (December 1984): 304.

52. Derek Benning, "The Emigrant Staffordshire Potters and Their Influence on the Recreative Patterns of Trenton, New Jersey, in the Nineteenth Century" (paper read at the Geographical Perspectives on Sport conference, University of Birmingham, July 7, 1983).

53. *Wilkes' Spirit* 12 (July 8, 1865): 301; newspaper clipping on the 1872 international match between the English twelve and the Philadelphia twenty-two, Chronicles of the Merion Cricket Club, 1865–1878, Scrapbook, Historical Society of Pennsylvania.

54. *Wilkes' Spirit* 18 (July 18, 1868): 397.

55. *Clipper* 16 (September 26, 1868): 199; *American Chronicle* 1 (July 23, 1868): 262.

56. *Clipper* 14 (October 13, 1866): 212.

57. *Clipper* 15 (September 7, 1867): 171.

58. *Wilkes' Spirit* 12 (July 1, 1865): 285; 13 (September 2, 1865): 13; (September 23, 1865): 55; (October 28, 1865): 140; 14 (July 21, 1866): 331; (July 28, 1866): 341; (August 25, 1866): 1866): 405; *Clipper* 14 (October 6, 1866): 203; (October 13, 1866): 212; (November 11, 1866): 242.

59. *Clipper* 15 (April 27, 1867): 20; (May 18, 1867): 43; (June 1, 1867): 59; *Philadelphia Sunday Mercury,* April 14, 1867; *Ball Players' Chronicle,* June 20, 1867; *Wilkes' Spirit* 16 (June 29, 1867): 327.

60. In 1869 a correspondent to Philadelphia's *Sunday Mercury* (December 12, 1869) called for a Pennsylvania state organization, and three years later in Philadelphia, delegates from the Germantown, Young America, Philadelphia, Merion, and Wakefield clubs convened to "simplify the game, shorten the time of playing, and make [cricket] suited to American business habits." The group approved proposals to determine the winner of a match when two innings could not be completed and to impose penalties for lateness. It called for an association of Philadelphia cricket clubs and a United States general convention. See a related newspaper clipping in a cricket scrapbook, C. Christopher Morris Cricket Library, Haverford College.

61. *Clipper* 13 (July 1, 1865): 92; 17 (October 2, 1869): 205; (October 30, 1869): 237; 18 (October 22, 1870): 226; *Spirit* 21 (September 25, 1869): 84; 23 (October 22, 1870): 145; *Philadelphia Sunday Mercury,* September 26, 1869.

62. J.S.B. to the editor, *Wilkes' Spirit* 12 (July 15, 1865): 317.

63. John I. Marder, *The International Series: The Story of the United States versus Canada at Cricket* (London, 1968), 67–73. The matches were played annually from 1879 to 1912 (except for 1887, 1889, and 1910), and a new series began in 1963.

64. *Clipper* 14 (August 25, 1866): 154–55; 16 (August 1, 1868): 131; (August 8, 1868): 143; 17 (May 15, 1869): 45; *Wilkes' Spirit* 15 (September 8, 1866): 18; 18 (July 18, 1868): 397; Park, "British Sports and Pastimes," 304.

65. *Official Report of the International Cricket Fetes at Philadelphia in 1868 and 1872* (Philadelphia, 1873), 3–4.

66. *Philadelphia Sunday Mercury,* August 23, 30, September 6, 1868.

67. *Clipper* 16 (May 16, 1868): 43; (August 29, 1868): 162; (September 19, 1868): 191; (September 26, 1868): 194.

68. *Clipper* 16 (October 17, 1868): 221.

69. This summary was compiled from *Clipper* 16 (September 26, 1868): 194; (October 3, 1868): 199, 202; (October 10, 1868): 210; (October 17, 1868): 221; (October 24, 1868): 227; *Spirit* 19 (September 19, 1868): 69; (October 3, 1868): 100; (October 10, 1868): 122; *New York Daily Tribune,* September 17–19, 1868; *New York Herald,* September 17–19, 1868; *New York Times,* September 17–19, 1868; *Philadelphia Sunday Mercury,* October 11, 18, 25, November 1, 1868; Chronicles of the Merion Cricket Club, 1865–1878; John A. Lester, ed., *A Century of Philadelphia Cricket* (Philadelphia, 1951), 34–36.

70. Newspaper clippings, Henry Chadwick's scrapbooks, vol. 1, Albert G. Spalding Collection, New York Public Library. For accounts of these international baseball matches, see *Spirit* 19 (October 3, 1868): 100; *Clipper* 16 (September 26, 1868): 199; (October 10, 1868): 213; (October 24, 1868): 227; (October 31, 1868): 237; *New York Herald,* September 19, 1868; *New York Times,* September 19, 1868; *Philadelphia Sunday Mercury,* October 18, 1868; *Philadelphia Public Ledger,* October 13, 1868.

71. R. A. Fitzgerald, *Wickets in the West: Or, The Twelve in America* (London, 1873), 209–10, 219–23. See also Lester, *Philadelphia Cricket,* 36–41; *Spirit* 27 (September 21, 1872): 81; *Clipper* 20 (September 21, 1872): 197; newspaper clippings in Satterthwaite scrapbooks, New Jersey Historical Society.

72. Fitzgerald, *Wickets in the West,* 264. See also *Chadwick's American Cricket Manual* (New York, 1873), 77; William H. Castle Scrapbooks, C. Christopher Morris Cricket Library, Haverford College.

73. Fitzgerald, *Wickets in the West,* 284.

74. The Philadelphia sponsoring clubs earned $2,550 and $1,500 for the 1868 and 1872 events, respectively. Both the *Clipper* and the *Spirit*

considered the 1868 Hudson City matches to be financial failures, but it is probable that the St. George club made at least a small profit. See *Official Report,* 3–4, 9; *Clipper* 16 (September 26, 1868): 194; *Spirit* 20 (March 6, 1969): 36. In 1872 the Dragon Slayers earned $877.39 from the Hoboken match, according to the club treasurer's report. See the St. George Cricket Club's annual reports for 1872 and 1873, Satterthwaite scrapbooks.

75. Fitzgerald, *Wickets in the West,* 302, 331–32 (reprinted from *Bell's Life in London*).

76. Newspaper clipping, undated, in a cricket scrapbook, C. Christopher Morris Cricket Library, Haverford College.

77. Quoted in the *Official Hand-Book for the International Cricket Fete, at Philadelphia, 1872* (Philadelphia, 1872).

78. *American Chronicle* 1 (March 19, 1868): 92; *Chadwick's Cricket Manual,* 83–104.

79. The migration of the St. George club from Hoboken to Bergen Heights (Hudson City), New Jersey, in 1867 and then back to Hoboken in 1871 is recounted in Satterthwaite scrapbooks. For more on New York City cricket during this period, see *Clipper* 12 (March 18, 1865): 386; (April 1, 1865): 402; 13 (May 6, 1865): 27; 14 (December 22, 1866): 291; 15 (April 20, 1867): 10; (April 27, 1867): 20; (May 4, 1867): 28; (August 10, 1867): 141; 16 (April 11, 1868): 2; *Wilkes' Spirit* 12 (April 8, 1865): 85; 14 (April 7, 1866): 84; *Spirit* 24 (April 15, 1871): 132; *Philadelphia Sunday Mercury,* February 11, 1866; March 31, 1867; *Chadwick's Cricket Manual,* 83; *Ball Players' Chronicle,* December 26, 1867; *American Chronicle* 1 (February 13, 1868): 49; Chadwick's scrapbooks, vol. 20; *New York Times,* July 28, 1871.

80. *Newark Daily Journal,* May 5, 1866; *Newark Daily Advertiser,* May 8, 10, 27, 29, July 31, August 1, 29, 1867; June 23, July 13, 1868; May 8, August 5, 7, October 8, 1869; May 16, 1870; *Wilkes' Spirit* 14 (April 21, 1866): 116; (May 19, 1866): 179; (June 23, 1866): 263; 16 (June 8, 1867): 277.

81. *Clipper* 13 (July 1, 1865): 92; (August 5, 1865): 131; *Wilkes' Spirit* 14 (May 26, 1866): 198; Haverford College Cricket Club Record Book, 1864–1921, C. Christopher Morris Cricket Library, Haverford College.

82. For detailed complaints about lack of attendance on practice days, members who did not pay dues, and problems with the Camden playing field, see the Minutes of the Philadelphia Cricket Club, vol. 2, 1865–79, Historical Society of Pennsylvania. See also Horace Mather Lippincott, *A History of the Philadelphia Cricket Club, 1854–1954* (n.p., 1954).

83. *Spirit* 23 (October 22, 1870): 151. See also *Philadelphia Sunday Mercury,* April 18, 1869; George M. Newhall, "The Cricket Grounds of Germantown and a Plea for the Game," *Site and Relic Society of Germantown Historical Addresses* (Germantown, 1910), 184–90; *The Merion Cricket Club, 1865–1965* (n.p., 1965); J. Thomas Jable, "Latter-day Cultural Imperialists: The British Influence on the Establishment of Cricket in Philadelphia, 1842–72," in J. A. Mangan, ed., *Pleasure, Profit, Proselytism: British Culture and Sport at Home and Abroad* (London, 1988), 73–98; scorebooks for the Germantown club are in the C. Christopher Morris Cricket Library, Haverford College.

84. *American Chronicle* 1 (March 19, 1868): 92; *Wilkes' Spirit* 12 (August 26, 1865): 403; 13 (February 24, 1866): 413; 14 (April 7, 1866): 84–85; (May 19, 1866): 179; (June 16, 1866): 247; (July 21, 1866): 331, 341; (August 25, 1866): 405; 18 (April 4, 1868): 100; *Clipper* 18 (September 3, 1870): 173; Chadwick's scrapbooks, vol. 20, p. 1.

85. *Clipper* 14 (September 15, 1866): 180.

CHAPTER

10

Baseball in Transition

BASEBALL'S phenomenal surge in popularity during the half decade following the Civil War generated a host of problems for the national game. Its startling success forced clubs, state organizations, and the National Association of Base Ball Players to adjust to new conditions and face new issues. Feature contests for local, state, regional, and even national championships stimulated mass excitement but also brought increased commercialism, professionalism, gambling, and crowd disorders, along with frequent hints of corruption involving betting rings and the bribery of players. While many lamented the passing of the old (more innocent) order of the prewar years, others proposed a variety of reforms to cure the ills of baseball. Despite the efforts of those who wished to retain the simplicity and idealism of the amateur era, baseball's future clearly belonged to commercialism and professionalism. The new sport was fast becoming a big business, tied to the booming economies and political machines of urban America in the Gilded Age.

With the advent of championship contests, commercialism, and professionalism—and their accompanying evils—came a backlash of sentiment against baseball. Parents worried about the influence of the new sport on their children. A subscriber to the *Cleveland Leader* attacked that newspaper for printing stories about "a pack of lazy devils going round the country playing ball for money" and sarcastically suggested that it "may as well crack up dog fights, bull fights, bull baiting, and 'seven up' for money, as professional baseball." A *Chicago Tribune* editorial, written partly in jest, despaired that baseball often led to "prevarication, deception, falsification, story-telling, backbiting, slandering, evil-speaking, and all untruthfulness." This conclusion was reached after a season of publishing the results of games between Chicago's amateur, junior, and boys' teams. The captains came from widely differing segments of Chicago society, but "each thought his position fully equal to that of the Superintendent of Police; each one thought Jim Wood [captain of the White Stockings] the greatest man alive, and each one damned the rival Captain with an exuberance and affluence of blasphemy."[1]

There is considerable evidence that many businessmen and journalists remained deeply suspicious of the compatibility of baseball and commercial, industrial, or professional careers. According to the secretary of the Irvington, New Jersey, club, "the invariable question put to young men applying for situations in New York is, whether they are members of ball clubs. If they answer in the affirmative, they are told their services will not be needed." The same was true in Philadelphia. And a Chicagoan stated that some players used fictitious names, fearing that their bosses might discharge them if it became known that they participated in baseball. He and others blamed the city's lack of a first-class nine on the prejudice of businessmen.[2] Catholic groups and other organizations in St. Louis encouraged Sunday ball play, but according to Henry Chadwick, baseball on the Sabbath worked "greatly against the interests of the game in the West," presumably because it offended the Protestant establishment. He also chastised businessmen for "not allowing their employees some time during one week day for healthy relaxation . . . as our business men of the North now do by closing up their stores at 3PM on Saturdays." A member of the Union club of St. Louis wrote in 1868: "We have struggled hard here in the last two years to get the support of the press and the mercantile community, and have met with much discouragement. The papers generally have taken no interest in us, and the business men have almost altogether frowned us down."[3]

Many men of influence supported baseball playing in moderation but warned against excessive involvement that could distract a person from the practical obligations of life. One Philadelphia employer appealed to young men to consider "whether they have not other duties devolving upon them of more importance concerning the future than the indulgence of a love of baseball." Few of his employees even bothered to request permission to play ball or watch a contest; they (and his sons) talked about little else save baseball. While he did not object to a "reasonable amount of recreation," he thought that "the matter of base ball is being run in the ground," with "serious injuries to its votaries."[4] When a group of New York merchants met in 1867 to consider the effects of the baseball mania, especially absenteeism and gambling, on their businesses and employees, they concluded that while baseball was an excellent diversion that should be encouraged as a means of physical exercise, "there was a point to which it might be pushed to an injurious excess." In the group's opinion it was "the duty of employers to do what could be done to impose upon [ball playing] a proper restraint."[5] Several daily and weekly newspapers warned against "Base Ball dissipation," and Baltimore and New Haven passed ordinances restricting the sport. Edwin A. Stevens supported the game but nonetheless prohibited major club matches on his grounds at Hoboken. Clearly, the growing enthusiasm for baseball in post–Civil War America was tempered by the problems of an evolving sport and a strong backlash from journalists, businessmen, professionals, and religious leaders.[6]

Championship competition at many levels brought out both the best and the worst in postwar baseball. Club rivalries within cities, states, and regions certainly raised the standard of play and stimulated enthusiasm among players and spectators, but these special contests also produced much ill will and controversy, in part because of the unofficial nature of the titles. Custom dictated that whichever nine won two out of three games from all of its rivals earned a championship. In the absence of any strong governing body to regulate challenges, resolve disputes, and designate a winner, controversies multiplied. By 1867 and 1868 the leading sporting journals were complaining at length of the bad effects of championship encounters. William Meeser, editor of Philadelphia's *Sunday Mercury*, reflected: "The evils growing out of the system of championship contests promised soon to demoralize the game, so much so as to endanger not only its reputation, but its permanency. Instead of legitimate trials of skill between clubs, in which the honor of winning the trophy was alone the incentive to exertion, we had conflicts in which animosities were engendered, gambling was fostered, and from which arose the effort to make ball-playing a regular business occupation." He urged the leading metropolitan clubs to drop their quest for the title of champion but continue their spirited, friendly rivalries.[7] The *Spirit* and Henry Chadwick's *Ball Players' Chronicle* echoed the charges that championship matches promoted discord, excessive commercialism and professionalism, and gambling.[8]

Despite these objections and warnings by journalists, the enthusiasm for championship events kept increasing in villages, towns, and cities across the United States. Ironically, the publicity provided by editorial criticism helped to heighten public excitement over title matches.[9] For example, the 1868 series between the Cincinnati Red Stockings and Buckeye club for the bragging rights to "Porkopolis" created much animosity in that Ohio city. According to the *Spirit,* "the Buckeye Club, ignoring all rules, shipped players from Washington to take part in this game, and even went so far, as stated by Cincinnati journals, as to drug some of the players of the Cincinnati Club and to bribe others."[10] In all fairness it should be stressed that Harry Wright's Red Stockings also recruited a few players from the East, no doubt contributing to the bad feeling as much as his club's victory did.

While a few state and regional associations did attempt to regulate championship play by establishing rules to govern competition, for the most part these efforts failed to reduce or eliminate the problems that plagued title matches. In 1866 the New England association offered a silver ball as the prize for its championship, but a flurry of disputes (especially between the Harvard and Lowell nines) disgusted its officers. The championship system was abolished in March 1868, and the association ordered that the silver ball be melted down and sold. The reigning champion Tri-Mountains gave up the trophy under protest; and the association's treasury was enriched by $19.50.[11] The 1870 meeting of the New Jersey association tabled a resolution that would have established rules for a state championship after hearing arguments "illustrating the ill-feeling and rivalry growing out of championship matters."[12]

Emotions intensified when clubs from rival cities played for the honor of being called the champion club of the United States. The most heated competition during the late 1860s involved the Brooklyn Atlantics, the Philadelphia Athletics, the New York Mutuals, and the Morrisania (Bronx) Unions. A dispute over gate receipts delayed the deciding game of the 1866 Atlantic-Athletic series until 1867. The Atlantics won that contest but then lost the first match of the 1867 series and refused to honor a contract to play the second game, pleading injuries to their leading players.[13] In 1868 Frank Queen offered a gold ball as a prize for the champion club of that year, along with nine gold medals to the best players at each position. He predicted that "the honor of winning the *Clipper Gold Ball* will cause the organizations who are aspirants for the championship honors to put forth extra exertions, and tend to stimulate honorable rivalry among the leading clubs of the country."[14]

Competition for the *Clipper* trophy did not turn out as Queen wished because of the difficulties of designating a winner. The Unions, who upset the Atlantics in 1867, lost their crown in 1868 to the Mutuals. The Athletics had the best overall season record in 1868 but were frustrated in their attempts to gain the title when the Mutuals refused to play a series with them until the following season. Queen withheld the gold ball until September 1869, when he finally awarded it to the Athletics for 1868. Philadelphia's players, fans, and journalists were all convinced that a New York–Brooklyn conspiracy deprived them of a fair chance at the title each of those years.[15] Queen and many others concluded that the NABBP or the top clubs should adopt rules to govern championship matches, "by which all trickery, collusion, and other dishonest practices may be rendered unavailable in the disposition of the title."[16] But the national conventions refused to establish a system to determine a champion for the United States.

Championship matches attracted large crowds throughout the 1860s, and it is not surprising that sporting entrepreneurs and club officials soon realized that spectators would pay to see their favorite nines compete. The commercialization of baseball followed naturally from the long-accepted practice of charging admission fees for popular amusements in general and sporting events (such as horse racing) in particular. There was even precedent for putting a price, ranging from ten to fifteen cents, on ball games—for example, at the 1858 Fashion Race Course New York versus Brooklyn all-star matches, the 1859 all-England cricket contests, the St. George Cricket Club's regular games in 1860, and the benefits held by cricket clubs to reward their professionals—but these were clearly exceptions to the prewar custom of free admission. After 1861, however, promoters translated the commercial potential of the new national game into profits.[17]

During the 1860s there were several ways of establishing a baseball business. The first involved capitalists who enclosed and improved a ground, which they offered rent-free to clubs in exchange for the right to charge an admission fee. William H. Cammeyer inaugurated this practice in 1862 when he drained his winter skating pond for summer baseball and opened the Union Grounds in Brooklyn's eastern district. His success prompted Messrs. Weed and Decker to follow his example. They converted their skating facility into the Capitoline Grounds in Brooklyn's western district in 1864. After the war a few entrepreneurs across the country organized all-star contests, charity events, or tournaments, offering prize money to the participating clubs and charging spectators to see the action.[18] A few clubs, like the Athletics and Olympics of Philadelphia, tried a third method of commercializing baseball when they purchased their own field, built a fence, and set an admission fee for matches.

Proponents of commercialized baseball pointed to several advantages of enclosed fields and admission fees. Chadwick, for example, was alarmed at the disappearance of suitable playgrounds in the cities as the postwar building boom gobbled up empty lots. He urged clubs to acquire a permanent ground and to collect gate receipts on match days to defray the expenses of purchasing and maintaining it. This new system increased the chances that feature contests would be played on a field clear of spectators, with fewer problems with crowd disturbances,[19] and also raised the caliber of competition. In 1868 Philadelphia's *Sunday Mercury* maintained that, "were it not for the admittance fee . . . which goes to sustain both grounds and players, the public would not have the opportunity of witnessing first-class nines contending on well cared for grounds."[20] Finally, commercialism facilitated charity and benefit contests, with all-star and feature club matches raising money for orphans, Southern war refugees, victims of mining disasters, and other needy people.[21]

Charging an admission fee restricted attendance to those who could pay, although people from the poorer classes still came to the grounds and congregated outside the fences. Critics of rowdy spectators applauded that result of commercialism. Chadwick, for one, admitted in 1867 that the twenty-five-cent charge for first-class contests was "not relished by the masses, but by the respectable portion of the community it is regarded as a desirable improvement, as by means of the increased price hundreds of blackguard boys and roughs generally are kept out, while the respectable patrons of the game are afforded better opportunites for enjoying a contest." He also noted "the blasphemy and obscenity of the language used by the hooting asemblage which congregate on the outside and peep through the fence holes at the players."[22] After an unruly mob forced the postponement of an encounter with their arch-rivals from Brooklyn, the Athletics erected a fence and charged a one-dollar fee for an 1866 game against the Atlantics.[23] That city's *Sunday Mercury* praised plans for a new, enclosed park in which "the visitor will not be annoyed by the gratuitous slang of the mob who generally congregate on important matches, and whose phraseology does not grate pleasantly upon polite ears."[24]

In addition to stabilizing club finances, raising the caliber of play, and reducing crowd disorders, commercialism in baseball also stimulated professionalism. Clubs that owned their own field spent a portion of their income to hire players, while others negotiated with park proprietors for a percentage of the gate receipts so they, too, could begin to pay players. (Clubs that collected gate receipts but refrained from paying participants still claimed to be amateur.) Regrettably, the attraction of admission fees offered a powerful incentive for a team to win the opener of a series and then lose the second game in order to increase excitement (and gate receipts) for the deciding third match. In Chadwick's words, "the primary evil of the gate-money system is the temptation it offers for dishonest practices in the way of getting up bogus matches, or of playing games on the 'hippodrome' principle."[25] The tendency of commercialism to foster both professionalism and corruption was clear by the late 1860s, as the leading clubs sought to strengthen their first nines by recruiting—and paying—skilled players.

Despite the NABBP's ban on payment to participants, before and during the Civil War such premier performers as James Creighton and Al Reach accepted some form of compensation, including gifts, jobs, or direct payments. Certain organizations also staged annual benefit contests, with the gate receipts distributed among the contestants. By the mid-1860s the sporting weeklies and daily papers were reporting that several clubs were subsidizing a few players through one means or another.[26] For the remainder of the decade participants and journalists debated the merits of professionalism.

Defenders of the new system justified it on the grounds that ball playing was a legitimate occupation and workers deserved remuneration for their toil. They did not see anything wrong with businessmen or politicians trying to promote their favorite nine or town by retaining athletes. Adrian "Cap" Anson recalled that in Iowa in the late 1860s, "It was generally the custom to import from abroad some player who had made a name for himself . . . and furnish him with a business situation." Anson continued: "So strong was the local pride taken in the success of the team that businessmen were not averse to furnishing such a man with a position when they were informed that it would be for the good of the home organization." A "green country lad" himself, Anson was also a rising star in the village of Marshalltown, as he signed with the Forest City nine of Rockford, Illinois, in 1870 for sixty-six dollars a month.[27]

Albert G. Spalding's account of his decision to accept a "semi-professional position" in baseball is illuminating. A star pitcher for the Forest City team, Spalding was employed at a small salary in a grocery. He recalled that his employer "affected to be quite proud of my efficiency as a pitcher" but "regularly 'docked' me when absent from the store." When he was then approached by a Chicago man, who offered him forty dollars a week to work in a wholesale grocery "with the understanding that my store duties would be nominal, a chance given to play ball frequently, without affecting my salary to reduce it," Spalding found the offer attractive but pondered its meaning and especially its moral aspects. He wondered if he would be "violating at least the spirit of that rule of the National Association . . . that forbade the payment of salaries to players." His mother was distressed at the idea of making "a business of ball playing." However, the president of the Forest City club advised him to accept the offer to join the Chicago Excelsiors, which he did, in 1867. Spalding justified his decision by noting that the NABBP rule was already moot. He did not understand "how it could be right to pay an actor, or a singer, or an instrumentalist for entertaining the public, and wrong to pay a ball player for doing exactly the same thing."[28] Ironically, the following spring the firm that had hired him went bankrupt and Spalding returned to Rockford, this time using his baseball connections to land positions at an insurance office and a newspaper.

By the late 1860s many other players and commentators endorsed this same viewpoint: as long as a player was loyal to his club and avoided gambling or taking bribes to lose a match, he should be free to receive both pay and respect. "A Professional" proclaimed in the columns of Chadwick's *American Chronicle* that a clerk or porter who earned twelve or fifteen dollars a week should be allowed to accept a higher salary for a clerkship that required playing ball for a particular club. He argued that "the rule prohibiting compensation to players is a rule which actually promotes the very evil it is designed to prevent, namely, getting in a class of men in ball matches *who will do anything for pay.*" This professional maintained that as long as he acted honestly he was "just as much entitled to the respect of my companions as the man who plays in the club for exercise and love of the sport only."[29] Chadwick himself endorsed the professional system as long as the players retained their integrity. He applauded the public's willingness to pay twenty-five cents to see professional matches and saw "no reason whatever why a professional ball player should be ashamed of his position, except when he gives way to the temptations offered by betting 'rings' and the gambling fraternity." Chadwick believed that if a player kept "in the honest path of the English cricket professional, he need not blush for his position."[30]

While Anson, Spalding, Chadwick and others came to accept and even welcome professional baseball, others had grave doubts about the new trend. Melvin Adelman correctly points out that some players and club officials initially opposed paying players because they feared that the wealthiest clubs would monopolize the best players and thereby destroy competitive balance. Moreover, most lovers of baseball still thought of the sport as primarily recreational. To them it was a means of escape from business worries, a healthful diversion from the business of life. But professional baseball required a scientific approach, much practice, and an emphasis on victory—all of which would transform baseball into a rigorous discipline and thereby render it unacceptable to those who, raised in a puritanical tradition, were deeply suspicious of turning play into serious work.[31] Philadelphia's *Sunday Mercury* expressed these concerns: "To hear some people talk, one would think that life had no other or higher aims than the frittering away of time in playing ball." Relating the story of a gentleman who refused to allow his son to join a base ball club and instead placed him in a business position, the paper concluded: "We are in favor of exercise, and plenty of it for young men; but we do not want to see them grow up professional ball-players."[32]

In addition to fears about competitive imbalance and excessive seriousness, there were also worries that professionalism would accelerate the disturbing trends toward gambling and corruption that had already appeared among the amateurs. Many observers believed that paid players would inevitably become the tools of gamblers. In 1865 the *Clipper* objected to a match arranged for the benefit of the Atlantics, on the grounds that paying the players made baseball a business instead of recreation, and "by and by, the game . . . will be played according to the regular hippodrome tactics of certain turf parties."[33] The following summer a correspondent to the *Clipper* declared that "a man who makes a *business of playing ball* is not a man to be relied upon in a match where great interests are centered, or on which a large among of money is pending."[34] Col. Thomas Fitzgerald, one of the founders of the Philadelphia Athletics, resigned as club president in 1866 to protest the new policy of hiring players. Editor of the *City Item,* he blasted the club's new officers for picking men who had been repeatedly arrested and confined for drunkenness and rioting. Fitzgerald championed the old amateur, recreational system and quit his club when it embraced the new era of championship contest, commercialism, and professionalism. The Athletics, in turn, expelled Fitzgerald from the club for what the membership viewed as "scurrilous attacks" on the organization.[35]

The advent of professionalism accelerated the trend toward open recruitment of players, as clubs that aspired to championships tried to acquire the best talent. Although lovers of baseball frowned upon this practice, the flagrant raiding of lesser nines by the most powerful teams became commonplace during the late 1860s. An NABBP rule prohibited multiple club memberships and required that a man wait thirty days after he resigned from one club before joining another.[36] While many honored this restriction, others resorted to subterfuge to circumvent it. In 1865 the *Jersey City Daily Times* reported that George Wright played under the name of Cohen for the New York Gothams in a victory over Newburg's Hudson City team while still a member of the Philadelphia Olympics.[37] "Cap" Anson recalled that he once accepted a fifty-dollar offer from a Clinton, Iowa, club to play for them in a game against their arch-rivals from Des Moines. To avoid recognition by the Des Moines players and spectators, he dyed his hair and stained his skin. Unfortunately for young Anson, his father penetrated his disguise, forbade him from going to Clinton, and soundly lectured him. Anson remembered the shame he felt and the hard time he had getting the dye out of his hair and the stain off his skin; he also recalled the fifty dollars he never received.[38]

Violations of the thirty-day rule became a heated issue by 1867, when several clubs acquired new men from other nines and played them immediately in contests that they declared were merely "social" or "exhibition" games as opposed to formal matches. When the Athletics toured New England in June of that year, they took with them Mr. Berry of Philadelphia's Keystone club and Mr. Radcliff of the Camden Unions. Although they received permission from their hosts to play these men, they were blasted by Henry Chadwick for imitating the New York Mutuals and other clubs that evaded the rule. He was concerned that importing outsiders reduced club loyalty as well as solidarity and argued that "the principal attraction in a contest between two clubs arises from the *esprit du corps* which attaches to rival organizations, and which leads them to strive their utmost to develop their club strength in a match, in order to excel their rivals." Chadwick also noted that one of the strongest objections to cricket in the United States was the English custom of having "half a dozen players in a strong club being found among the contesting elevens of half a dozen other clubs, thereby depriving a contest between them of all the interest that would naturally attach to it if it was a *bona fide* trial of skill between regular players of but one club."[39] The *Spirit* criticized these exhibitions as "Speculation Games," played only for the gate, whereby "the public are made to pay the fiddler for the privilege of witnessing a sham dance."[40] However, Philadelphia's *Sunday Mercury* and the *Clipper* defended these "social" contests that included players ineligible for matches under the NABBP rules.[41]

The practice of players jumping from one club to another, which was known as the "revolver" system, had other negative consequences. First, it diminished the opportunity for regular members to compete on their club's first nine. Second, the raiding of certain clubs knocked them out of the ranks of contending nines. In Chadwick's words, "One of the most injurious results of this importing system is the demoralization of native and home talent which is sure to ensue. Promising young players thereby find their ambitious hopes blasted, and their field of promise occupied by strangers; and it very naturally follows that they cease to take an interest in their club, and in many instances in the game itself." He concluded that "in the place of a club having for its main object the encouragement of an enjoyable recreation and an exciting exercise, an organization is created which looks chiefly to the pecuniary results of contests as the principal object in view."[42]

The "revolver" system also hurt teams that would not or could not spend the money to keep their best men. In 1867 the third baseman of the New Jersey Irvingtons accepted a $1,200 clerkship under Boss Tweed and joined New York's (and Tweed's) Mutual club. Despite (or perhaps because of) their success that year, the Irvingtons were decimated by 1868, as six of their starting nine departed for greener pastures, including two to the Cincinnati Buckeyes, one to the Washington Nationals, and three to their arch-rivals, the Mutuals. The Eurekas of Newark suffered similar defections. Several Newark natives starred for the famed Cincinnati Red Stockings during their glory years, 1869–70.[43]

By the late 1860s the leading professional clubs were actively bargaining for the best players, some of whom were pledging their services and accepting money from one organization and then jumping to another. One of the most notorious cases was that of John Radcliff, who played for the Athletics until July 1868, when he switched to the Mutuals. A Philadelphian enticed him back to the Athletics by paying off his New York debts and refunding the one-hundred-dollar bonus the Mutuals had given him. Radcliff signed a contract with the Athletics in January 1869 but then joined the Cincinnati Red Stockings. The Athletics promptly expelled him, but when the Red Stockings decided to drop him as well, he moved back to Philadelphia and accepted money to compete for the Keystones. In the end he quit the Keystones and was readmitted into the Athletics after acknowledging his wrongdoing.[44] Philadelphia's *Sunday Mercury* had urged the Athletics to recruit "native amateur talent" rather than "professional players from rival cities, who cannot be expected to have the welfare of the club at heart as much as our own men." According to that paper, the "revolving" players "go in a gambling spirit for what they can get, caring little for the higher attributes of the ball player." The *Clipper* expressed disgust at the number of players who broke their contracts and asked: "If neither the pledged word or written agreement of players can bind them, can we place any faith in their playing? Would they not be just as liable to sell a game as to sell a club?"[45]

By the spring of 1869 professional baseball had come of age, with at least ten clubs compensating part or all of their first nines through one means or another. In the New York area these clubs included the Mutuals, the Eckfords, the Atlantics, and the Unions; they were joined by the Philadelphia Athletics, the Unions of Lansingburg, New York, and the Baltimore Marylands in the East and by clubs in Chicago, Pittsburgh, Cincinnati, Fort Wayne, and Columbus, all of which experimented with hired players. Earnings from gate receipts and salary probably netted participants on the better nines anywhere from $600 to $1,500 a year.[46]

The professional baseball fever took hold in two prominent midwestern cities, Cincinnati and Chicago. In the former, a local booster and a transplanted New Yorker combined to create the first all-salaried team with players under yearly contracts. The Cincinnati Red Stockings, reorganized in 1867 by Aaron B. Champion and a group of lawyers and businessmen, shared a grounds lease with the city's Union Cricket Club and had a bitter rivalry with the local Buckeye nine. Determined to outshine his competitors, Champion raised $26,000 over two years to improve the grounds and sign players. Thanks to successful raids on several eastern clubs and the Buckeyes, the Red Stockings fielded a team in 1869 that featured many of the best players in the United States.

Top talent did not guarantee success on the field, however. It was up to the manager, Harry Wright, to train the nine that would become baseball's first legendary team. As the son of the cricket professional for New York's St. George club, Wright had been schooled in team sports since his boyhood. Experienced in baseball as well as cricket, he came to Cincinnati after the war to serve as bowler and professional for the Union Cricket Club. Once the baseball mania engulfed the city, however, he concentrated on the more popular pastime and by 1868 was well known for his managerial skills, especially his insistence upon discipline and teamwork. Although Chadwick and others praised his methods, some native easterners resented the tactics of a British-born field captain who was now spearheading a western assault on the East.[47]

Champion's investments and Wright's recruitment and training of his players paid handsome dividends on the field and at the box office. During the 1869 season the Red Stockings demolished their eastern rivals and rolled up victory after victory on extended tours across the country. The final triumphant trip to California climaxed a summer and fall that featured fifty-seven victories, one disputed tie with the Troy (N.Y.) Haymakers, and no defeats. The *Clipper* estimated that the Red Stockings had traveled 10,879 miles by rail and steamboat and had performed before 179,500 spectators.[48] The team began the 1870 campaign with twenty-seven victories before losing an eleven-inning thriller to the Atlantics, 8–7.[49]

The success of the Cincinnati Red Stockings irritated the baseball and commercial communities of Chicago, who despised being second best in the West to the sportsmen of "Porkopolis." In 1868 the hometown Excelsiors failed to win with local talent supplemented by New York imports, and one Chicagoan complained that his city "had no interest in a club virtually from New York State; and even when these men came here they could not uphold the good name of the club, but, by carelessness and dissipation, were beaten on every hand." He suggested a remedy: the consolidation of "six or eight fifth class ball clubs in Chicago" into two "No. 1 clubs."[50] Instead of following that strategy, a new Chicago club began to solicit outsiders in November 1869. The *Chicago Post* poked fun at this scheme: "Of course the players will all be Chicago men; although just now they are all 'visiting' other parts of the world. These gentlemen are to be invited to come 'home,' and are to be paid a sufficient sum to make the invitation effective. Chicago . . . has got the material for the best base ball club in the world. Just now that material is a little 'scattered.' All that is needed is a little judicious 'concentration.'"[51] The eastern press ridiculed the "Garden City's" attempt to capture the national championship, but by the late fall of 1870 the sportswriters were impressed with the success of the White Stockings.[52]

Championship contests, hired players, "revolving," and professional nines aside, there was one unwelcome trend that threatened to destroy early baseball just as it was passing through its adolescence: gambling. Journalists, clergymen, and advocates of Victorian values condemned the widespread wagering on first-class matches, which both reflected and fed the baseball mania of the late 1860s. These critics believed that it was intrinsically immoral to bet on a ball game; that it corrupted an innocent amusement and was the major cause of crowd disorders and bad feeling among clubs. Editorials in dozens of daily and weekly periodicals warned that gambling was tarnishing baseball's reputation and dragging the sport down to the level of boxing, horse racing, or even blood sports such as cock-fighting. In 1868 the *Albany Evening Journal* declared that "the manly and noble sport of ball playing has . . . become perverted to the base uses of gaming. Betting has become a concomitant of the sport, as assuredly as that which attends horse-racing." The next year it remarked that baseball clubs were supposed to be "missionary organizations, preaching the new gospel of health," but now they competed for other purposes that were "unworthy and discreditable." The paper warned that "if the baseball arena is to become a sporting ring . . . then respectable people must cease to give it countenance, and the field will be abandoned, as the trotting course has . . . to blacklegs and sharpers."[53]

In arguing that the "disgraceful disturbances" that marred many matches were not caused by "great partisan feeling," the *Newark Daily Advertiser* pointed to "the sums of money which are staked on the issue by those who make betting a business, and who have no attachment for either club, but examine the good points of each, just as they would those of a race horse."[54] The *New York Times* called for the preservation of baseball "from the contamination which must assuredly ensue if it is to be prostituted into a mere occasion of reckless 'plunging' for professional gamblers, and an invidious form of temptation to its youthful and ardent admirers to commence a 'sporting' career." The paper continued: "Surely, there is scope enough for gentry of a certain class to exercise their vocation in connection with prize fighting, faro saloons, rat killings, sham pedestrians, cock fighting and the like, without corrupting a game designed, and admirably suited, to afford healthful relaxation to our youth of all conditions and circumstances."[55]

For promoters of the national pastime, the greatest threat to the integrity of the sport was the fixing of matches by gamblers and bribed players. In 1865 a special investigating committee of New York's Mutual club accused William Wansley of splitting one hundred dollars with two teammates, Edward Duffy and Thomas Devyr. Devyr admitted that before the contest against the Brooklyn Eckfords, Wansley asked him to join in the conspiracy for thirty dollars. He testified that Wansley said, "We can lose this game without doing the Club any harm, and win the home-and-home game. . . . Now, you ain't got a cent, nor neither has Duffy; you can make this money without any one being a bit the wiser of it." After Wansley assured Devyr that he would not have to do the actual "heaving" of the match himself, the latter agreed. The three men were subsequently expelled from the club but were reinstated in 1867 (Devyr), 1868 (Duffy), and 1870 (Wansley).[56]

While this incident remains the only documented example of a fixed contest during this period, there was much suspicion that many matches might have been lost intentionally. The sporting and daily newspapers of the half decade following the Civil War are filled with speculation that the Atlantics, the Athletics, the Mutuals, and other prominent teams sometimes dropped games to set up a third, deciding contest, which would bring higher gate receipts and more bets. Some people charged that these clubs sold games outright for the benefit of gamblers' rings. But since the outcome of these games was so uncertain, and since it was so difficult to obtain proof of wrongdoing, the extent of corruption was never clear.[57] In a rather sarcastic 1869 editorial the *Clipper* declared: "It cannot be expected that a club can win *every* game; and if they *should* lose a game or two when the odds are the biggest in their favor, it does not *always* follow that the 'thing' was fixed." Admitting that it was impossible to say if all games were fairly contested, the paper jokingly reminded the "croakers" that "base ball players have no ring—*they* play on the square." Of all the opponents of gambling and bribery, however, none was more outspoken or energetic than Henry Chadwick. He supported the honest professional player but conceded that by "making the game a means of livelihood, he becomes a more prominent object for the attack of the blacklegs." Chadwick's solution was "to prohibit betting of large sums in connection with every fairly contested game."[58] Of course, neither the NABBP nor any other organization had the power to stop or control wagering on baseball.

While Chadwick and other journalists condemned the evils of gambling, there were a few commentators who downplayed its supposed ill effects on baseball. In 1868 *Wilkes' Spirit* expressed regret over the damage that "moral sermons" had done to the baseball fraternity.

> What is it that makes base-ball, or any other pastime, popular with all classes? Just this: If one cannot play at it himself, he can bet his money, and thereby enjoy the excitement more keenly than even the players themselves. . . . Is it believed that ten in a hundred of all that now practice or behold this delightful game care a grot whether or not money be staked on its issue? In truth, to deprive it of this feature would be to render it as tame a pastime as pitching buttons to any but the actual players themselves.

In another editorial that journal maintained, "There is no immorality in a bet. . . . it is merely a question of prudence, because money is put at risk."[59] A correspondent ("Old Chalk") to Philadelphia's *Sunday Mercury* could not see the difference "between betting a hundred or even a thousand dollars on a ball match . . . and of entering into stock gambling at the Gold Room or Board of Brokers." He wrote: "The efforts of brokers to 'bull' and 'bear' the market, are no less fraudulent than are the actions of the gamblers in base ball who strive to induce nines to lose games for betting purposes."[60]

By the late 1860s the increasing problems of the new system of commercial and professional baseball forced many sportsmen to reevaluate the latest developments. They expressed dissatisfaction with the escalating expense of player contracts and the growing evidence of "revolving," the spector of gambling and corruption, the loss of playing opportunities for regular club members, inter-club ill will, and an emphasis on championship matches. Club officers and members had to decide whether the gate receipts and fame earned by a paid nine were worth the costs and the headaches, or whether their organization should return to the simpler recreation of early amateur baseball. Philadelphia's *Sunday Dispatch* complained in 1866 that baseball was supposed to be a pastime for young men engaged in sedentary pursuits, but instead "the rivalries which exist between clubs and players soon absorb all the attention of those interested, and those who would like to play an occasional game merely for recreation are precluded from doing so." It added that "all the base ball clubs of any prominence give up their grounds entirely to the first nine, and out of several hundred members they are the only ones who derive any benefit whatever from the game."[61] In 1869 the *Spirit* declared that the tendency of the leading teams to rent private fields "broke up the second nines of first-class clubs, destroyed all social practice, and converted the great clubs into 'great nines.'" The original club members "found that the exhultation attending the success of their particular club did not repay for the abuse thrown at them by the paid members, and they resolved either that they must drop their own names from the list, or the old order of things be again brought about."[62]

Some organizations either resisted the temptations of commercialism and professionalism or briefly flirted with them before returning to the old ways. New York's Knickerbocker club played ball because members loved it, as did that city's Eagles and Empires.[63] The Brooklyn Excelsiors and the Philadelphia Olympics stopped paying players after the war and were satisfied with amateurism. Philadelphia's *Sunday Mercury* applauded their choice, stating: "The salvation of the game depends upon just such organizations. . . . the reprehensible behavior of certain clubs on the ball field is losing the game the support of the very parties whose interest it is most desirable to retain." It was hoped that "a brighter day is dawning, and that the game will be as it was in its infancy—an innocent, healthful means of amusement to thousands who take no interest in other out-door exercises."[64]

In New Jersey, the Newark Eurekas tried the professional system for one season, became disgusted with it, and reorganized a new first nine with amateurs only. In 1868 they paid the price when the Atlantics destroyed them, 45–8; in 1869 they stopped playing regular matches, although they still met for practice. The *Clipper* reported that "the once champion club of New Jersey are now but a shadow of their former greatness," adding that several of their stars "have evidently become disgusted with the huckstering now going on among clubs and players, and given up a pastime which is not as it used to be."[65] By contrast, the Unions of Morrisania, former champions, decided to return to amateurism in 1869. The result was a revival among the old guard, more members, and a stronger treasury. According to the *Clipper*, "those who love the game for the game itself are now the best friends of the club." The *Spirit* reported that "the boys played only to win the games and the sweet smiles of the dames." But apparently one faction wished to return to the "big time," for early in 1870 the Unions announced plans for a new professional nine.[66]

The revolt against professionalism also reached Cincinnati, when first the Buckeyes in 1869 and then the Red Stockings in 1870 dropped the new system. A Buckeye explained: "One year's experience with an imported nine was sufficient; home players were debarred from playing or even practicing, while their pockets were taxed for those whose only interest in the club was their weekly salary. You may rest assured that the Buckeyes will not be troubled with 'revolvers,' who carry their pockets filled with offers from clubs, thereby keeping a club in a 'stew' from the beginning to the end of a season."[67] More surprising, however, was the announcement that the powerful Red Stockings would not hire players for the next campaign. The *Spirit* commented that the "fun and the glory, as well as the wages, all went to the professional nine. The amateurs at Cincinnati had the pleasure of footing the bills and seeing 'Red Stockings' in the newspapers." The victories of the Red Stockings "only made the poor play of the real club at home more glaring by the strong contrast, and thus discouraged the young men and striplings who played upon their home grounds."[68] A vocal minority of the club believed that fielding an amateur squad would better serve the original purposes and true interests of the national game in Cincinnati. Its executive committee, which balked at the prospect of doubling its payroll from its 1870 level of $6,000–8,000, maintained that "the payment of large salaries leads to extravagance, dissipation, and jealousies among the players, and worse than that, such a course would plunge the club into debt, or make too heavy a draw on the members." The decision sparked a stormy meeting at which a majority voted to reinstitute professionalism. The club's officers then quit, but the membership refused to accept their resignations, and in the end no action was taken to renew the existing contracts or sign new players.[69]

Along with the amateur revival among senior clubs, junior, school, and college baseball teams proliferated in 1869 and 1870. Undergraduate ball flourished at Harvard, Yale, Williams, Amherst, Princeton, Fordham, Manhattan, Brown, Virginia, Seton Hall, Columbia, Tufts, Hobart, Hamilton, the U.S. Naval Academy, and many other schools. The Harvard nine was the strongest of that era, defeating nearly all of its amateur opponents as well as several professional clubs while on tour in the East and Midwest. The *New York Times* found college ball playing particularly attractive, observing that while professionals sometimes did not "exert themselves to their utmost to win," this was not the case for college nines, "for the *esprit du corps,* and the natural rivalry between leading colleges to carry off the palm for their *Alma Mater,* must necessarily lead to legitimate efforts to win in every contest."[70]

With professional baseball's problems on the rise, and as more clubs stopped hiring players, the sporting fraternity attempted to define precisely the differences between professional and amateur ball playing. Delegates to state and national conventions debated the merits of formally separating the two. Those who supported the idea of paying players believed that if professionalism were openly endorsed, many of its abuses could be eliminated. In 1866 the *Clipper* argued, "Far better it is that this making a business of ball playing be guided into a legitimate channel, than that it should be allowed to be carried on in the underhanded style in which it has been of late years." The paper recommended that professionals be hired to teach novices and that they be barred from club contests but allowed to compete among themselves.[71] Those who were most disgusted with professionalism wanted to check its growth or eliminate it. Failing that, they wished to divorce themselves from it entirely.

In December 1868 the National Association of Base Ball Players recognized that its ban on hiring players had become moot and voted to officially recognize two classes, professionals and amateurs, with state associations governing their relations. The press interpreted this to mean that clubs could now advertise for players and that the latter could solicit employment. Amateur groups who wanted to remain in that class could hire an expert to take care of the grounds and to teach, but he could join in a match only if the other team also agreed to include a professional. The *New York Times* applauded this move, noting that "custom will now rank every club as a professional organization which has a majority of its nine composed of professional players." It predicted both "an amateur revival" and "increased interest in the contests of professional clubs, as now all their efforts to excel can be made openly and honorably."[72]

The year 1869 witnessed the creation of the first team with all of its men on contracts, and it also brought more confusion over the exact meaning of professionalism. In November, delegates at the New York state association meeting engaged in a long debate over what constituted a professional club, finally passing a resolution that "a club receiving gate money, so long as it was not devoted to remunerating players, was not a professional." They also instructed delegates to the NABBP convention to obtain a proper definition from that body. In New Jersey delegates voted unanimously to require that their NABBP representatives take measures to eject all professional clubs from the national association, while the Pennsylvania state association told its emissaries to do the opposite.[73] When the NABBP convened in Boston in December, delegates voted to strike the section that distinguished between amateurs and professionals. The *Clipper* blamed the outcome on the political influence of professional players and stridently declared: "By this, not only are all clubs placed on the same level as regards playing strength, but all that has been previously done to place professional ball playing upon a reputable footing has been nullfied."[74]

Tensions between proponents of professionalism and amateurism increased throughout the 1870 season and climaxed at the NABBP's annual meeting on November 30 during a "spicey debate" as to whether or not "the custom of publicly hiring men to play the game of base ball [is] reprehensible and injurious to the best interests of the game." Two-thirds of the delegates voted against this resolution, which, according to the *Clipper,* demonstrated that "the last feather had been placed on the camel's back, and under the pressure of the control of a clique of professional managers the National Association gave up the ghost, and after a reputable existence of ten years and a decline in health during the last three, it adjourned *sine die.*"[75] The amateurs then proceeded to launch their own organization, bolstered by the Knickerbockers, who had withdrawn from the parent body several months earlier.

In December 1870 the Brooklyn Excelsiors issued a call for an amateur convention, and delegates from thirty-three clubs from New York, Brooklyn, Philadelphia, Boston, Baltimore, and other towns convened at the Excelsiors' meeting rooms in March 1871. Their collective purpose was to redeem baseball "from the odium attached to it by the evils introduced under the abuses of the worst phases of professional ball playing" and to restore "the old status of base-ball playing." The group invited participation by clubs "which engage in the game for recreative exercise only, and not for gate money, receipts, or for pecuniary benefit only"; it also planned to establish rules that would repudiate "all countenancy of playing baseball for money." Delegates adopted the 1867 constitution and 1870 rules of the NABBP, endorsed dividing the baseball fraternity into two classes, and prohibited amateur clubs from playing against professionals.[76] (It is ironic that the Excelsiors led this revolt, for that club was perhaps the first to hire a player, when it enlisted James Creighton in 1860.) The one issue that threatened to divide the amateurs at the outset—gate money—was left unresolved. The Brooklyn Stars wished to continue to play on enclosed grounds and collect gate receipts; the Knickerbockers strongly opposed these practices. In the end, "tacit consent" was given to admission fees when a club was on tour or needed funds to pay for their grounds, although it was agreed that this money could never be used to compensate players "in any shape or form."[77]

Clearly, the primary purpose of this group was to revive the customs of the 1850s and early 1860s, which many men who had been prominent players, club officers, or national association officials during that time viewed as the golden age of baseball. In his call for the amateur convention, Dr. Jones of the Excelsiors had praised the sport's health benefits and fondly recalled the days when the participants included "the mechanic, the merchant, the professional classes, the school children, the collegiates, the aged and the young, the church member and minister, the public official, the private affluent member of society." He blamed England's paid cricket players for beginning the corruption of the American sport and condemned the professionals who took over control of baseball. His appeal was made to those who wished "to restore this pastime to its former high status . . . to eradicate the evils that have, by the machinations of the unprincipled, ambitious, or the money seeker, been fostered upon the game."[78]

Jones's plea represented an exaggerated, idyllic view of an antebellum era marked by class harmony and ball playing for fun and recreation only. Warren Goldstein has argued that there never was a golden age of baseball and that the amateur attack on professionalism represented an upper-class refusal to accept the legitimacy of paid, skilled workers—in this case, ball players—who toiled in their trade. While there is some validity to this interpretation, it is more correct to state that the early years did witness increased emphasis on exercise for all classes, socializing after ball games, and wholesome amusement for participants and spectators. Jones and his colleagues were traditionalists who wished to retain the best elements of early baseball while eliminating the worst. Many of them respected working-class ball players but hated the gamblers and others who corrupted their pastime. Their objections to professionalism lay not so much in the hiring of players as in the growth of commercialism, wagering, and the fixing of games. While there certainly was a class element in their hostility toward professionalism, it was not the most important factor.[79]

The founding of the new association signaled an amateur revival in baseball during the early 1870s. One newspaper praised the positive aspects of the movement, stressing that there was no longer "any just cause for amateurs retiring from base ball playing for fear of being classed as professional or hired ball tossers." While it conceded that professional ball playing was not necessarily "a degrading position," the paper stated that "the majority prefer, for business reasons, to be considered as only participating in the game for recreative purposes." Professional clubs were good for baseball because, among other things, they served "to attract from amateur contests the class of 'sports' who have introduced all the evils connected with professional playing."[80]

One reporter estimated that legitimate amateur nines numbered in the hundreds, yet attendance was sparse at the amateur association meetings on December 13, 1871, and again the following March, when ten clubs sent delegates and sixteen others paid their dues but were not represented. It is not surprising, then, that the amateur association lasted only until 1874 and that the players who followed its rules soon faced many of the problems confronted by professionals. Tensions remained over the question of gate money as well as the issues of whether or not to go on tour or to play against professionals. Some amateur nines practiced diligently, took their pastime as seriously as professional teams, and gained glory on the diamond. Others, like the Boston Lowells, limped along for a few years and then disbanded.[81] A few, like the Knickerbockers, stuck to the old ways. They practiced, played intrasquad games and matches against those clubs that shared their philosophy, and partied much as they had done before the Civil War.

The defection of the amateurs did not disturb the professionals, who simultaneously organized themselves into the National Association of Professional Base Ball Players in March 1871. Agents from ten clubs adopted the 1870 NABBP constitution and bylaws, arranged tours, set rules of championship competition, and began the task of rationalizing baseball into a business. Harry Wright and other founders of this association were determined to demonstrate that professional baseball could be exciting, entertaining, wholesome, and honest. While their amateur counterparts experimented with a trip back in time, these modernizers launched what would become a major new entertainment industry in the United States.[82]

The formation of the professional association signaled both the end of baseball's transition era and the beginning of a new one for the national pastime. By then baseball's popularity was assured among most classes and throughout virtually all regions of the nation. The participation of so many thousands (perhaps even millions) of players and spectators, coupled with commercialism and professionalism for the most talented, proved that the sport was deeply ingrained in American culture only a decade and a half after its first growth spurt. Baseball was now a thriving industry in the business world of the Gilded Age; it also entered the mainstream of urban politics in American cities, as party bosses brought the amusement under their influence.

Proof that baseball had become a booming business was evident in the growth of the sporting goods industry, the proliferation of retail stores that sold equipment and supplies, the rise in gate receipts, and the first attempts of the federal government to tax professional matches. In 1871 a *New York Times* reporter toured his city's "grand emporium of baseball" on Nassau Street, where one company produced sixteen kinds of balls. He estimated that one New York manufacturer supplied 162,000 balls in 1870 and that the whole country would require a half million in 1871. The sale of bats was also tremendous, with one firm running two mills all year to meet the demand. The 1870 census found another huge baseball supply town at Natick, Massachusetts, with two companies making 33,000 dozen balls per year and paying $21,750 in wages.[83] Scores of small and larger retail sporting goods stores across the land sold these items, plus bases, spikes, uniforms, scorebooks, rule books, magazines, tobacco, and much more. One of the most successful was Al Reach's Base Ball Depot at 404 Chestnut Street, Philadelphia, where the baseball fraternity congregated to gossip and to buy the latest implements and clothing.[84]

At the professional level, baseball's business aspects were expanding and growing more complex each year. Some clubs sold shares of stock to investors eager for dividends and used the cash to pay salaries and traveling expenses. As early as 1868 the *New York Times* estimated that over 200,000 people gathered to watch feature contests across the United States, generating gate receipts of $100,000. These figures skyrocketed over the next two years, with the spectacular success of the Cincinnati Red Stockings and their rivals.[85] Such developments did not escape the notice of the federal internal revenue office in Washington, D.C. In 1869 a tax collector ruled that baseball clubs that charged an admission fee must purchase a ten-dollar license and pay 2 percent of their receipts to the federal government.[86]

The links between baseball and urban politics, first forged before the Civil War, were strengthened after 1865. Republican and Democratic party machines assisted in the formation of several prominent clubs, often by recruiting men from volunteer fire companies and other private associations. Public officials occasionally secured suitable playing grounds and often arranged for police to keep order at feature matches. The popularity of the national pastime impressed politicians, who often tried to use baseball clubs to boost their own standing in their communities. Candidates for local offices and bosses of urban machines frequently were elected as club officers, while prominent players used fame earned on the ball field to gain public office. Boss Tweed's affiliation with the New York Mutuals is the best known example of this phenomenon. The president of the Mutuals, John Wildey, who served a term as chief executive of the NABBP, was also the New York City coroner.[87]

In Philadelphia the ties between ball players and politics were also close. The *Sunday Mercury* warned in 1867 that when organizations chose their officers "clubs should sternly reprove the efforts being made to exalt mere politicians to these positions, whose only aim is their own political preferment, and who would use club and members for this purpose."[88] Boston provided perhaps the most dramatic example of the power of baseball in politics when, in 1869, the city fathers plowed up part of Boston Common, thus depriving the Lowells and other nines of the use of their favorite field. Incensed, the Lowells and their friends backed candidates for mayor and aldermen who pledged support for athletics in general and a new baseball ground in particular. On election day the baseball party ran a special ticket marked by a large red ball. It won about 3,000 votes and swept its men into office.[89]

By 1871 baseball was an integral part of American life, thanks in part to its intrinsic appeal but also because of the boost provided by the professionals. The *Spirit* observed that without their influence, the sport "would never have attained the eminence it now enjoys; it certainly would never have fallen into a state of desuetude, but the well known apathetic habits of amateurs would have done little more than keep it alive." The paper called for harmony between amateurs and professionals so that the national pastime would continue to flourish.[90] But some old-timers continued to lament the passing of the old order. A correspondent to Chadwick's *American Chronicle*, who called himself "Old Peto Brine," contrasted "the class of men who now fix up your matches" with "the fair and square style of men who controlled your clubs in the good old times of base ball." He urged an end to heavy betting and the influence of politicians, lamenting, "You're in for 'biz' in playing your matches now, and have forgotten the time when your club's name stood higher as a fair and square club than it does now. . . . we used to play matches for the honor of the thing in my young ball days, now clubs play for gate money and the betting rings."[91]

"Old Peto Brine" no doubt had a rather romantic and selective memory of his ball-playing past, yet he did express the common feeling that the professional era lacked the innocence, honesty, sportsmanship, and club loyalty of antebellum baseball. By 1871, however, more people were playing, the level of competition was higher, and the baseball business was booming. There was no turning back the clock. America's pastime had left the antebellum era behind and was marching on toward the twentieth century.

NOTES

1. Quoted in *Philadelphia Sunday Mercury*, August 26, 1866; *Chicago Tribune*, July 24, November 27, 1870.

2. *Philadelphia Sunday Mercury*, February 17, 1867; *Chicago Tribune*, July 29, September 9, 1869.

3. *American Chronicle* 1 (February 27, 1868): 68; *Ball Players' Chronicle*, August 1, 1867; *Clipper* 16 (May 2, 1868): 26.

4. *Philadelphia Sunday Mercury*, June 23, 1867.

5. Quoted in *Philadelphia Sunday Mercury*, October 13, 1867.

6. *Clipper* 15 (September 28, 1867): 194; 18 (September 24, 1870): 195; (November 12, 1870): 253; *Ball Players' Chronicle*, June 6, August 1, 1867; *American Chronicle* 1 (April 23, 1868): 129.

7. *Philadelphia Sunday Mercury*, February 17, 1867.

8. *Spirit* 19 (November 21, 1868): 211; *Ball Players' Chronicle*, October 3, 1867.

9. There is a similarity between newspaper coverage of boxing and baseball. Editorials condemned gambling and other abuses in each sport, but the extensive stories seem to have stimulated greater public interest

and participation in betting. For example, see the *New York Times*'s coverage of the international boxing match between John Heenan and Tom Sayers during the spring of 1860.

10. *Spirit* 19 (November 21, 1868): 211.

11. *Wilkes' Spirit* 18 (March 24, 1868): 55; (April 7, 1868): 85; *American Chronicle* 1 (March 19, 1868): 90; *Clipper* 15 (March 21, 1868): 395; 16 (November 21, 1868): 258.

12. *Newark Daily Advertiser,* November 7, 1868.

13. *Clipper* 14 (October 27, 1866): 226; (November 3, 1866): 235; 15 (September 21, 1867): 187; (September 28, 1867): 194; (October 5, 1867): 202; (October 12, 1867): 210; (October 19, 1867): 220; *Ball Players' Chronicle,* October 3, 1867.

14. *Clipper* 16 (April 25, 1868): 180.

15. *Clipper* 16 (May 2, 1868): 26; (November 14, 1868): 250; (January 2, 1869): 306; 17 (September 25, 1869): 194; *Philadelphia Sunday Mercury,* October 25, November 15, 1868; September 26, 1869.

16. *Clipper* 16 (December 5, 1868): 274.

17. Melvin L. Adelman, *A Sporting Time: New York City and the Rise of Modern Athletics, 1820–70* (Urbana, Ill., 1986): 148–50.

18. *Wilkes' Spirit* 13 (December 30, 1865): 285; 17 (September 21, 1867): 83; (October 19, 1867): 167; *Clipper* 15 (July 27, 1867): 125; (November 16, 1867): 250; *Newark Daily Advertiser,* November 2, 1867.

19. *Ball Players' Chronicle,* June 6, 27, 1867; *American Chronicle* 1 (February 20, 1868): 60.

20. *Philadelphia Sunday Mercury,* August 9, 1868.

21. *Wilkes' Spirit* 13 (December 30, 1865): 285; 17 (September 21, 1867): 83; (October 19, 1867): 167; *Philadelphia Sunday Mercury,* June 2, 1867; September 26, 1869; *Clipper* 15 (July 27, 1867): 125.

22. *Ball Players' Chronicle,* August 22, 1867.

23. *Clipper* 14 (November 3, 1866): 235.

24. *Philadelphia Sunday Mercury,* May 6, 27, 1866.

25. *American Chronicle* 1 (February 20, 1868): 60.

26. *Brooklyn Daily Eagle,* August 27, 1863; May 4, August 17, 1864; September 3, 1866; *Clipper* 13 (December 9, 1865): 274.

27. Adrian C. Anson, *A Ball Player's Career* (Chicago, 1900), 29, 45. See also David Porter, "Cap Anson of Marshalltown: Baseball's First Superstar," *Palimpsest* 61 (August 1980): 98–107.

28. Albert G. Spalding, *America's National Game* (New York, 1911), 119–23 (quotes on pp. 119, 120, 123).

29. *American Chronicle* 1 (February 13, 1868): 50. See also an editorial from the *Brooklyn Union* reprinted in *Philadelphia Sunday Mercury,* November 8, 1868.

30. *American Chronicle* 1 (April 30, 1868): 137.
31. Adelman, *A Sporting Time,* 152–54.
32. *Philadelphia Sunday Mercury,* July 26, 1868.
33. *Clipper* 13 (December 9, 1865): 274.
34. *Clipper* 14 (August 18, 1866): 146.
35. The Fitzgerald controversy was reported in *Wilkes' Spirit* 15 (September 8, 1866): 28; *Clipper* 14 (September 8, 1866): 170; (September 15, 1866): 179; *Philadelphia Sunday Mercury,* May 27, September 9, 1866.
36. *Clipper* 12 (March 25, 1865): 394; *Wilkes' Spirit* 12 (April 8, 1865): 85.
37. *Jersey City Daily Times,* August 9, 1865.
38. Anson, *A Ball Player's Career,* 44–45.
39. *Ball Players' Chronicle,* June 20, 1867. See also *Ball Players' Chronicle,* June 27, 1867; *American Chronicle* 1 (July 2, 1868): 226.
40. *Spirit* 20 (July 10, 1869): 329.
41. *Philadelphia Sunday Mercury,* June 23, 1867; *Clipper* 15 (June 29, 1867): 91.
42. *American Chronicle* 1 (July 23, 1868): 262.
43. *Newark Daily Advertiser,* June 17, 24, July 15, 1867; July 23, August 10–11, 13, September 30, October 2, 1868; June 9, 1869; April 29, 1870; *Spirit* 19 (August 15, 1868): 471; *Clipper* 17 (October 2, 1869): 204.
44. *Philadelphia Sunday Mercury,* March 14, April 4, May 23, 30, June 13, 1869.
45. *Philadelphia Sunday Mercury,* January 24, 1869; *Clipper* 17 (March 19, 1870): 397. For other cases of "revolvers," including John Hatfield's expulsion from the Red Stockings, see *Philadelphia Sunday Mercury,* April 18, 1869; *Clipper* 15 (February 20, 1868): 363; 16 (March 20, 1869): 395, 397; 17 (April 17, 1869): 10.
46. Adelman, *A Sporting Time,* 157, 160; David Q. Voigt, *American Baseball,* vol. 1 (Norman, Okla., 1966), 18–22; *Philadelphia Sunday Mercury,* August 18, 1869.
47. For example, see Charles Graffen's criticism of Wright's system and his feeling that Philadelphia's Athletics "felt ashamed to see Americans being bamboozled in their own game, and that by a Britisher," in *Philadelphia Sunday Mercury,* August 2, 1868.
48. *Clipper* 17 (December 18, 1869): 293.
49. Voigt, *American Baseball,* 23–34; *Spirit* 20 (June 19, 1869): 278, 281; (June 26, 1869); 296; (July 10, 1869): 325; *Clipper* 16 (April 18, 1868): 11; (October 24, 1868): 227; (October 31, 1868): 234; (March 13, 1869): 387; (April 3, 1869): 411; 17 (June 12, 1869): 74; (June 19,

1869): 82; (June 26, 1869): 91, 92; (July 3, 1869): 99; (July 10, 1869): 106; (July 17, 1869): 116; (October 2, 1869): 204; *Philadelphia Sunday Mercury,* June 27, 1869; *Newark Daily Advertiser,* June 17, 21, 1870.

50. Quoted in *Philadelphia Sunday Mercury,* August 2, 1868; *Spirit* 20 (August 7, 1869): 391.

51. Quoted in *Philadelphia Sunday Mercury,* December 5, 1869.

52. *Spirit* 21 (October 9, 1869): 119; 22 (April 23, 1870): 154; (July 9, 1870): 323–24; *Philadelphia Sunday Mercury,* October 17, December 5, 1869; *Clipper* 17 (October 16, 1869): 219; (October 30, 1864): 237; (December 18, 1869): 291; 18 (October 29, 1870): 237.

53. Quoted in *Philadelphia Sunday Mercury,* August 16, 1869; *Clipper* 17 (October 2, 1869): 205.

54. *Newark Daily Advertiser,* August 23, 1867.

55. *New York Times,* June 24, 1869.

56. *Wilkes' Spirit* 13 (November 11, 1865): 166; *Clipper* 13 (November 11, 1865): 242. For reports and commentaries on the national association's judiciary committee hearings on the reinstatements of Devyr and Duffy, see *Clipper* 15 (April 27, 1867): 21; (May 18, 1867): 43; (October 19, 1867): 220; (October 26, 1867): 227; (November 9, 1867): 243; *Ball Players' Chronicle,* October 10, 24, 31, November 7, 1867; *Philadelphia Sunday Mercury,* October 18, 1868.

57. For examples of suspicion of bribery in baseball, see *Wilkes' Spirit* 16 (July 6, 1867): 348; 17 (August 31, 1867): 27; (September 28, 1867): 108; *Spirit* 21 (October 2, 1869): 106; *Philadelphia Sunday Dispatch,* November 4, 1866; *Newark Daily Advertiser,* September 2, 1867; *Clipper* 15 (November 16, 1867): 250; 16 (September 26, 1868): 195; *Philadelphia Sunday Mercury,* October 7, 1866; September 22, 1867; October 17, 1869.

58. *Clipper* 17 (August 14, 1869): 146; 18 (August 20, 1870): 154; *Ball Players' Chronicle,* December 12, 1867. See also *Ball Players' Chronicle,* August 8, September 5, 1867; *American Chronicle* 1 (April 16, 1868): 124.

59. *Wilkes' Spirit* 18 (April 25, 1868): 148; *Spirit* 19 (September 26, 1868): 89.

60. *Philadelphia Sunday Mercury,* November 8, 1868.

61. *Philadelphia Sunday Dispatch,* October 7, 1866.

62. *Spirit* 19 (January 23, 1869): 359.

63. *Wilkes' Spirit* 12 (April 8, 1865): 84; 14 (May 19, 1866): 178; 18 (April 11, 1868): 115.

64. *Philadelphia Sunday Mercury,* August 23, 1868.

65. *Clipper* 16 (April 11, 1868): 2; (June 6, 1868): 69; *Newark Daily Advertiser,* May 15, 1868; May 19, 1869.

66. *Clipper* 17 (April 17, 1869): 13; (January 15, 1870): 323; *Spirit* 20 (August 14, 1869): 407.

67. Quoted in *Philadelphia Sunday Mercury,* February 7, 1869.

68. *Spirit* 23 (November 26, 1870): 232.

69. Reported in *Clipper* 18 (August 13, 1870): 148; (August 27, 1870): 163; (December 3, 1870): 275; (December 17, 1870): 291; *Spirit* 23 (November 26, 1870): 235; *New York Times,* November 27, 1870; newspaper clipping from the *Cincinnati Times,* Henry Chadwick's scrapbooks, vol. 19, Albert G. Spalding Collection, New York Public Library.

70. *New York Times,* April 10, 1869. See also *American Chronicle* 1 (June 25, 1868): 214; *Wilkes' Spirit* 14 (May 19, 1866): 178; *Clipper* 17 (May 29, 1869): 58; (April 2, 1870): 413; 18 (August 27, 1870): 165.

71. *Clipper* 14 (December 15, 1866): 282.

72. *New York Times,* April 10, 1869; *Clipper* 16 (December 19, 1868): 293; (January 23, 1869): 333.

73. *Clipper* 17 (November 20, 1869): 261; *Philadelphia Sunday Mercury,* November 14, 21, 1869; *Spirit* 21 (November 13, 1869): 199.

74. *Clipper* 17 (December 18, 1869): 290–91; *New York Times,* December 9, 1869.

75. *Clipper* 18 (December 10, 1870): 285; *New York Times,* December 1, 1870; *Spirit* 23 (December 3, 1870): 245.

76. *Clipper* 18 (July 9, 1870): 107; (December 10, 1870): 283; (December 24, 1870): 299; *New York Times,* January 16, March 1, 17, 1871; *Philadelphia Sunday Mercury,* February 19, March 26, 1871.

77. *Clipper* 18 (March 25, 1871): 405.

78. *Clipper* 18 (February 18, 1871): 365.

79. Warren Jay Goldstein, "Playing for Keeps: A History of American Baseball, 1857–1876" (unpublished Ph.D. dissertation, Yale University, 1983), 235–58.

80. Newspaper clippings, Chadwick's scrapbooks, vol. 1 (1871, 1872).

81. Newspaper clippings, Chadwick's scrapbooks, vol. 1 (1871, 1872); *New York Times,* April 13, 1871; James D'Wolf Lovett, *Old Boston Boys and the Games They Played* (Boston, 1907), 203–4.

82. *New York Times,* March 1, 6, 13, 1871; *Philadelphia Sunday Mercury,* March 19, 1871; *Clipper* 18 (January 28, 1871): 338; (February 4, 1871): 348; (March 18, 1871): 394; (March 25, 1871): 402; *Spirit* 24 (March 25, 1871): 84.

83. *New York Times,* April 30, 1871. See also *Ball Players' Chronicle,* June 27, 1867.

84. *Philadelphia Sunday Mercury,* April 7, 1867; *Clipper* 15 (April 13, 1867): 3.

85. *Spirit* 23 (November 12, 1870): 197; *New York Times,* April 10, 1869.

86. *Ball Players' Chronicle,* November 14, 1867; *Spirit* 20 (August 14, 1869): 373; *Clipper* 17 (September 4, 1869): 173.

87. *Wilkes' Spirit* 14 (April 21, 1866): 116; *Clipper* 13 (August 5, 1865): 131; *Ball Players' Chronicle,* November 14, 1867.

88. *Philadelphia Sunday Mercury,* September 9, 1866; January 27, 1867.

89. Lovett, *Old Boston Boys,* 197–200; *Clipper* 17 (January 1, 1870): 307.

90. *Spirit* 23 (December 24, 1870): 292. See also *Spirit* 20 (April 24, 1869): 146; 24 (March 4, 1871): 48.

91. *American Chronicle* 1 (January 9, 1868): 10. "Old Peto Brine" is a play on the name of Peter O'Brien, one of the best players on the Atlantics during their early years. For a different perspective on this letter, see Goldstein, "Playing for Keeps," 105–11.

Conclusion

THE respective fates of baseball and cricket in America had already been established by the early 1870s, and they continued their sharp divergence during the last quarter of the nineteenth century. Baseball increasingly became an integral part of American culture, earning a significant presence and even prominence in the country's economic, political, social, and cultural life. By contrast, cricket experienced a modest revival during these years, especially in Philadelphia, various English immigrant communities, and scattered working-class towns where the game had taken root during the Civil War era. But the British sport remained distinctly marginal to the recreational life of the vast majority of Americans, especially after the rise of the more popular team sports of football and basketball.

In the economic arena, baseball flourished in the Gilded Age as owners schemed to turn the national pastime into a profitable business. While professionalism and commercialism swept through the nation's major and minor cities and towns, very few clubs made money and entrepreneurs discovered that the expense of constructing new ball parks and paying player salaries was often greater than the income generated by admission fees. Retaining and disciplining recalcitrant or "revolving" athletes proved to be a major headache until the National League, founded in 1876, developed the structure of a loosely organized cartel. That association eventually restricted competition among franchises through the use of the reserve clause in player contracts. While baseball bosses struggled to show a profit, sporting goods magnates like Albert G. Spalding and Al Reach accumulated fortunes in the manufacture of balls, bases, uniforms, and other materials for a growing market of amateurs and professionals who were wild about playing ball.

The national pastime also extended into the political world of the country's burgeoning cities and even rode the new wave of American imperialism that appeared around the turn of the century. The ties between baseball and urban political machines grew stronger as owners turned to politicians for favors such as choice sites for the location of ball parks, timely arrangements with the transit lines that brought customers to their gates, and police protection for crowd control. Owners also struggled with the issue of Sunday baseball, which was tolerated in the West but still was banned in most parts of the Northeast. Moreover, the sport's boosters did not limit their efforts to the United States. Spalding, Charles Comiskey, and other missionaries of America's favorite pastime tried to plant the game around the world. While their much-publicized tours were flops, American soldiers, sailors, clergymen, and businessmen succeeded in popularizing the sport in Asia and the Caribbean.

Perhaps most important, during this era baseball established itself as a powerful force in the social and cultural worlds of the American people. Its publicists promoted the sport as a democratic game that offered all classes and ethnic groups an opportunity to play, at least on the sandlot level if not in the professional leagues. Immigrants learned that competing on the diamond was one way of joining the mainstream of society. The sport built upon its early popularity among factory and shop hands, petty proprietors, clerks, and office workers and became the game of the masses. Its place in the American imagination was already secure in 1888 when Ernest Lawrence Thayer dramatized in verse Mighty Casey striking out for the Mudville Nine. Thayer's piece was an early contribution to what became a vast body of baseball prose and poetry, as the national pastime generated its distinctive myths, legends, symbols, and folklore.[1]

In 1872 American cricket was on the eve of a new era of growth that marked the second phase of the English game in the United

States. Most sport historians have traditionally pointed to cricket's decline in America after the Civil War, but this interpretation is misleading because it ignores the revival that lasted from the mid-1870s to World War I. While a thorough investigation of that period in the saga of American cricket lies beyond the scope of this study, it is appropriate to offer a few observations on the fate of the English pastime during those years.

Although the enthusiasm for cricket remained centered in Philadelphia, it did extend to several other metropolitan regions and factory towns in New England, New York, New Jersey, Maryland, and the Midwest. The year 1874 witnessed the beginning of the sport's second stage of development when a Philadelphia twelve won a tournament in Halifax, Nova Scotia. The gentlemen presented their trophy for local competition from 1880 to 1926, when the battle for the Halifax Cup was a highlight of each sporting and social season in Philadelphia society. The appearance of the *American Cricketer* in 1877 gave the sport an organ that would promote the game for fifty years. The outstanding performance of eleven Americans against a touring Australian team in 1878 created great excitement in the City of Brotherly Love and contributed to the founding that year of the Cricketers Association of the United States. In 1879 that body renewed the annual United States versus Canada series. The next three decades featured a flowering of intercollegiate cricket and several international challenges between British and American sides.

The golden age of American cricket began in the late 1880s, when Philadelphia teams earned a string of victories against British elevens. Although it ended with the World War I, that catastrophe was not the major cause of the sport's decline in the United States. More important were changing recreational trends, especially for the youth in Philadelphia and other upper-class subcultures. Country clubs adopted new British sports such as tennis and golf, which became more popular than cricket because of their greater appeal to participants and spectators. The growing popularity of the automobile and the advent of scouting and summer camps also drew boys away from the cricket fields. Many privileged young men who came of age in the 1920s were not reared in the culture of cricket, as their fathers and grandfathers had been. As the elite abandoned the game, the English working-class immigrants were unable by themselves to sustain the previous standing of the sport. A few American college and private clubs kept the sport alive for a time, but ultimately cricket's status in America depended upon East and West Indian newcomers whose countries had once been part of the British Empire. Yet its influence on baseball, and its social, cultural, and athletic significance for its adherents made cricket an important part of the sport history of nineteenth-century America.[2]

NOTES

1. For late nineteenth-century baseball see Peter Levine, *A. G. Spalding and the Rise of Baseball* (New York, 1985); Steven Riess, *Touching Base: Professional Baseball and American Culture in the Progressive Era* (Westport, Conn., 1980); Ted Vincent, *Mudville's Revenge: The Rise and Fall of American Sport* (New York, 1981), chaps. 4–7; Harold Seymour, *Baseball: The Early Years* (New York, 1960); David Q.Voigt, *American Baseball,* vol. 1: *From Gentleman's Sport to the Commissioner System,* 2d ed. (University Park, Pa., 1983); Lee Lowenfish and Tony Lupien, *The Imperfect Diamond* (New York, 1980), part 2; Warren J. Goldstein, "Playing for Keeps: A History of American Baseball, 1857-1876" (unpublished Ph.D. dissertation, Yale University, 1983), chap. 5.

2. John I. Marder, *The International Series: The Story of the United States versus Canada at Cricket* (London, 1968), 73–75; John A. Lester, *A Century of Philadelphia Cricket* (Philadelphia, 1951), 272–91.

Methodological Note

THE demographic analyses of players and clubs presented in Chapters 6 and 7 are based on information gathered from books, newspapers, magazines, pamphlets, club records, city directories, federal censuses, and other sources. For a variety of reasons, the percentages, means, and medians should not be viewed as precise figures but rather as close approximations that incorporate some degree of error. This is unavoidable because of the nature of the sources and the difficulties inherent in identifying players and linking their names to city directories and census manuscripts. I have made every effort to minimize the degree of error.

I began this project by collecting names primarily from box scores and newspaper reports. Officers, delegates to conventions, and active players constituted the bulk of my original sample of about 2,000 players from five New Jersey cities and towns and Philadelphia. Nearly two-thirds of these men could not be identified in city directories because of missing first names or initials or because they were not heads of households. For those who were found, the city directories listed their occupation, home address, and (in some cases) place of work.[1] Since the directories usually omitted many from the lower classes and most who were not heads of households, they are not ideal sources for demographic studies. However, as Melvin Adelman has noted, newspaper and other qualitative sources suggest that very few men from the bottom ranks of society participated in the formally organized clubs (although many no doubt participated in street or informal ball play). It is true that many of the young and single men who joined junior or senior clubs were not listed in the directories. Since street addresses were required to find people in the census manuscripts, those players who were not heads of households generally could also not be identified in the latter source and thus could not be included in this study. If more men in this category could have been included, it probably would have lowered the mean and median ages and property holdings of each group significantly, but the results for birthplace, occupation, and residence probably would not have changed very much.[2]

By consulting the United States census manuscripts I was able to check data on occupation and residence and collect additional information on birthplace, age, and wealth (real and personal estates).[3] Using the federal census on population for New Jersey was extraordinarily difficult because of the lack of any useful indexes and the failure of the census takers to follow any clear street pattern in their coverage of each ward. The Philadelphia research was easier and more fruitful because I was able to use the vast resources of the Philadelphia Social History Project at the University of Pennsylvania.[4] I also benefited from the invaluable assistance of Thomas Jable, with whom I collaborated on a joint study of Philadelphia athletic club members.

NOTES

1. Most of the names for my original sample came from the *New York Clipper* (1855–70), the *Spirit of the Times* (1855–60), *Porter's Spirit of the Times* (1856–60), and *Wilkes' Spirit of the Times* (1859–68). I used the following city directories: *Directory of the City of Newark*, B. T. Pierson, comp. (Newark, N.J., 1855–61); *Directory of Jersey City*, James Gopsill, comp. (Jersey City, N.J., 1855–61); *McElroy's Philadelphia City Directory* (Philadelphia, 1860–70); *Gopsill's Philadelphia City Directory* (Philadelphia, 1860–70).

2. Melvin L. Adelman, *A Sporting Time: New York City and the Rise of Modern Athletics, 1820–70* (Urbana, Ill., 1986), 287–89.

3. For the New Jersey sample I used microfilm copies of the 1850 and 1860 schedules of the seventh and eighth censuses of population, United

States Bureau of the Census. For the Philadelphia sample I used the eighth and ninth censuses, 1860 and 1870.

4. For the methodology and studies of the Philadelphia Social History Project, see *Historical Methods Newsletter* 9 (March/June 1976): 41–184; for the problems of record linkage, see pp. 137–63.

Bibliographical Note

THE most important primary sources consulted for this study were newspapers and collections of manuscripts, scorebooks, guidebooks, minute books, pamphlets, and related materials. Newspapers are the most significant repository of information about early team sports, but they are difficult to use because there were no sports pages or sections or reliable indexes during the period. The leading national sporting journals that I read, all published in New York City, were: the *Spirit of the Times* (1838–60); *Porter's Spirit of the Times* (1856–60); *Wilkes' Spirit of the Times* (1859–72), which changed its name to *Spirit of the Times* in June 1868; and the *New York Clipper* (1853–72). I also used Henry Chadwick's *American Chronicle of Sports and Pastimes,* which began as the *Ball Players' Chronicle* (1867–68); the *New York Times* (1858–72); the *Brooklyn Daily Eagle* (1858–72); the *Newark Daily Advertiser* (1845–72); the *Newark Evening Journal* (1855–61); the *Jersey City Daily Courier and Advertiser* (1855–61); the *Philadelphia Sunday Mercury* (1867–72); and the *Chicago Tribune* (1868–71). I consulted as well select issues of several other newspapers from Boston, New York, Newark, Jersey City, Philadelphia, and Chicago.

Several libraries have excellent holdings for nineteenth-century baseball and cricket. The Albert G. Spalding Collection at the New York Public Library contains Spalding's own scrapbooks, Henry

Chadwick's diaries and scrapbooks, Harry Wright's correspondence, notes, and account books, the scorebooks of the St. George Cricket Club and the Cincinnati Red Stockings, the scorebooks and minute books of the Knickerbocker Base Ball Club, and assorted pamphlets, guidebooks, and other materials. The National Baseball Library at Cooperstown, New York, has several scrapbooks and pamphlets pertaining to the amateur era but is strongest on the professional leagues that began in 1871. The most extensive cricket repository in North America is the C. Christopher Morris Cricket Library and Collection at the Haverford College Library, Haverford, Pennsylvania. That library is best for the period 1880–1920, but it also has some materials on the early years of American cricket. The Historical Society of Pennsylvania has the records and correspondence of the Pythian Base Ball Club, which includes a wealth of information about black voluntary associations and sports clubs for the 1860s. The Society also has minute books and records of the Philadelphia Cricket Club, as well as scrapbooks and other materials pertaining to the leading Philadelphia cricket clubs. The New Jersey Historical Society owns the Satterthwaite scrapbooks, which include much material on cricket and other sports in New Jersey. A smaller collection of pamphlets and scorebooks is at the New-York Historical Society.

Index

A Note on the Author

George B. Kirsch, professor of history at Manhattan College, has an A.B. degree from Cornell University and M.A. and Ph.D. degrees from Columbia University. He is the author of *Jeremy Belknap: A Biography* and has published in the *New England Quarterly*, the *Journal of Sport History*, *New Jersey History*, and the *Journal of Regional Cultures*.